The State of the Jews

The State of the Jews
A Critical Appraisal

Edward Alexander

Transaction Publishers
New Brunswick (U.S.A.) and London (U.K.)

Copyright © 2012 by Transaction Publishers, New Brunswick, New Jersey.

All rights reserved under International and Pan-American Copyright Conventions. No part of this book may be reproduced or transmitted in any form or by any means, electronic or mechanical, including photocopy, recording, or any information storage and retrieval system, without prior permission in writing from the publisher. All inquiries should be addressed to Transaction Publishers, Rutgers—The State University of New Jersey, 35 Berrue Circle, Piscataway, New Jersey 08854-8042. www.transactionpub.com

This book is printed on acid-free paper that meets the American National Standard for Permanence of Paper for Printed Library Materials.

Library of Congress Catalog Number: 2011032331
ISBN: 978-1-4128-4614-1
Printed in the United States of America

Library of Congress Cataloging-in-Publication Data

Alexander, Edward, 1936-
 The state of the Jews : a critical appraisal / Edward Alexander.
   p. cm.
 ISBN 978-1-4128-4614-1
 1. Jews—History. 2. Judaism—History. 3. Jews—Politics and government—20th century. 4. Jews—Politics and government—21st century. 5. Jews in literature. 6. Trilling, Lionel, 1905–1975—Political and social views. I. Title.
  DS117.A618 2012
  305.892'4—dc23

2011032331

IN MEMORIAM
Lucy S. Dawidowicz
Emil and Rose Fackenheim
Sol and Lizzie Fox
Josef Hadar
Anna Levy
Lew and Rose Levy
Roy and Dagmar McClement
Bernard and Eleanor M. Saffran
Marie Syrkin

The hand of the LORD was upon me, and carried me out in the spirit of the LORD, and set me down in the midst of the valley which was full of bones...

And he said unto me, Son of man, can these bones live? And I answered, O Lord GOD, thou knowest...

Then said he unto me, Prophesy unto the wind, prophesy, son of man, and say to the wind, Thus saith the Lord GOD; Come from the four winds, O breath, and breathe upon these slain, that they may live.

So I prophesied as he commanded me, and the breath came into them, and they lived, and stood up upon their feet, an exceeding great army.

Then he said unto me, Son of man, these bones are the whole house of Israel: behold, they say, Our bones are dried, and our hope is lost: we are cut off for our parts.

Therefore prophesy and say unto them, Thus saith the Lord GOD; Behold, O my people, I will open your graves, and cause you to come up out of your graves, and bring you into the land of Israel.

And ye shall know that I am the LORD, when I have opened your graves, O my people, and brought you up out of your graves.

And shall put my spirit in you, and ye shall live, and I shall place you in your own land; then shall ye know that I the LORD have spoken it, and performed it.

—Ezekiel, 37

Contents

Preamble: A Walk through the Table of Contents—and
a Linguistic Alert ... xiii

Acknowledgments ... xv

Introduction ... 1

I The Victorian Background ... 13

    Dr. Arnold, Matthew Arnold, and John Stuart Mill ... 15

II History ... 41

    Britannia Waives the Rules: Antisemitism,
    English-Style ... 43

    British Philosemitism: A Thing of the Past? ... 53

    Medieval Zionism: Yehuda Halevi ... 59

    Hitler's American Professors ... 65

    Hitler's (Palestinian) Arabs ... 71

    Beethoven and the Holocaust in Hungary ... 75

    Israel's "Original Sin": The Refugees of 1948 ... 81

    "If I Am Not for Myself, Who Will Be for Me?"
    The History of *Commentary* Magazine ... 87

    End of the Holocaust? ... 95

III Politics — 103

Survival Precedes Definition: Ruth Wisse's Moral Imperative — 105

"Pharaoh Who Knew Not Joseph": Obama Demotes the Jews — 113

The Meaning of Criticism — 123

Professors for Suicide Bombing: The Explosive Power of Boredom — 129

Back to 1933: How the Academic Boycott of Israel Began — 139

Afrocentrism, Liberal Dogmatism, and Antisemitism at Wellesley College — 145

Tom Paulin: Poetaster of Murder — 151

Jewish Israel-Haters Convert Their Dead Grandmothers: A New Mormonism? — 159

The Antisemitism of Liberals: A Gentile's View — 165

IV Literature — 171

Lionel Trilling: The (Jewish) Road Not Taken — 173

Metaphor and Memory in Cynthia Ozick: Pro and Con — 181

Foreign Bodies: Americans Abroad in Post-Holocaust Europe — 195

Saul Bellow's Jewish Letters — 201

Lublin Before It Became Majdanek: Jacob Glatstein's Autobiography — 207

Abba Kovner: Partisan, Poet, Curator, Avenger	213
Ashamed Jews: *The Finkler Question*	219
Daniel Deronda: "The Zionist Fate in English Hands" and "The Liberal Betrayal of the Jews"	227
Index	241

Preamble: A Walk through the Table of Contents—and a Linguistic Alert

My old teacher Lionel Trilling mischievously entitled one of his collections of essays *A Gathering of Fugitives*, by which he meant that they were in flight from unity, as perhaps all collections of essays, going back to Montaigne's *Essais* of 1580, must be in some degree. I have arranged the essays and reviews in the present collection in four sections, not logically parallel to one another. Because so much of the present ideological assault on Israel and Zionism emanates from liberals, the very people Thomas Carlyle used mockingly to call "friends of the species," I begin the book with a lengthy background essay that examines antisemitic and philosemitic strains in three prominent and influential Victorian liberals: Dr. Thomas Arnold, his son Matthew Arnold, and John Stuart Mill. Those terms, as applied here, are anachronistic. Both are German coinages of the 1870s, and both, as Gertrude Himmelfarb has pointed out, were invented by antisemites, "antisemitism used approvingly, philosemitism disparagingly."[1] The former term was invented by people who felt the need for a more antiseptic term than "Jew-hatred" and came up with this pseudoscientific euphemism. Today when Israel-haters still brazenly insist that, as champions of those Semites called Arabs, they can hardly be "anti-Semites," one must keep repeating that antisemites hate Jews, not "semites." The second term, philosemites, presents a more complicated problem; John Milton and numerous other admirers (and literate interpreters) of Hebraism could also be strident haters of Judaism and Jews. But Matthew Arnold, author of three ambitious books about religion as well as the famous "Hebraism and Hellenism" chapter of *Culture and Anarchy* (1869), was a (relatively) straightforward philosemite, just as his father had been an unqualified antisemite; and Jewish editors of the Bible text (like J. H. Hertz) who occasionally annotated it with his readings were justified in doing so. (Arnold was also the first serious critic of the Bible as a literary work, and held that Isaiah was equal in literary power to Homer, superior to Shakespeare and Milton.) John Stuart Mill was neither antisemite nor philosemite, but a *tertium quid* foreshadowing a political type of more immediacy to my subject than the two Arnolds themselves.

The main body of the book is divided according to genre: history, politics, and literature; the book's subtitle—"A Critical Appraisal"—is meant to invoke Matthew Arnold's famous definition of criticism as "the endeavour, in all branches of knowledge, theology, philosophy, history, art, science, to see the object as in itself it really is." It is *not* the endeavor to destroy the object. Here too I write in defense of language as well as the Jews, and seek to reclaim and rescue the word "criticism" from the ravages of Israel's ideological enemies. These linguistic desperadoes (who appear often in the pages that follow) have long done battle with that straw man they call "Zionists who want to silence all criticism of Israel," mythical creatures nobody has ever been able to identify—unless we agree that calls to throw Israel into the sea, or to "turn the Mediterranean red with Jewish blood," or to "shoot settlers dead" (thus the English poetaster Tom Paulin) or (this the linguistic enlargement of a Jewish leftist named Derfner) "to kill Israelis" generally are to be accounted "criticism," as their authors claim.

I also emulate Arnold in removing the qualifier "literary" from the term "criticism." Given the unity and integrity of knowledge, the criticism of literature leads naturally, and I hope tactfully, into the discussion of history and politics—creating the organic filaments that bind together the book's three sections.

Note

1. Gertrude Himmelfarb, *The People of the Book: Philosemitism in England, From Cromwell to Churchill* (New York and London: Encounter Books, 2011), 5.

Acknowledgments

For help and suggestions of various kinds that I received in writing this book, I am grateful to Rebecca Alexander, Paul Bogdanor, David Brumer, Werner Cohn, Joel Fishman, Irving Louis Horowitz, Menachem Kellner, Isi Leibler, Steve Plaut, and Doug Wertheimer.

I am grateful to the following journals for permission to reprint articles and reviews, in whole or in part.

Claremont Review of Books
"First, Survive," Fall 2008.

Standpoint
"The Unfinished Journey of Lionel Trilling," August 2008.

The Weekly Standard
"History Defiled," May 30, 2011.

Modern Judaism
Review of Benjamin Balint, *Running Commentary*, February 2011.

Harvard University Center for Jewish Studies
"*Daniel Deronda*: 'The Zionist Fate in English Hands' and 'The Liberal Betrayal of the Jews'" in *Arguing the Modern Jewish Canon: Essays on Literature and Culture in Honor of Ruth R. Wisse* (Harvard University Press, 2008).

Society
"John Stuart Mill and the Jews," 38, November/December 2000.

Midstream
"The Antisemitism of Liberals," September/October 2007.

Nativ
"Tom Paulin: Poetaster of Murder," April 2004.

Jewish Press
"Jewish Israel-Bashers and Dead Grandmothers: A New Mormonism?" January 28, 2011.

Judaism
"Dr. Arnold, Matthew Arnold, and the Jews," Spring 2002.

Academic Questions
Review of Mary Lefkowitz, *History Lesson: A Race Odyssey*, Fall 2008.

Chicago Jewish Star
Review of Jennie Lebel, *The Mufti of Jerusalem: Haj-Amin el-Husseini and National Socialism*, April 18, 2008.
"Obama's European Constituency," August 15, 2008.
"Obama Demotes the Jews," April 24, 2009.
Review of Stephen Norwood, *The Third Reich in the Ivory Tower*, November 20, 2009.
Review of Anthony Julius, *Trials of the Diaspora*, April 30, 2010.
Review of Howard Jacobson, *The Finkler Question*, December 10, 2010.
Review of Cynthia Ozick, *Foreign Bodies*, January 14, 2011.
Review of Jacob Glatstein, *The Glatstein Chronicles*, April 15, 2011.
Review of Alvin Rosenfeld, *The End of the Holocaust*, June 10, 2011.
Review of Jerold Auerbach, *Brothers at War*, July 29, 2011.
Review of Harold Bloom, *The Shadow of a Great Rock*, December 9, 2011.

Jerusalem Post
"The Academic Boycott of Israel: Back to 1933?" January 2003.
"Professors for Suicide Bombing," January 2003.

Introduction

The only visible result [of the Dreyfus Affair] was that it gave birth to the Zionist movement—the only political answer Jews have ever found to antisemitism and the only ideology in which they have ever taken seriously a hostility that would place them in the center of world events.
—Hannah Arendt, *Antisemitism* (1951)

The subject of all this talk is, ultimately, survival—the survival of the decent society, created in Israel within a few decades.... The Jews, because they are Jews, have never been able to take the right to live as a natural right.
—Saul Bellow, *To Jerusalem and Back* (1976)

By *The State of the Jews* I mean the Land of Israel, the condition of the people Israel, and the relation between the two. That relation is a very old subject, defined in its most dramatic and accusatory form by Moses himself: "And Moses said unto the children of Gad and the children of Reuben: 'Shall your brethren go to the war, and shall ye sit here?'" (Numbers 32:6). When European Jews were being persecuted and murdered by the Nazis and their collaborators during the years 1933–1945, what, if anything, were their brethren sitting far from that war doing to save them? That should have been the besetting question for Jewish intellectuals during Hitler's war against the Jews, but for most of them it was not. Moses' question should be the pressing one for Diaspora Jewry today, when the international noose grows ever tighter about Israel's throat. But is it?

Long after World War II had ended, William Phillips (born William Litvinsky), cofounder of *Partisan Review* with Philip Rahv (born Ivan Greenbaum), recalled that Irving Howe (born Irving Horenstein), the most astute political mind among the New York Intellectuals (and the one who had made the gravest political mistakes about World

War II itself), "was haunted by the question of why our intellectual community... had paid so little attention to the Holocaust in the early 1940s.... He asked me why we had written and talked so little about the Holocaust at the time it was taking place." One may, for example, search the pages of *Partisan Review* from its founding in 1937 through the summer of 1939 without finding a single mention of Hitler or Nazism. When Howe was working on his autobiographical *A Margin of Hope*, he looked through the old issues of his own journal *Labor Action* to see how, or indeed whether, he and his socialist comrades had responded to the Holocaust. But he found the experience painful, and concluded that the Trotskyists, including himself, were only the best of a bad lot of leftist sects, people who had been disabled by their virtues. He told Phillips that this inattention to the destruction of European Jewry was "a serious instance of moral failure on our part."[1]

Not all American-Jewish intellectuals had been guilty of this moral failure. Marie Syrkin, the title of whose 1980 book I have borrowed for the present volume, belonged to what her biographer Carole Kessner has called "The 'Other' New York Jewish Intellectuals."[2] By that she meant that Syrkin, along with such figures as Hayim Greenberg, Maurice Samuel, and Ben Halpern, and in sharp contrast to the far more celebrated (now as then) Howe, Lionel Trilling, and Saul Bellow, paid attention to what was happening to the Jews of Europe and also of Palestine during the late thirties and forties, "fostered a real sense of community with the Jewish world in those troubled times."[3] and asked what they could do besides "sitting here."

Syrkin's *The State of the Jews* alluded simultaneously to the polity called Israel, and to the condition of Jews in the Diaspora. Its guiding premise was that the Jews may be a dispersed people, but they are not a dismembered one. Syrkin (like her father Nachman Syrkin) was a great figure in the Labor Zionist movement and close friend of Golda Meir. She was a talented essayist and poet, and a prescient observer of the dark forces of European antisemitism in the Hitler era. She was one of the first people to recognize that Hitler's chief war aim was the destruction of European Jewry and its civilization, and to say so—in the pages of the Labor Zionist monthly *Jewish Frontier* in November 1942. (She worked there for thirty-five years without any pay.) Writing with the clarity that could come only from courage, and spurning the gullible *disbelief* misnamed "common sense," she (and coeditor Hayim Greenberg) wrote: "In the occupied countries of Europe a policy is now being put into effect whose avowed object is the extermination of a whole people. It is a policy of systematic murder of innocent civilians which in its ferocity, its dimensions and its organization is unique in the history of mankind.... We print this somber record to acquaint the free world with these facts and to call on the governments of the Allied Nations to do whatever may be done to prevent the fulfillment of the horror that broods over the blood-engulfed continent of Europe."

That call, as everybody now knows, was not heeded. But if there was no doubt about the ignominious role of America and the other democracies during the war against the Jews, just what did the Jews far from the field of conflict do to prevent the complete destruction of European Jewish civilization? What did the Zionists do? Syrkin's colleague Hayim Greenberg denounced American Jewry in a *Jewish Frontier* article of February 1943 titled "Bankrupt," in which he attacked every Jewish organization and party, from the Zionist American Jewish Congress to the American Jewish Committee, from Jabotinsky Revisionists to the Leftist Bund, for failure to unite in a common program. "Never before in history have we displayed such shamefully strong nerves as we do now in the days of our greatest catastrophe..." Yet, Greenberg himself confessed helplessness: "If it is still possible to do anything then I do not know who should do it and how it should be done. I only know that we are—all five million of us, with all our organizations and committees and leaders—politically and morally bankrupt."[4]

Syrkin did not share Greenberg's fury at the Jewish organizations. She believed, perhaps mistakenly, that American-Jewish political activism on behalf of European Jewry would have made Roosevelt even less inclined to attempt their rescue than he already was. But in the postwar era she unleashed her anger at other Jews—Hannah Arendt in particular for her *New Yorker* reports on the Eichmann Trial (permeated by "blinding animus" toward Israel and "vast ignorance"[5]) and the New York intellectuals in general for their appalling indifference to "all that has so recently been endured and achieved." Events of biblical magnitude had occurred within a single decade: a few years after the destruction of European Jewry, the Jewish people had created the state of Israel. This was a sequence of events that has been called "a more hopeful augury than the dove's reappearance to Noah with an olive leaf after the flood."[6] Yet, American-Jewish intellectuals, Syrkin charged in 1960, "keep drawing further away from the forces which shaped them and from identification with a Jewish future...."[7]

The moral failure of ignoring the Holocaust was now compounded by a related failure: having averted their eyes from the destruction of European Jewry, they now looked away from one of the most impressive assertions of the will to live that a martyred people has ever made. No more damning comment on the continued inattention, indifference, immoral thoughtlessness—of the New York Jewish Intellectuals to the fate of the Jews can be found than that of Ruth Wisse: "Rather than exposing themselves to the storm, the New York intellectuals . . . spent the 1940's as a Jewish *arrière-garde*, sheltered by the conviction that they were serving a higher purpose. Only decades later did some of them suddenly discover the Jewish state, which had meanwhile transformed world politics and culture."[8] This too was in striking contrast to Syrkin and her circle, including Ludwig Lewisohn and Charles Reznikoff, who in the thirties and forties riveted their attention upon (and put their pens at the service of) the embattled Jews not only of Europe but also of Palestine. Their now far more famous contemporaries in the world of intellectual Jewry had been immersed in the twists and turns of literary modernism, in the fate of socialism in the USSR and the United States, and of course—perhaps most of all—in themselves, especially in their "alienation" not only from America but from Judaism, Jewishness, and Jews. Indeed, as Kessner observes, "they defined themselves Jewishly *through* their alienation from their Jewishness"[9] (just as their contemporary successors define themselves *through* their alienation from Israel).

Here again, just as he had done with respect to "inattention" to the Holocaust, the fiercely honest Howe confessed his malfeasance:

> I wasn't one of those who danced in the streets when Ben Gurion made his famous pronouncement that the Jews, like other peoples, now had a state of their own. I did feel an underglow of satisfaction, but my biases kept me from open joy. Old mistakes cling to the mind like pitch to skin . . . It took some time to realize that being happy about the establishment of Israel . . . didn't necessarily signify a conversion to Zionist ideology . . . And suppose a little Zionism *did* creep into one's heart?[10]

In one sense, the Trillings, Howes, and Rahvs were the (embarrassed) prototypes, if not exactly the progenitors, of the numerous "anti-Zionist" Jews discussed in many of the essays in this book.[11] But the "alienation" of which many New York Jewish intellectuals belatedly grew ashamed has now become the boast of the Tony Judts, Tony

Kushners, Noam Chomskys, Jacqueline Roses, and Judith Butlers. These are people who do not merely "sit here" while their brothers go to war. Some of them take the side of their brothers' enemies and proclaim cowardly treachery to be courage; others, more cautious and scholarly, discover that the Jewish state which most Europeans now blame for all the world's miseries (with the possible exception of global warming) should never have come into existence in the first place, and that "the [non-Zionist] roads not taken" would have brought (and may yet bring) a "new" Diaspora Golden Age. They are forever organizing kangaroo courts (called "academic conferences") on "Alternative Histories within and beyond Zionism"[12]; or else they are churning out articles or monographs or novels celebrating those roads not taken; or they are "public intellectuals" breathlessly recommending a one-state solution or a binational solution or a no-state solution or (this from the tone-deaf George Steiner) "a final solution."[13]

Their strategy is at once timely and timeless. At the very time that their liberal, progressive colleagues insist that the nation-state is itself obsolete and that Israel is its most pernicious example, these Jewish academicians excavate from relative obscurity long-dead Jewish thinkers (Hans Kohn, Simon Rawidowicz, and Mordechai Kaplan) who opposed Zionism altogether or opposed political Zionism (a Jewish state). Truly a wonderful coincidence! But in another sense these academics (often employed in Jewish Studies programs that came into existence largely because of Israel's victory in the Six Day War) are ahistorical and disdainful of time: they write as if there were no difference between Jewish opposition to a conjectural Jewish state seventy or eighty years ago and opposition to a living entity of almost six million souls facing constant siege by genocidal fanatics.

The Jewish "identity" of these deep thinkers rests almost entirely upon their repudiation of the Jewish state.[14] In 1942, a character named Yudka ("little Jew") in Haim Hazaz's famous Hebrew short story "The Sermon" says that "when a man can no longer be a Jew, he becomes a Zionist." But the unnatural progeny of the New York intellectuals embody a new, darker reality: "when a man can no longer be a Jew, he becomes an *anti*-Zionist." They have turned on its head the old slogan of assimilationism, which was "Be a Jew at home, but a man in the street." Their slogan is: "Be a man at home, but a Jew in public." By the time Howe and Trilling and Bellow came to recognize that their lack of concern with Jewish survival had indeed been a "moral failure," a new generation of Jewish intellectuals was already proclaiming it as a virtue entitling them to put on the long robes and long faces of biblical prophets. Their prodigious work in painting Israel black as Gehenna and the pit of hell has forced a small yet crucial revision of Orwell's famous pronouncement about moral obtuseness and the ignorance of the learned: "Some ideas are so stupid that only [Jewish] intellectuals could believe them."

What then is the ultimate meaning of this blindness of the visionaries? Saul Bellow, in a letter of 1987 to Cynthia Ozick, reflected on the failure of the New York Jewish intellectuals during the Holocaust:

> It's perfectly true that 'Jewish Writers in America'... missed what should have been for them the central event of their time, the destruction of European Jewry. I can't say how our responsibility can be assessed. We ... should have reckoned more fully, more deeply with it. Nobody in America seriously took this on and only a few Jews elsewhere (like Primo Levi) were able to comprehend it all. The Jews as a people reacted justly to it. So we have Israel, but in the matter of higher comprehension ... there were no minds *fit* to comprehend. And intellectuals[...] are trained to expect and demand from art what intellect is unable to do. All parties then are passing the buck and every honest conscience feels the disgrace of it. I was too busy becoming a novelist to take note of what was happening in the Forties.... or, like my pals of the *Partisan Review*, with modernism, Marxism, New Criticism, with Eliot, Yeats, Proust, etc.—with anything except the terrible events in Poland. Growing slowly aware of this unspeakable evasion I didn't even know how to begin to admit it into my inner life. Not a particle of this can be denied.[15]

For Bellow, the "moral failure" to heed the injunction to be your brother's keeper or (to change metaphors) to keep your own vineyard (instead of meddling, incompetently, with everybody else's) or—to shun metaphor altogether—to keep the Jews of Europe alive, was a disgrace, an "unspeakable evasion." His book of 1976, *To Jerusalem and Back*, demonstrated complete understanding that the real subject of all the rhetorical fireworks he witnessed during his stay in Israel was "survival," and all the allegations of anti-Zionist Jews like George Steiner that Zionism had drawn its inspiration from Prussian models nothing more than flatulent wind. Zionism, Bellow retorted, came into being not because Jews worshiped Germanic *Blut und Eisen* "but because they alone, amongst the peoples of the earth, had not established a natural right to exist unquestioned in the lands of their birth.

That right is still clearly not granted them, not even in the liberal West."[16] What even Bellow did not quite grasp was that a new generation of Jewish intellectuals would not only disavow their moral responsibility to preserve the state of the Jews, the last remaining center of Jewish civilization, but would lead the campaign to hoot it down, indeed to act as accessories before the fact to the genocidal aims of Iran and its allies and client states on Israel's borders. Irving Howe, who (as we have seen) was even more contrite than Bellow about his moral failure during the Holocaust, foresaw what was coming as early as 1970—the treachery of the younger generation of Jewish intellectuals, which for Howe was *literally* unspeakable:

> Jewish boys and girls, children of the generation that saw Auschwitz, hate democratic Israel and celebrate as 'revolutionary' the Egyptian dictatorship; . . . a few go so far as to collect money for Al Fatah, which pledges to take Tel Aviv. About this, I cannot say more; it is simply too painful.[17]

These "Jewish boys and girls" are by now, a great many of them, well-established figures in the journalistic and academic worlds, tigers of wrath who became tenured and heavily petted insurrectionaries warming themselves in endowed university chairs, or established columnists for the *New York Times* or *New York Review of Books*, or editors of the *New Yorker*—changed in almost every way except their hatred of "democratic Israel." They have succeeded in destroying the consensus that, just two decades ago, united virtually all Jews except fanatical ideologues of the far right and the far left: namely, that Israel, whose creation was one of the few redeeming elements of a century of blood and shame, must be helped and kept alive, that its survival is a necessity, and not for Jews alone. Winston Churchill, addressing the House of Commons in January 1949, declared:

> The coming into being of a Jewish state in Palestine is an event in world history to be viewed in the perspective, not of a generation or a century, but in the perspective of a thousand, two thousand or even three thousand years. That is a standard of temporal values or time-values which seems very much out of accord with the perpetual click-clack of our rapidly changing moods and of the age in which we live. This is an event in world history.[18]

A later British Prime Minister, Harold Macmillan, saw Israel's victory in the June 1967 war as confirmation of Churchill's recognition of the Jewish state's meaning for the nations, including the British nation. Asked by the *Saturday Review* in 1968 whether Great Britain should aspire to be like Athens or like Sweden, he rejected Athens because it lived on slavery and was overtaken by decay and death, and Sweden for reasons he felt it undignified to enumerate. He continued, as follows:

> No, the future I hope for Britain is more like that of Israel. In the time of Elizabeth we were only two million people, in the time of Marlborough only five or six million, in the time of Napoleon only ten million. The other day, while the world debated, Israel's three millions imposed their will on their enemies. They had what any great people need—resolution, courage, determination, pride. These are what really count in men and nations.[19]

My emphasis upon the role played by Jews in the war of ideas against the state of the Jews, the latest version of that "hostility" which, in Hannah Arendt's prescient formulation, continues to place them "in the center of world events," is not meant to scant the role played by non-Jews in this sordid enterprise. They receive their just deserts and are amply represented in this volume. The multitudinous ranks of British antisemites, for example, almost comprise a book within a book: they are discussed in "Britannia Waives the Rules: Antisemitism, English-Style," "Tom Paulin: Poetaster of Murder," "*Daniel Deronda*: 'The Zionist Fate in English Hands' and 'The Liberal Betrayal of the Jews,'" "The Antisemitism of Liberals: A Gentile's View," "Back to 1933: How the Academic Boycott of Israel Began," "Professors for Suicide Bombing: The Explosive Power of Boredom," and "Ashamed Jews: *The Finkler Question*." Neither do I ignore such Muslim collaborators with Hitler as Haj Amin el-Husseini or assorted American university professors and administrators who sympathized with the Third Reich. The forces now ranged against Israel also include, as does this book, the more diplomatic but far more important "demotion" of the Jews as well as the state of Israel and its leaders by Barack Hussein Obama, the most hostile American president Israel has had to face since its founding in 1948.

If the Jewish enemies of the Jewish state appear in this book to get disproportionate attention, it is for the same reason that Samuel Johnson likened women preachers to dogs walking on their hind legs: "It is not done well, but you are surprised to find it done at all." The analogy is, of course, inexact because the element of surprise is now

Introduction

(for those who judge by empirical evidence rather than moral logic) almost gone from Jewish vilification of the Jewish state. Indeed, nothing is more common than the uniquely Jewish combination of worn-out Bolshevist politics with public declarations that "I am Jewish, but I abhor Israel and Zionism." Or, for no extra charge, this version: "I am a Jewish descendant of Holocaust survivors/victims; I am sure that, were they still alive, they would abhor, as I do, Zionism and the state of Israel, which should never have come into existence . . ."

Notice again that, while lamenting the moral and intellectual failure of Jewish writers to face the Holocaust, Bellow observed that "The Jews as a people reacted justly to it. And so we have Israel . . ." So it would appear that, as Bellow had written elsewhere, "Maybe an unexamined life is not worth living. But a man's examined life can make him wish he was dead." Jewish intellectuals keep asking themselves "Why are we Jews?" "Who is a Jew anyway?" "What reason is there for us to remain Jews?" They do not generally ask whether there is any mandate in Jewish religion for their liberalism, or whether, without that liberalism, Jews would continue to think of themselves as Jews. But they do ask whether Israel should be the chief alternative to assimilation for those Jews who are nonreligious. They do complain that Zionism enables American Jews to postpone that inner reconsideration of "Jewishness" which the American condition requires. By contrast, the "Jews as a people" have not asked whether "working for Israel" established them as Jews, or whether their commitment to Israel's survival is contingent upon Israel's being more just and moral than every other nation that exists or ever existed. Unlike their intellectual betters, they have understood that survival precedes definition, that to be moral (or Jewish) you need to be alive. If that "postponement" of self-examination was an evasion, it was instinctively felt to be (unlike the one to which Bellow confessed) a worthy and an honorable one. And so it is throughout this book.

Notes

1. William Phillips, *A Partisan View* (New York: Stein and Day, 1983), 123. The Holocaust and also the prospect of a second Holocaust and the failure of Jewish intellectuals to confront both subjects are treated in essays in each of the three sections of this book. The Holocaust itself is dealt with in the portrait of Abba Kovner, commander of the Vilna Ghetto uprising, in the essays on Zsuzsanna Ozsvath's stunning memoir of the Holocaust in Hungary, in Jacob Glatstein's account of his return to Lublin before it became the killing center called Majdanek, and in the discussion of Cynthia

Ozick's novel, *Foreign Bodies*, set (in part) in Europe in the immediate aftermath of the Holocaust. The role of Israel-hating Jewish intellectuals in tightening the noose around the neck of the Jewish state is the burden of "Back to 1933: How the Academic Boycott of Israel Began," "Ashamed Jews: *The Finkler Question*," Ruth Wisse's study of the Jews' troubled relation to political power, and "The End of the Holocaust?"

2. Carole S. Kessner, *The "Other" New York Jewish Intellectuals* (New York: NYU Press, 1994).
3. Ibid.
4. Marie Syrkin, "What American Jews Did During the Holocaust," *Midstream* 84 (October 1982): 4. See, on the subject of the timid reluctance of American Jewish leaders to speak out during the Nazi era, Gulie Arad, *America, Its Jews, and the Rise of Nazism* (Bloomington: Indiana University Press, 2000).
5. Marie Syrkin, *The State of the Jews* (Washington, DC: New Republic Books, 1980), 196.
6. Ruth R. Wisse, *Jews and Power* (New York: Schocken Books, 2007), xiv.
7. "Have American Jews a Jewish Future?" in *State of the Jews*, 269.
8. Ruth R. Wisse, "The New York (Jewish) Intellectuals," *Commentary* 84 (November 1987): 36.
9. Kessner, *'Other' New York Jewish Intellectuals*, 3. (My italics)
10. *A Margin of Hope* (New York: Harcourt Brace, 1982), 276. The first issue of *Commentary*, in November 1945, stressed that the center of gravity of the Jewish world had shifted from Europe to America; the *yishuv* in Palestine was not mentioned. Neither Elliott Cohen nor anyone on his staff could speak Hebrew.
11. See, for example, "Britannia Waives the Rules," "Ashamed Jews," and "The New Mormons."
12. "Alternative Histories Within and Beyond Zionism," at the University of California, Santa Cruz, in March 2007. See Tammi Rossman-Benjamin, "The Academic Legitimization of Anti-Zionism and the Efforts to Combat It: A Case Study," in *Antisemitism on the Campus: Past & Present*, ed. Eunice G. Pollack (Boston, MA: Academic Studies Press, 2011), 393–413.
13. "Might the Christian West and Islam live more humanely, more at ease with themselves, if the Jewish problem were indeed 'resolved' (that *endlosung* or 'final solution')?"—George Steiner, *Errata: An Examined Life* (London: Weidenfeld and Nicolson, 1997), 52.
14. See, on this subject, Allan Arkush, "Roads Not Taken," *Jewish Review of Books* 6 (Summer 2011): 10–14.
15. *Saul Bellow: Letters*, ed. Benjamin Taylor (New York: Viking Penguin, 2010), 438–39.
16. *To Jerusalem and Back* (New York: The Viking Press, 1976), 26.
17. Irving Howe, "Political Terrorism: Hysteria on the Left," *New York Times Magazine*, April 12, 1970: 25–27, 124–28. On the continuities and also discontinuities between the New York Jewish intellectuals and contemporary Jewish leaders of the ideological war on Israel, see Alvin Rosenfeld, "Modern

Jewish Intellectual Failure: A Brief History," in *The Jewish Divide over Israel: Accusers and Defenders*, ed. Edward Alexander and Paul Bogdanor (New Brunswick, NJ: Transaction Publishers, 2006), 7–32.
18. Speech in the House of Commons, January 26, 1949.
19. *Saturday Review* 51 (1968): 26.

I
The Victorian Background

Dr. Arnold, Matthew Arnold, and John Stuart Mill

Dr. Thomas Arnold

Perhaps the Reverend Dr Arnold, Head Master of Rugby School near Birmingham, would be a proper person. He is one of the most enlightened and liberal of our clergy. . . . (John Stuart Mill, letter of December 6, 1831)[1]

On April 5, 1830, in his maiden speech to the House of Commons, Thomas Macaulay spoke eloquently in favor of Robert Grant's bill for the removal of Jewish disabilities. Alluding to but not actually naming, Nathan Rothschild (who had financed the Allied armies ranged against Napoleon), Macaulay noted that "as things now stand, a Jew may be the richest man in England. . . . The influence of a Jew may be of the first consequences in a war which shakes Europe to the centre," and yet the Jews have no legal right to vote or to sit in Parliament. "Three hundred years ago they had no legal right to the teeth in their heads."[2] If some members of the House thought it indecent of Macaulay to dredge up this nasty old business about King John extracting gold teeth from Jewish heads, certain opponents of Jewish emancipation found it still much the best policy. According to J. A. Froude (his biographer), Thomas Carlyle, standing in front of Rothschild's great house at Hyde Park Corner, exclaimed: "I do not mean that I want King John back again, but if you ask me which mode of treating these people to have been nearest to the will of the Almighty about them—to build them palaces like that, or to take The pincers for them, I declare for the pincers." Carlyle even fancied himself in the role of a Victorian King John, with Baron Rothschild at his mercy: "Now, Sir, the State requires some of these millions you have heaped together with your financing work. 'You won't? Very well'—and the speaker gave a twist with his wrist—'Now will you?'—and then another twist till the millions were yielded."[3]

Although Macaulay was a liberal, he did not speak for all liberals, some of whom stood much closer to Carlyle on the Jewish question. One of these was Thomas Arnold, the famous headmaster of Rugby and intellectual leader of the liberal or Broad Church branch of the Church of England. Arnold set himself against conservatism as the most dangerously revolutionary of principles: "there is nothing so unnatural and so convulsive to society as the strain to keep things fixed, when all the world is by the very law of its creation in eternal progress."[4] When John Henry Newman, leader of the Anglo-Catholic (or "High") branch of the Church of England, declared that liberalism was "the enemy," and that by liberalism he meant "the Antidogmatic Principle," Arnold was among the principal culprits he had in mind, particularly "some free views of Arnold about the Old Testament."[5]

But Arnold's preference of improvement to preservation and of free views to dogma drew up short where the Jews were concerned. He might excoriate the High Church party for having, throughout English history, opposed improving measures of any kind, but he shared with his Anglo-Catholic adversaries the conviction that Christianity must be the law of the land. In 1834 (a year after the Jewish Emancipation Bill had been passed by the Commons but rejected by the Lords), Arnold insisted that he "must petition against the Jew Bill" because it is based on "that low Jacobinical notion of citizenship, that a man acquires a right to it by the accident of his being littered *inter quatuor maria* [on the nation's soil] or because he pays taxes."[6] That indelicate word "littered" suggests that Arnold's opposition to Jewish emancipation was not purely doctrinal, but had a strong admixture of compulsive nastiness (or worse).

Arnold took the view that the world is made up of Christians and non-Christians; with the former, unity was essential, with the latter, impossible or, where possible, deplorable. Parliament should be thanked for having achieved the great liberal desideratum of doing away with distinctions between Christian and Christian. But "I would pray that distinctions be kept up between Christian and non-Christian." Jews, Arnold argued, had no claim whatever to political rights because "the Jews are strangers in England, and have no more claim to legislate for it, than a lodger has to share with the landlord in the management of his house . . . England is the land of Englishmen, not of Jews . . . my German friends agree with me."[7]

The only way in which Jews could claim English citizenship was by becoming Christians. "They . . . have no claim to become citizens but by conforming to our moral law, which is the Gospel." Arnold even speculated about deporting the Jews from England, "to a land where they might live by themselves Independent." Indeed, he would even feel morally obligated to make a financial contribution to the costs of deportation.[8] If the Jews were to be accorded citizenship, Arnold feared, they might one day become magistrates or judges, an appalling prospect.

Since Arnold's hostility to Jews was obsessive and irrational, not merely doctrinal, it could burst forth in the most unlikely places. In a letter of May 9, 1836, for example, Arnold appears to be discussing the relative importance of scientific and moral subjects in education, one of his favorite hobby-horses. "Rather than have [physical science] the principal thing in my son's mind, I would gladly have him think that the sun went round the earth, and that the stars were so many spangles set in the bright blue firmament." So far, so good, especially since Arnold here sounds a note that will be played, with many embellishments and variations, by his son Matthew. But by the next sentence the eternal enemy has crossed and disturbed his field of vision. "Surely the one thing needful for a Christian and an Englishman to study is Christian and moral and political philosophy, and then we should see our way a little more clearly without falling into Judaism or Toryism, or Jacobinism or any other ism whatever."[9]

Insofar as it can be rationally defined, what Arnold means by "Judaism" in such passages is the High Church party of John Henry Newman and Edward B. Pusey. Of all the abusive epithets Arnold hurled at his Anglo-Catholic enemies—"the Oxford Malignants," "White Jacobins," Romanizers, the most spiteful and (in his view) damning was "formalist, Judaizing fanatics."[10] Arnold saw in "the Jews and Judaizers of the New Testament" the forerunners of the High Churchmen of Oxford.[11] (One reason why Arnold took up the defense of the appointment of Renn Dickson Hampden to the Regius Professorship of Divinity at Oxford in 1836 was that Conservatives [including the High Church party] objected to Hampden's support for the abolition of religious tests for admission to Oxford. Two years later, Arnold would insist on the religious test for Jews at London University. Needless to say, he failed to see any irony or contradiction in his position.) When Arnold beheld

17

the Oxford high churchmen contending for the apostolic succession or sacerdotal authority, his mind's eye was riveted upon "the zealots of circumcision and the ceremonies of the law." It was in the Jewish "enemies and revilers" of Jesus, "and in these alone," that the Oxford "conspirators" found their perfect prototype. But the Jews serve not merely as polemical counters with which Arnold can taint the Christian purity of the High Church critics of his friend Hampden. His venom against Judaism itself bursts forth more than once in his essay. "The poisonous plant of Judaism was cut down or withered away; but the root was left in the ground; and thus, when its season returned, it sprung up again, and is now growing rankly."[12] (So insistent was Arnold in designating the High Church party as Jewish that there must have been more than a little rebelliousness or filial impiety in his son Matthew's later [indeed, after his father was dead] insistence that the puritan nonconformist dissenters, the polar opposites of the Oxford Party, were "Hebraizers.")

Arnold's unswerving conviction that, as he wrote in April 1837, "'Religion,' in the king's mouth, can mean only Christianity," was central to his idea of education and its establishments. When he found that he could not turn the Society for the Diffusion of Useful Knowledge (an organization formed in 1827 whose executive committee included such militant secularists as James Mill) into a Christian organization, he abandoned it. Then, as a member of the first senate of the newly chartered London University, Arnold found himself up against "fierce" opposition to his insistence on examining all students in the New Testament. He had been a supporter of the new university in large part because (unlike Oxford and Cambridge) it was to be open to all Christians, including Dissenters, "which in common speech does not mean, I think, Dissenters from Christianity." But he soon found that "every single member of the Senate except myself was convinced of the necessity, according to the Charter, of giving the Jews Degrees."[13]

A university, in Arnold's view, can aid the cause of general education only if it has a Christian character.[14] This means, among other things, that all students must be examined in the New Testament, for Christianity is no mere branch of knowledge but its very basis. When he tried to imagine examining a Jewish student in a sacred history "of which he would not admit a single fact," or tried to imagine having to abstain "from calling our Lord by any other name than Jesus" (because for the Jews, of course, Jesus was not "the Christ"), he rebelled. Who would be served by ripping out the core of education? "Are we really for the sake of a few Jews . . . who may like to have a Degree in Arts to destroy our only chance of our being even either useful or respected as an Institution of national education?. . . . It would be the first time that education in England was avowedly unchristianized for the sake of accommodating Jews. . . ."[15] Finding himself the sole member of the London University senate opposed to giving Jews degrees (and exempting them from New Testament examinations), Arnold resigned his position.

The objections to Arnold's position hardly need to be emphasized. His stress on the Christian character of English education and citizenship was inseparable from a racial idea of English character and an obvious distaste for Jewish people. It was clear (even to Arnold himself) that it was not only "a few Jews" (and "one or two Muslims") who would be excluded from his "non-sectarian" Christian university, but also a large and growing number of home-grown English unbelievers, especially those who had been touched by the criticism of the New Testament which tended to support "Jewish" views of Jesus as an observant Jew who neither was nor aspired to be a Messiah, especially in the sense Christians give to that term.

To English Jews, Thomas Arnold must have seemed a Hesperidean dragon trying to preserve what Tennyson called, in a poem of 1832, "the treasure/Of the wisdom of the West" from barbarous intruders, a bigot denying them full rights of academic citizenship. Yet one must note, if only in passing, that Arnold's exclusiveness rested on a grasp, albeit a partial one, of a truth that Jews eager for "emancipation" and "enlightenment" tended to miss altogether: namely, that when you study western history and literature, you are studying not just revolutions and poems, but the mind of western Christianity. Arnold knew, far better than the Jews did, that anyone who studied English history and literature, even at a nonsectarian London University, must perforce submit to a whole world of assumptions that were alien and presumably offensive to him: namely, that the "Jewish God" is a fierce, tribal deity who was supplanted in the progressive movement of the world by the gentle and "universal" Christian one; that the Jews had rejected Jesus' more "spiritual" teaching because they were attached to the old law and could not see that his message of love and forgiveness had made it obsolete; that although their Bible had foretold his birth, death, resurrection, etc., they rejected him as their Messiah because they found his claim to divinity blasphemous and condemned him to death; that what Jews call Torah is an "Old Testament" that had to be edited, interpreted, complemented, fulfilled, superseded, by the New Testament; and that Jewish collective existence since the inception of Christianity was a prolonged illustration of the spiritual blindness derided in the Gospels.[16]

Even without the compulsory examination in New Testament that Arnold so much insisted on, the education Jews would receive at London University exacted a price for national citizenship in the form of a distortion and narrowing of Jewish self-definition. Paradoxically, Jews might have been better off, as Jews, had the exclusionist Arnold and not his more liberal and secular opponents won the struggle over university admissions. Nearly a century later, Morris Joseph, addressing Jewish students at Cambridge, pointed to the snares that awaited Jewish undergraduates at the great English universities. These included not only what seemed (especially to those—an ever-growing multitude—ignorant of traditional Jewish learning, from the *siddur* [prayer book] to the Talmud) to be a wider learning and culture than that of their ancestors, but even the physical surroundings. Gothic architecture, as Pugin had argued in the 1830s, was essentially Christian architecture, even if the buildings were not (and many of them were) chapels. The Jewish student, said Joseph, "is set in an intensely Christian atmosphere, all the more potent because of the historic associations that go to the making of it; and the simple services of the plain brick structure that does duty for a synagogue present a glaring contrast to the impressive form and environment of the public worship of the University churches."[17]

The risks that university life entailed for Jews may be measured in part by the experience of those whom Dr. Arnold did not consider "dissenters from Christianity" and to whom churches and chapels, Gothic and otherwise, were not alien. Todd Endelman has pointed out that Nonconformists, that is, Protestants who did not belong to the Established Church, had experiences at universities during the Victorian period that were similar to that of the Jews. They often became Anglicans in order to overcome their sense of being outsiders and to embrace the culture (and career possibilities) of the dominant majority. Catholics, also outside the Established Church, would have faced similar dangers at the English universities, but their church, drawing upon its greater fund of worldly experience and political wisdom, showed no interest in having the universities opened to their young people. Indeed, a writer in the Catholic journal *The Rambler* wrote in 1851: "Thanks be to God, the Protestantism of England has shut out Catholics from Oxford, and with few exceptions indeed, from Cambridge also."[18]

Matthew Arnold

> In spite of all which in them and in their character is unattractive, nay, repellent,—in spite of their shortcomings even in righteousness itself and their insignificance in everything else,—this petty, unsuccessful, unamiable people, without politics, without science, without art, without charm, deserve their great place in the world's regard, and are likely to have it more, as the world goes on, rather than less.[19]

The question of how important and advantageous it is to belong to an established church, wedded to the state, and to be absorbed by its institutions was a central concern of Dr. Arnold's son, the poet and critic Matthew Arnold. "In my notions about the State," he wrote to his mother in February 1864, "I am quite papa's son, and his continuator."[20] Continuator perhaps he was, but with respect to the Jews, in a far more discriminating, complicated, and indeed attractive form.

In his introduction to *Culture and Anarchy* (1869), Arnold, by way of explaining his opposition to proposals by the religious Nonconformists and Liberal statesmen to disestablish the Church of Ireland (that is, the Church of England in Ireland), argues that the great figures of European civilization have all belonged to or been trained in Establishments. The seminal figures of the English Puritan tradition that wars against the Established Church were, Arnold insists, themselves trained within its pale, and he cites as examples Milton, Baxter, and Wesley. He grants but two exceptions to his iron rule, two religious disciplines that "seem exempted, or comparatively exempted, from the operation of the law which appears to forbid the rearing, outside of national Churches, of men of the highest spiritual significance." These two are the Roman Catholic and the Jewish. But the contradiction is more apparent than real, for these "rest on Establishments, which, though not indeed national, are cosmopolitan." Catholics and Jews do not, therefore, lose in their intellectual culture what English Nonconformists do by being outside the Established Church, but the States of which they are citizens lose something because the conditions in which Jews and Catholics are reared make them, in a spiritual sense, less than full citizens. (Unlike his father, Matthew Arnold never suggests denying the Jews English citizenship.)

For Arnold, religious establishments are the existential realizations of the idea of integration into the main stream of human life, than which nothing is more important for a human being. Christianity, he believed, at its inception uprooted its various adherents from their foundations in Jewish and Greek culture, and would have lost itself in "a multitude of hole-and-corner churches like the churches of English Nonconformity" if Constantine had not established it as the official religion of the Roman Empire in the fourth century. From that act of establishment (which for John Stuart Mill marked the decline of Christianity) flowed "the main stream of human life" in Europe; to have been cut off or to have separated oneself from that mainstream is to have been irreparably damaged.

To illustrate his meaning, Arnold invokes the speculations of a French Protestant theologian named Albert Réville, who had very "advanced" views for his age.

> M. Albert Réville, whose religious writings are always interesting, says that the conception which cultivated and philosophical Jews now entertain of Christianity and its Founder, is probably destined to become the conception which Christians themselves will entertain. . . . Now, even if this were true, it would still have been better for a man, during the last eighteen hundred years, to have been a Christian and a member of one of the great Christian communions, than to have been a Jew because the being in contact with the mainstream of human life is of more moment for a man's total spiritual growth, and for his bringing to perfection the gifts committed to him . . . than any speculative opinion which he may hold or think he holds.[21]

For Arnold, 1,800 years of Jewish existence, the collective life of millions of people bound by covenant to the living God and by history to one another, was nothing more than "speculative opinion." Had Arnold forgotten that people do not live and die for speculative opinions? They live and die for realities. Although Arnold had (as would become evident from his religious books of the following decade) already discarded several of the central doctrines of Christianity, he still in 1869 adhered to a secularized and softened version of the Christian myth. According to this myth, the Jews, because they had rejected and killed Christ, were in turn rejected as God's chosen people, who in future would be drawn from the Gentiles. The Jews would be preserved but in misery. In one sense, Arnold is so far removed from the old Christian myth that he does not even feel it necessary to spring to the defense of the Christian doctrine of Jesus' Messiahship. Yet his insistence that Jewish existence is mere "speculative opinion," and that Jewish life since the appearance of Jesus has been a diversionary ripple leading its adherents away from the "main stream" into dusty irrelevance shows the tenacity of the myth. Judaism is no longer presented, as traditionally it was in Christian iconography, as blind to the truth, but as blind to the future course of civilization's development, "inveterate," as Arnold would say in a later work, "in its fated isolation."[22]

But there is another side to all this. Arnold had far more experience of Jews and Jewish convictions than his father did. His position as an inspector of schools frequently brought him to Jewish institutions such as the Jews' Free School in London, and he treated them with sympathy and respect.[23] He came to know several members of the Rothschild family, and was a particular friend (some believe more than a friend) of Lady Louisa de Rothschild. He claimed, in a letter of December 23, 1871, to have made enough progress in Hebrew to want to acquire a Hebrew Bible.[24] He read such ex-Jews as Benedict Spinoza and Heinrich Heine with a sharp eye out for their "Jewish" characteristics, plausibly in the case of Heine (in an Oxford lecture of June 1863):

> No account of Heine is complete which does not notice the Jewish element in him. His race [Heine] treated with the same freedom with which he treated everything else, but he derived a great force from it. . . . He has excellently pointed out how in the sixteenth century there was a double renaissance—a Hellenic renaissance and a Hebrew renaissance—and how both have been great powers ever since. He himself had in him both the spirit of Greece and the spirit of Judaea . . . the Greek spirit by beauty, the Hebrew spirit by sublimity. By his perfection of literary form, by his love of clearness, by his love of beauty, Heine is Greek; by his intensity, by his untameableness, by his "longing which cannot be uttered," he is Hebrew.

Arnold went on to quote from Heine's *Hebrew Melodies* the poem about Yehuda Halevi now considered a central text of Zionist literature.[25] Although he celebrated Heine as a warrior against Philistinism (in its modern incarnation), Arnold also lamented a "want of moral balance" resulting (ironically) from his lack of what Arnold a few years later would famously define as "Hebraism."

Indeed, in the "Hebraism and Hellenism" chapter (IV) of *Culture and Anarchy*, Heine gets a slap on the wrist for his blind worship of

Hellenism and disparagement of Hebraism. This is less paradoxical than it at first seems because, as Milton Himmelfarb observed in a splendid essay, Arnold was not really much concerned with Jews and Judaism at all in *Culture and Anarchy*, but with the excesses (as he saw them) of English Puritanism. "Arnold was defining the spirit, as he understood it, of sectarian Protestantism in nineteenth-century England. His Hebraism keeps pointing to sectarian Protestant bibliolatry . . ."[26] Arnold knew that bibliolatry was not among the failings of the Jews.

Arnold was definitely concerned with Jews and Judaism in his encounter with Emanuel Deutsch. He met and read some of the work of Deutsch, known to him and other Victorians open to Jewish influences as "the Talmud man."[27] Arnold wrote to Lady de Rothschild in 1867 that "the abundance of Christian doctrine and dispositions present in Judaism toward the time of the Christian era, and such phenomena as Hillel's ownership of the Golden Rule, for instance—I knew already, from the writings of the Strasburg school . . . But the long extracts from the Talmud itself were quite fresh to me, and gave me huge satisfaction." He even surmised that the English people, from constitution and training, were far more likely to be brought to "a more philosophical conception of religion" through Judaism than through Hellenism.[28] This is one of the rare occasions on which Arnold proposed that English Protestantism was in greater need of leavening by Hebraism of a sort than by Hellenism—but one must remember that his correspondent was a Jew, even if one whose intellectual culture was not much above the (modest) level of most English Jews of the upper class.

Arnold's attitude toward the prospect of bringing Jews into the educational system while respecting the integrity of their religious culture stands in sharp contrast to that of his father. He praised the French system of education, for example, because it accepted, without necessarily encouraging, religious division. The spirit of sect, Arnold observed, was noxious, but less noxious than the spirit of religious persecution. The French, with a population of thirty-six million, recognized three, and three only, religious divisions for educational purposes: "Protestantism, Roman Catholicism, Judaism." The English system, despite England's smaller population of twenty-one million, recognized no less than seven religious divisions—six Protestant, one Catholic, none Jewish.[29] Matthew Arnold's ideas about the place of Jews in higher education also diverged sharply from his father's.

Again, he praised France as "a model of reason and justice" because, unlike Prussia, which, "keeping in view the *christlichen Grundcharakter* of itself and its public schools," barred Jews from the office of public teacher. "In a country where the Jews are so many and so able, this exclusion makes itself felt." As for the universities in Prussia, Jews could hold professorships in medicine and mathematics, but not in history or philosophy. "France," he concluded "is in all these matters a model of reason and justice, and as much ahead of Germany as she is of England." He applauded the French for leaving religious instruction in their schools to clergymen and "ask[ing] no other instructor any questions about his religious persuasion."[30]

But the most striking example of Arnold's breaking away from the prejudices of his father (and indeed of his class) with respect to Jews and Judaism is to be found in his religious books of the seventies. *St. Paul and Protestantism* (1871) treats "the great mediaeval Jewish school of Biblical critics" with a respect rare among Victorian Christian writers, mainly because they provide support for Arnold's view that the Bible is a work of literature and not of (exploded) science. The medieval Jewish commentators enunciated "the admirable maxim," forgotten for centuries by virtually all Christian exegetes, that "The Law speaks with the tongue of the children of men,—a maxim which is the very foundation of all sane Biblical criticism."[31]

In Arnold's next book, *Literature and Dogma: An Essay Towards A Better Appreciation of the Bible*, first published in 1873, "Jewish" concerns play a central role. In this formidable work, Arnold tried to convince literate Englishmen that the main prerequisite for understanding the Bible was tact, a talent of literary critics rather than of "scientific" theologians. His declared aim was to demonstrate only the effect of their religion upon the language of the Jews who were the authors and protagonists of the Hebrew Bible. But in pursuit of this aim he spread his net much wider and at least came close to allowing that Jews had (and have) a religious culture and inner world of their own.

He begins, to be sure, with a linguistic matter, namely, the Hebrew people's mode of naming God. The name they used, Arnold insists, was "The Eternal" and not Jehovah, "which gives us the notion of a mere mythological deity, or by a wrong translation, Lord, which gives us the notion of a magnified and non-natural man" (182). What they meant by this name, Arnold argues, was "the Eternal righteous, who loveth righteousness." Arnold thus makes the (Biblical) Jews into a foil for certain

"Archbishops of York," who import into the Bible extraneous notions of moral philosophy when they expand "the Eternal" into "the Eternal cause." No, the Jews "had dwelt upon the thought of conduct, and of right and wrong, until the not ourselves, which is in us and all around us, became to them . . . a power which makes for righteousness . . . and is therefore called The Eternal."[32]

Arnold's crucial encounter with Biblical Judaism comes in the fifth part of Chapter I. Here he argues that literary tact and a fair mind will show that all the standard objections to the Hebrew people of the Bible are shallow and mistaken. First, he rebuts those who ask why, if the Hebrews of the Bible really had the unique sense for righteousness that Arnold ascribes to them, "does it not equally distinguish the Jews now?" (196). Using the concessive rhetoric that was a hallmark of his argumentative prose, Arnold allows that "a change of circumstances may change a people's character," but he then asks whether "the modern Jews lost more of what distinguished their ancestors, or even so much, as the modern Greeks of what distinguished theirs?" To those who claim that the Jews' God was not in fact the eternal power that makes for righteousness but merely their tribal God, Arnold replies with a question: "How, then, comes their literature to be full of such things as 'Shew me thy ways, O Eternal, and teach me thy paths; let integrity and uprightness preserve me, for I put my trust in thee! if I incline unto wickedness with my heart, the Eternal will not hear me.'" To Christian polemicists who say that the Jews' divine law was a merely traditional and external code, kept in superstitious dread of the almighty, Arnold retorts by citing yet more proof texts: "Teach me thy statutes, Teach me thy way, Show thou me the way that I shall walk in, Open Mine eyes, Make me to understand wisdom secretly!"[33] Why, if the law already stood, stark and written before their eyes, would they repeatedly say such things?

True, Arnold does not (how could he and still remain a Christian?) entirely abandon the spirit of Christian triumphalism over the "old" law. Although genuine, the Jewish conception of righteousness was, he says, often "narrow" until the prophets brought into play the more profound elements of personal religion such as conscience. In fact, says Arnold, "Every time that the words contrition or humility drop from the lips of prophet or psalmist, Christianity appears."[34] This may remind us of Arnold's contemporary John Ruskin, an intensely Protestant figure, trying to explain his attraction to architectural ornaments on medieval

Catholic buildings: he calls them budding Protestantism, trying to burst forth from the constricting hold of Rome—thereby licentiously applying a religious label he likes to a style of art that he likes.

But for the most part Arnold's discussion is a defense lawyer's brief for the accused, indeed accursed, Jews. He insists that they had a unique sense of the natural and necessary link between conduct and happiness, and will therefore always be the signal embodiment of this endowment of human nature. Arnold's ringing declaration is one of the most amazing things in the whole body of his voluminous writings: "as long as the world lasts, all who want to make progress in righteousness will come to Israel for inspiration, as to the people who have had the sense for righteousness most glowing and strongest...."[35]

Perhaps Arnold is only referring to the Jews of the Bible here, but there are also hints that—whether rightly or wrongly—he was intrigued by the possibility that there was more than a thread of continuity between those Jews of long ago and the politically debased Jews whom his father wanted to harry out of the country. Samuel Taylor Coleridge wrote in his *Table-Talk* entry for August 14, 1833: "The two images farthest removed from each other which can be comprehended under one term, are, I think, Isaiah—'Hear, O heavens, and give ear, O earth!'—and Levi of Holywell Street—'Old Clothes!'—both of them Jews, you'll observe." Coleridge's conclusion, rendered in a burst of Latin, was *immane quantum discrepant* (how great is the difference). Arnold, to his credit, could never be quite sure that it was, and he was more likely than Coleridge to know that Levi could read Isaiah in the original.

John Stuart Mill

In the second chapter of his autobiography, shortly after describing how his father taught him to believe that the *ne plus ultra* of wickedness was embodied in the creed of Christianity as commonly understood, John Stuart Mill declared that he was "one of the very few examples, in this country, of one who has, not thrown off religious belief, but never had it" and grew up with a wholly negative view of it. Seeking to set himself apart from all those Victorians who looked back nostalgically to the lost Christianity of their youth, Mill said that "I looked upon the modern exactly as I did upon the ancient religion, as something which in no way concerned me. It did not seem to me more strange that English people should believe what I did not, than that the men whom I read of in Herodotus should have done so."[36]

In fact, Mill (writing in the 1850s) overstates the extent of his separation from his Christian contemporaries. The posthumous publication (in 1874) of the *Three Essays on Religion,* two written between 1850 and 1858, the third between 1868 and 1870, revealed—to the consternation of many of his agnostic followers—that Mill was by no means the dogmatically secular "saint of rationalism" that many had supposed him to be. Neither had he been, in earlier years, as free of the premises (and prejudices) of Christendom as he later declared himself to be. This is evident in his (now astonishing) statement in the *Westminster Review* of July 1824, when he was supposed to be a devout Benthamite rationalist, that "Christianity is the only true faith in our opinion," in his remarkably sympathetic letters to the *Morning Chronicle* in 1842 about the Tractarians, in his 1840 essay on Coleridge, and even in the assumptions that pervade *On Liberty* about the superiority of "the West" to "the East." But nowhere is the unacknowledged Christian substratum of Mill's thought more apparent than in his remarks about Judaism and Jews.

Most of his allusions to the Jews participate in the common Christian practice of self-congratulatory observations on the ethical inferiority of Jewish biblical practices to those of Christianity. In *Utilitarianism* (1861), for example, Mill expresses the cliché disapproval of the Jews' (supposed) commitment to the retaliatory morality of "an eye for an eye." "No rule on this subject recommends itself so strongly to the primitive and spontaneous sentiment of justice, as the *lex talionis*, an eye for an eye and a tooth for a tooth. Though this principle of the Jewish and of the Mahomedan law has been generally abandoned in Europe as a practical maxim, there is, I suspect, in most minds, a secret hankering after it. . . ."[37] Mill's words show no awareness that (as Numbers 35:31 indicates) this law of retaliation was carried out literally only in the case of murder, and they contain only the faintest hint that in actuality corporal punishment played a far larger role among the Christians than among the Jews of Europe. It goes without saying that Mill neglects to mention that even for Jews in ancient times "eye for an eye" meant, for physical injuries that were not fatal, a monetary payment rather than a literally retaliatory one, i.e., was a step forward not backward in moral history.

Invariably, Mill assumes Christianity—even if (as *On Liberty* argues) it falls short of his own "secular" ethical ideals—to be the highest form of religion, the culmination of a long evolutionary process in which

Judaism is (at best) a stepping-stone to higher things. Christianity is always regarded by Mill (as by the ministers of Christianity whom he so often scorned) as the ultimate development of "Monotheism." Moreover, he insists, whenever the topic arises, that the reception of Hebrew monotheism by Gentiles "was only rendered possible by the slow preparation which the human mind had undergone from the philosophers" (CW, X, 274–75).

So firmly fixed in Mill's mind was the familiar Christian dogma that Christianity is a more fully realized and "developed" form of Judaism that when it happened upon incontrovertible evidence to the contrary he ignored it or relegated it to a bashful footnote. For example—in a passage in *Three Essays on Religion* so optimistic that if it had been written by a lesser eminence one would call it obtuse—Mill argues that the greatest moral truths of the past, of "the best and foremost portion of our species" (i.e., West Europeans) are so deeply imbedded in the intellect and feelings of all good people that there is no danger of their being forgotten or ceasing to work on the human conscience; such a danger "may be pronounced, once for all, impossible." In the course of this sanguine argument, Mill cites as illustrative of the highest moral goodness the precept in the gospel of John (13:34): "The 'new' commandment to love one another." But here Mill's intellectual conscience and better than average knowledge of the Bible obliged him to add, albeit in a footnote: "Not, however, a new commandment. In justice to the great Hebrew lawgiver, it should always be remembered that the precept, to love thy neighbour as thyself, already existed in the Pentateuch; and [he feels compelled to add] very surprising it is to find it there" [Leviticus, 19:18]. Given Mill's prejudices, very surprising indeed. Needless to add that, if Mill were of a mind to look for them, there are scores of such "surprises," but an anthology of them would throw a monkey wrench into the argument for relentless progress from the Pentateuch to the Prophets to the New Testament (CW, X, 416). One finds something similar in *The Subjection of Women*, where Mill commends the Stoics for being the first to incorporate in their ethical system the moral obligations to slaves—"the first (except so far as the Jewish law constitutes an exception)" (CW, XXI, 266).

In his essay "The Utility of Religion," Mill implies that the Jews were ethically inferior not only to the Christians who succeeded to their inheritance but even to the Romans who bested them in combat. In order to buttress his assertion that religious sanctions not backed by the sanctions of public opinion have very rarely had much influence, Mill invokes the history of the Jews. "If ever any people were taught that they were under a divine government, and that unfaithfulness to their religion and law would be visited from above with temporal chastisement, the Jews were so. Yet their history was a mere succession of lapses into Paganism. Their prophets and historians . . . never ceased to complain that their countrymen turned a deaf ear to their vaticinations; and hence, with the faith they held in a divine government operating by temporal penalties, they could not fail to anticipate . . . *la culbute générale*; an expectation which, luckily for the credit of their prophetic powers, was fulfilled . . ." (CW, X, 412).

Thus Mill reads the fact that the prophetic voices of Israel blamed the defeat and exile of their people not upon their enemies or upon a God who had proved to be ineffectual, but upon themselves, as a sign that the Jews were morally inferior to other peoples of the ancient Near East who also suffered defeat and exile at the hands of their enemies but blamed their misfortunes either upon those enemies or upon the inadequacy of their national gods. Since Mill, once again operating on the same premises that his Christian neighbors accepted unquestioningly, did not acknowledge that Judaism continued to exist and develop after the arrival of Christianity, he never asks what should be the obvious question: why did the Jews and Judaism survive in exile when other peoples of the ancient Near East who suffered a similar fate disappeared? Had Mill ever encountered a Hittite or a Girgashite or a Jebusite on his daily walks to and from work at the East India Company? Probably not—but in any case the fact did not prompt him to ask whether the Jews' habit of accepting responsibility for what had befallen them might not explain why they, unlike their fellows in misfortune, remained loyal to their God even after they had been punished for their sins by being sent into exile. Neither does he see that the real drama inherent in prophetic censoriousness of a wayward people lies not in its threat of divine punishment of their unfaithfulness to religion and religious law. Rather, it resides in the paradox of chosenness itself: "You only have I known among all the families of the earth; therefore, I will visit upon you all your iniquities" (Amos 3:2).

Mill makes the naive assumption that prophetic condemnation of Jewish misbehavior means little more than that the Jews behaved very badly indeed. When there is scant historical evidence of such misbehavior, Mill simply takes it for granted and relies on surmise—as in the case of the law of the sabbatical year in Leviticus. "By the Jewish law property in immovables was only a temporary concession; on the Sabbatical year it returned to the common stock to be redistributed; though we may surmise that in the historical times of the Jewish state this rule may have been successfully evaded" (CW, V, 751, 254). (Although we might expect that a text which, like that outlining the laws of the sabbatical, culminates in the exhortation to "proclaim [in the jubilee year] liberty throughout the land unto all the inhabitants thereof," would strike a responsive chord in the author of *On Liberty*, it evokes no comment whatever from Mill.)

Neither does Mill here demonstrate a clear understanding of biblical prophecy itself. A biblical prophet is successful when his "predictions" are *not* fulfilled, i.e., when the people he exhorts to abandon their evil ways return to the Lord. (The book of Jonah is a classic example.) Mill does acknowledge that he is aware of this, but only in private correspondence. In a letter of November 4, 1863, for example, he says that there really is no such thing as biblical prophecy in the sense of prediction. "With regard to prophecies, in the sense attached to the word by modern theologians I do not believe that any such ever were made. The splendid religious & patriotic poetry of Isaiah, Jeremiah & others so far as it contains any predictions of future events contains only such as are made by Carlyle or anybody who argues that moral degeneracy in a people must lead to a catastrophe" (CW XV, 895–96).

At one point in his life Mill announced that he was revising his earlier, mistaken views about Jews and Judaism. In a letter of September 1842 to F. D. Maurice, he declares that he has recently been "cured of many of my crude notions about [the Jews]." This is an important document for understanding Mill's views on Jewish history, but less important than it would be if we knew more about what those views had been prior to 1842; the disease must have been virulent indeed if the views herein expressed represent a cure. The agent of Mill's cure was, he reports, "the writings of Salvador, a Jew by race and by national feeling, a Frenchman by birth, and a rationalist of the school of Paulus by opinion, whose book on the Mosaic institutions and on the Jewish people though somewhat ludicrous in its adaptation of Moses to a Voltairian public and in its attempts to prove that the Jews were Constitutional Liberals and Utilitarians is yet so full of strong facts and even arguments that it made a great impression on me when I read it a year or two ago" (CW, XVII, 1998).

The author in question is Joseph Salvador (1796–1873), who wrote *Jésus-Christ et sa doctrine: Histoire de la naissance de l'Église, de son organisation et de ses progrès pendant le premier siècle* (Paris, 1838) and *l'Histoire des Institutions de Moise et du peuple hebreu* (Paris, 1828). In fact, Salvador, being born of a Catholic mother, was only "half-Jewish" by "race" and could not have been Jewish at all according to Jewish religious law unless he had been converted, which he was not. Not only did Mill know nothing of the inner life of Jews, he was so ignorant of Judaism that he appears to have been unaware of the fact that Jewish identity is determined matrilineally. Salvador, who had a medical degree, was known for his scholarly interest in the history of religions. He applied the methods of historical criticism to the study of religion in general and to Jesus in particular, thus becoming a forerunner of German scholarship. He tried to outline a "universal" creed, founded on a kind of reformed Judaism, or on the fusion of Judaism and Christianity into a single doctrine of "progress." He imagined that the center of this syncretistic religion would be Jerusalem, and saw this ultimate faith as the lineal outgrowth of what he imagined classical Judaism to have been.

In another letter earlier in the same year to Gustave D'Eichthal, who as the baptized son of Jewish parents who had converted to Catholicism was typical of the few "Jews" he knew, Mill reports a mixed impression of Salvador's earlier work and a "wholly favourable" one of the Jesus book. The latter, he says, "is nearer the truth than even Strauss. Altogether it is a grand book & I have instigated several people to read it" (CW, XIII, 496–97).

Although the first book made Mill think, or so he claims, in a new and unexpected way about "the Hebrew people & polity," he found laughable Salvador's strained arguments (apparently an early version of the belief of American Jewish liberals that Judaism follows an arrow-straight course from Sinai to the left wing of the Democratic Party) to "recommend poor Moses to the Constitutional Opposition & to shew that the Jews were liberals, political economists & Utilitarians, that they had properly speaking no religion . . . & were . . . worthy sons of the 18th century." He mentions Salvador's argument that the liberty of prophesying was equivalent in the Jewish polity to liberty of the press. Later in the same letter Mill complains that Salvador has not been translated or even heard of in England, where nobody is ripe for serious philosophical discussion of the Bible. "We are all either bigots or Voltairians" (CW, XIII, 496–97).

Since we know so little of Mill's ideas about Jews prior to 1842, it is hard to say what difference his reading of this "grand book" by Salvador brought about. Perhaps the best evidence of Salvador's influence on Mill is to be found in *Considerations on Representative Government*, a work of 1861. Here, in the course of a discussion of how to determine the form of government that is best suited to a particular people, Mill introduces, by way of contrast to the Egyptians and Chinese, "the example of an opposite character afforded by another and a comparatively insignificant Oriental people—the Jews." Although they too had an absolute monarchy and a hierarchy, and organized institutions of "sacerdotal origin," neither their kings nor their priests obtained, as they did in Egypt and China, the exclusive power to mould their monarchy and hierarchy; their religion forbade that. "Their religion, which enabled persons of genius and a high religious tone to be regarded and to regard themselves as inspired from heaven, gave existence to an inestimably precious unorganized institution—the Order ... of Prophets." These prophets became a formidable power in the nation, "often more than a match for kings and priests, and kept up, in that little corner of the earth, the antagonism of influences which is the only real security for continued progress" (CW, XIX, 396–97).

This belief in progression resulting from contraries is, of course, standard Mill doctrine, going back before 1842 at least to the Bentham and Coleridge essays of 1838 and 1840. But the 1861 passage is nevertheless striking because here, for once, religion is not, as generally Mill views it, "a consecration of all that was once established, and a barrier against further improvement." He graciously attributes this notion about the Jews to the remark of "a distinguished Hebrew, M. Salvador, that the Prophets were, in Church and State, the equivalent of the modern liberty of the press." He proceeds to call this notion just, even if not fully adequate to explain "the part fulfilled in national and universal history by this great element of Jewish life." Admitting the legitimacy of prophecy was, Mill asserts, equivalent to admitting that the canon of inspiration was never complete, but always in process of development. The formal validation of prophecy meant that "the persons most eminent in genius and moral feeling could not only denounce and reprobate, with the direct authority of the Almighty, whatever appeared to them deserving of such treatment, but could give forth better and higher interpretations of the national religion, which thenceforth became part of the religion." Thus, if one can rid himself of the habit of reading the Bible as if it were a single book (an error Mill imputes to Christians as well as to unbelievers), he will see "with admiration the vast interval between the morality and religion of the

Pentateuch, or even of the historical books (the unmistakable work of Hebrew Conservatives of the sacerdotal order), and the morality and religion of the Prophecies: a distance as wide as between these last and the Gospels" (CW, XIX, 397) .

This historical scheme does give the Jews a high place among Mill's heroes of progression. They created conditions very favorable to progress as understood by him: . . . " the Jews, instead of being stationary like other Asiatics, were, next to the Greeks, the most progressive people of antiquity, and, jointly with them, have been the starting-point and main propelling agency of modern cultivation." Nevertheless, Mill, just like his Christian neighbors in Victorian England, assumes an evolutionary progression from the Pentateuch and the "historical books" to the Prophets and thence to—the culminating point—Christianity. Given the drift of his discussion of the Hebrew prophets up to this point, one might expect Mill now to ask what, if any, countervailing power to that of the priests and monarchs of Christendom received the legitimacy that the prophets had in ancient Israel. Instead, Mill falls back upon the well-worn clichés of Christian supercessionists and accepts without question or hesitation the assumption that the morality of the prophets (presumably including the prophet Samuel, who instructed Saul to "spare no one, but kill alike men and women, infants and sucklings" [I Samuel 15:3]) is a great advance over the morality of the narrator of the Binding of Isaac and, in turn, that Matthew 10:34 ("Do not think that I have come to bring peace on earth; I have not come to bring peace, but a sword.") is as superior ethically to Isaiah 2:4 ("Nation shall not lift up sword against nation / Neither shall they learn war any more.") as Isaiah was to Leviticus. In his book on Comte (1865), Mill explicitly calls Christianity "the highest form of Monotheism" (CW, X, 274).

Since Mill took the view that Christianity represented an advance over Judaism in most things he valued, it is not surprising that, despite his liberalism, he is very sparing of sympathy toward the travails of the Jews in their postbiblical existence. In one of his early historical essays ("Modern French Historical Works," 1826), Mill takes rather a cool and detached attitude toward the persecution of the Jews in medieval England. "The celebrated anecdote of King John and the Jew's teeth, as it has, besides the cruelty, something whimsical in it, fixes itself in the memory; and is perpetually quoted as an extraordinary instance of the cruel treatment to which the Jews were subject in that reign. Yet what is this, compared to what we here see practised by one seigneur upon another" (CW, XX, 29). This is not quite in the class of Carlyle's praise of King John for ripping the gold teeth out of Jewish mouths (and imagining himself doing the same to Lord Rothschild). But in referring to this barbaric act as "whimsy" and making it a minor cruelty when compared with the torture of one landed proprietor of knightly caste by another in feudal Europe, Mill shows—how should one put it?—a slight deficiency of sympathy in the Jewish direction.

And what was his attitude toward the Jews of his own time and country? Jews had been banished from England from 1290 until the 1650s, and their struggle to gain some measure of civic equality with their Christian neighbors was laborious and slow. But Mill showed little interest in Jewish emancipation, though he did not, of course, oppose it. In 1849, he was incensed by Lord John Russell's "Bill to Alter the Oaths to Be Taken by Members of the Two Houses of Parliament Not Professing the Roman Catholic Religion." The bill's immediate purpose, as Mill well knew, was to admit Jews into Parliament. But for him it was a "piece of meanness" because it reinserted in the new oath the words "on the true faith of a Christian" for all persons except Jews. Mill's anger was not, to be sure, about the admission of Jews but about the exclusion of those non-Christians who did not declare themselves to be Jews. Lord Russell, Mill complains, "opens the door of parliament just wide enough to allow one particular class of dissenters from Christianity to slip in, and closes it . . . against all others." The admission of Jews was not for Mill a sufficiently weighty matter to justify trampling on the rights of atheists. "We say nothing about Jews, whom this very measure is intended to let in." A similar hardheartedness with respect to his Jewish contemporaries is evident in *The Subjection of Women*, where Mill asserts, astonishingly, in Chapter One that only in the case of women is any group still legally discriminated against on grounds of birth: "even religious disabilities (besides that in England and in Europe they have practically almost ceased to exist) do not close any career to the disqualified person in case of conversion" (CW, XXI, 275). If only the Jews would become Christians, all careers would be open to them.

Still more indicative of a certain moral blindness to the predicament of Jews in Christendom is Mill's treatment of them in *On Liberty*. Every reader of that work recalls just where the Jews come into view. They supply, in Chapter Two ("Of the Liberty of Thought and Discussion") one illustration of the folly of established authority acting on the premise of its infallibility to silence dissenting opinion. Mill comments on the paradox that that those who are shocked by the behavior of the Jewish high priestly authorities toward Jesus would have acted precisely as the (now despised) Jews did had they been alive then and born Jews. These Jewish priests, says Mill, were "not bad men . . . but rather the contrary; men who possessed in a full, or somewhat more than a full measure, the religious, moral, and patriotic feelings of their time and people" (CW, X, 65). Most of the Christians who now shudder at the conduct of the high priest described in Matthew (26:55) would have done exactly as he did.

Here the Jews of late antiquity supply the epitome of those who, committing the sin of supposing themselves infallible, do terrible mischief. But at the very time Mill was composing his great treatise in favor of liberty and against the assumption of infallibility, it was precisely the Jews who were being victimized by the invocation of infallibility, in a case that in its time was as momentous a scandal as the Dreyfus affair would be at century's end. In June 1858, Edgardo Mortara, a six-year-old child of a Jewish family in Bologna, was, by order of the Inquisition, kidnapped by the papal police from his parents and taken to Rome, where he was confined in the House of Catechumens. The rationale for the kidnapping was that the child had been secretly baptized five years earlier by a Christian servant who believed him to be seriously ill and in danger of dying. Although the Roman Church had sanctioned numerous previous kidnappings of this sort, the Mortara affair seemed to many Europeans, especially those of a liberal bent, a particularly flagrant invocation of the ancient dogma of the infallibility of the Church. In this case, after all, that alleged infallibility had been given precedence by the Inquisition—this in 1858!—and Pope Pius IX over parental rights and religious freedom and, some argued, natural law itself. Emperor Napoleon III was one of those who protested the Church's actions, and the Mortara affair led to the founding of the Alliance Israelite Universelle in 1860 to "defend the civil rights and religious freedom of the Jews." It seems very likely that the uproar contributed to the end of the church's secular power and the loss of its territories a decade later, though also—in reaction to the prospect of losing that power—to the new dogma of the infallibility of the pope. But of all this, Mill has not a single word to say in *On Liberty*, where the Jews appear as the exponents and not the victims of the mistaken belief in infallibility.

But there is a still more serious deficiency in *On Liberty* with respect to the Jews, one that was noticed by no less formidable a contemporary of Mill's than George Eliot. As we have seen, Mill fell readily into the habit of his Christian countrymen of celebrating and espousing the "universalism" of Christianity in opposition to the particularism of Judaism (and several other religions). In his essay on Sedgwick, for example, he wrote that "Christianity does not deliver a code of morals, any more than a code of laws. Its practical morality is altogether indefinite, and was meant to be so. This indefiniteness has been considered by some of the ablest defenders of Christianity as one of its most signal merits, and among the strongest proofs of its divine origin: being the quality which fits it to be an universal religion, and distinguishes it both from the Jewish dispensation, and from all other religions. . . ." But the drift of *On Liberty* is entirely contrary to such "universalism," for it proclaims the undesirability of unanimity and insists vigorously on the importance of variety, possibility, eccentricity, even going so far as to say that if opponents of all important doctrines do not exist, it is necessary to invent them. Eliot recognized clearly the Jewish blind spot in Mill's magnum opus: "A modern book on liberty has maintained that from the freedom of individual men to persist in idiosyncrasies the world may be enriched. Why should we not apply this argument to the idiosyncrasy of a nation, and pause in our haste to hoot it down? There is still a great function for the steadfastness of the Jew . . ." If the logic of *On Liberty* is transferred from individuals to nations, then liberals should recognize in the Jewish people a "beneficent individuality among the nations."

Elsewhere in "The Modern Hep! Hep! Hep!", the essay of 1878 in which this remark about *On Liberty* appears, George Eliot suggests that liberals as a group have a "Jewish problem." Among her contemporaries, she charges, "anti-Judaic advocates usually belong to a party which has felt itself glorified in winning for Jews the full privileges of citizenship." Paradoxically, however, "these liberal gentlemen, too late enlightened by disagreeable events," routinely blame the Jews themselves for the inability of liberalism to protect them. Eliot's generalization does not really cover Mill: on the one hand, he was only mildly interested in winning civil rights for Jews; on the other he tended simply to avert his eyes from the troubles of the Jews rather than blaming them for the malignance of their enemies. But Eliot's observations about the inability of liberals to deal with the Jewish problem, coming as they do in close proximity to her remarks about Mill's magnum opus, prompt us to ask whether the inadequacy of his treatment of Jews and Judaism was not a foreshadowing of the failures of his intellectual inheritors.

Perhaps too the inability of the outstanding liberal thinker of the Victorian period to get beyond the assumptions about Judaism of the very Christianity he believed himself freed from by his heterodox education casts an ironic light upon the assumption of so many modern Jews that liberalism is the essence of Judaism itself.

Notes

1. *Earlier Letters of John Stuart Mill: 1812–1848*, ed. F. E. Mineka (Toronto and London: University of Toronto Press, 1963), I, 92.
2. G. O. Trevelyan, *Life and Letters of Lord Macaulay*, 2 vols. (London: Oxford University Press, 1961), I, 148.
3. Montagu Frank Modder, *The Jew in the Literature of England* (Philadelphia, PA: Jewish Publication Society, 1960), 171–72.
4. Arthur Penrhyn Stanley, *Life of Thomas Arnold, D. D.* (London: J. Murray, 1904), 249.
5. J. H. Newman, *Apologia pro Vita Sua* (London: Longmans, 1864), Chapter One and the Note on Liberalism.
6. Stanley, *Life of Thomas Arnold, D. D.*, I, 341.
7. Ibid., II, 32–33.
8. Ibid., II, 33, 35.
9. Ibid., II, 37.
10. "The Oxford Malignants and Dr. Hampden," in *Victorian Literature: Prose*, ed. G. B. Tennyson and D. J. Gray (New York: Macmillan, 1976), 17.
11. One reason why Arnold took up the defense of the appointment of Renn Dickson Hampden to the Regius Professorship of Divinity at Oxford in 1836 was that Conservatives (including the High Church party) objected to Hampden's support for the abolition of religious tests for admission to Oxford. Two years later, Arnold would insist on the religious test for Jews at London University. Needless to say, he failed to see any irony or contradiction in his position.
12. "Oxford Malignants," 18–19.
13. Stanley, *Life of Thomas Arnold, D. D.*, II, 84, 94, 105.
14. It might be interesting to compare the liberal Arnold's views on this matter with those of his "conservative" adversary John Henry Newman, who in *Idea of a University* is at pains to point out that the liberal education imparted by a university produces neither the Catholic nor the Christian, but the gentleman. (This is not to say that Newman was any more inclined than Arnold to countenance the presence of Jews in the university. London University, in fact, was for him the epitome of what a university should *not* be partly because it admitted Jews and Dissenters.)
15. Stanley, *Life of Thomas Arnold, D. D.*, II, 93.
16. See on this subject Cynthia Ozick's "Still Another Autobiography of an Assimilated Jew," *New York Times*, December 28, 1978.
17. Todd Endelman, *Radical Assimilation in English Jewish History, 1656–1945* (Bloomington: Indiana University Press, 1990), 109.
18. Ibid., 112.

19. "Literature and Dogma (1873)," in *Dissent and Dogma*, ed. R. H. Super (Ann Arbor: University of Michigan Press, 1968), 199.
20. *Letters of Matthew Arnold: 1848-1888*, 2 vols., ed. G. W. E. Russell (London and New York: Macmillan, 1900), I, 263.
21. *Culture and Anarchy*, ed. J. Dover Wilson (Cambridge: Cambridge University Press, 1932), 29–30.
22. *Democratic Education*, ed. R. H. Super (Ann Arbor: University of Michigan Press, 1962), 143.
23. See, e.g., his speech at a banquet for the school on May 21, 1884, printed in the appendix to volume X of Super's edition of Arnold's prose works.
24. *Letters of Matthew Arnold*, II, 86.
25. Arnold's "Heinrich Heine" first appeared in the *Cornhill Magazine* for August 1863. The essay is reprinted in R. H. Super's *Lectures and Essays in Criticism* (Ann Arbor: University of Michigan Press, 1962), 107–32.
26. Milton Himmelfarb, "Hebraism and Hellenism Now," *The Jews of Modernity* (Philadelphia, PA: Jewish Publication Society, 1973), 299.
27. Ibid., II, 59.
28. Ibid., I, 434.
29. *Democratic Education*, 142–43.
30. *Schools and Universities on the Continent*, ed. R. H. Super (Ann Arbor: University of Michigan Press, 1964), 232.
31. "St. Paul and Protestantism," in *Dissent and Dogma*, 21.
32. "Literature and Dogma," in *Dissent and Dogma*, 183.
33. Ibid., 196–97.
34. Ibid., 197.
35. Ibid., 199.
36. *Autobiography and Other Writings*, ed. Jack Stillinger (Boston, MA: Houghton Mifflin, 1969), 27–28.
37. See *Collected Works of John Stuart Mill*, vol. X (*Essays on Ethics, Religion, and Society*), ed. John M. Robson (Toronto: University of Toronto Press, 1969), 253. (Hereinafter referred to as CW and cited in parentheses within the text.)

II
History

Britannia Waives the Rules: Antisemitism, English-Style

In a now famous letter of October 1838 to his friend John Forster, Charles Dickens wrote that "the Jew" (Fagin), who dominates a novel (*Oliver Twist*) named after a far less interesting character than himself, is "such an out and outer that I don't know what to make of him." At first, the remark sounds odd: if the writer who made Fagin does not know "what to make of him," who should? But Dickens, in a very real sense, did *not* make Fagin, a character (or rather a figure or a force) who emanates from historical myth and was dredged up by Dickens out of the English folk imagination. Fagin is an archetypal figure—with hammering insistence he is called "the Jew" in the original (1837–1839) version of the novel—coming out of centuries of myth, hatred, and fear. Fagin, "a loathsome reptile" with red hair, is the descendant not only of Satan and Judas but also, especially for Dickens' English audience, of Shakespeare's Shylock, just as Shylock is the descendant of the "cursed Jew" in Chaucer's "Prioress' Tale." The perfectly innocent boy Oliver Twist, rejected by respectable society, is taken in by the criminal Fagin, who seeks to corrupt and capture his soul, and whose menace registers in "little Oliver's blood." Oliver also descends directly from the seven-year-old boy who in Chaucer's version of the Norwich blood libel makes the fatal error of singing a hymn in praise of the Virgin while walking through the Jewish ghetto, where his throat is cut and his body dumped in an open pit.

English antisemites, the subject of Anthony Julius' magisterial, judicious, and comprehensive *Trials of the Diaspora: A History of Anti-Semitism in England* have been extraordinarily fortunate in having three of the preeminent authors of their country's literary canon also shine forth as the preeminent authors of England's literary antisemitic canon.[1] His book handsomely illustrates the old adage that "nonsense is nonsense, but the study of nonsense is scholarship," especially when the nonsense has proved infectious and deadly. It is an open secret, visible to everybody (perhaps even to Julius' indifferent Cambridge English professors of 1974–1977) and yet seen by very few, that Chaucer, Shakespeare, and Dickens are among the greatest writers in a great literary tradition and also its most flagrant promoters of antisemitism. This literary insight—and Anthony Julius, hitherto best known not as the author of a book on T. S. Eliot but as the lawyer of Princess Diana in her divorce proceedings and of Deborah Lipstadt in her legal contest with David Irving, the Hitler-loving English historian, is a literary critic of great insight and nearly perfect pitch—is, both literally and figuratively, at the core of *Trials of the Diaspora*. Indeed, the book's many pages on English *literary* antisemitism (not only in the aforementioned Big Three but in such eminences as John Donne, Thomas Carlyle, W. M. Thackeray, Anthony Trollope, T. S. Eliot, and such dwarfs as Caryl Churchill and Tom Paulin) could stand as a separate volume. Needless to say, what has been the best of British luck for Albion's Jew-haters has been the worst for Anglo-Jewry, who to this day inhabit what Julius calls a Shylock–Fagin "character prison" from which they are unlikely ever to escape. Literature, as we must always be reminded, has the power not only to elevate and transform but to degrade and damage; so we should not be surprised when the elevation and degradation exist side by side.

According to Julius, there have been, since medieval times (where his narrative begins) three dominant anti-Jewish libels: (1) the blood libel, (2) the conspiracy libel, and (3) the economic libel. The earliest English narrative of Jewish ritual murder, itself a work of literary distinction, is Thomas of Monmouth's *Life and Miracles of St. William of Norwich* (1173); its author, Julius perspicaciously observes, was at once the inventor of the blood libel and of the equally English genre known as the detective story; its clerical detective discovers that—but of course!—it is the Jews who are guilty of William's murder. The blood libel alleges that Jews have homicidal intentions toward Gentiles, and that Jewish ritual law supports these intentions. The conspiracy libel holds that Jews always, despite surface appearances to the contrary, act as one, and in pursuit of goals inimical to the interests of Gentiles. It is exemplified in the *Protocols of the Elders of Zion*, regurgitated in recent years by the late Tony Judt, an English expatriate who was constantly warning Americans that "there are a set of Jewish organizations, who do work, both in front of the scenes and behind the scenes, to prevent certain kinds of conversations, certain kinds of criticism . . . a *de facto* kind of conspiracy . . . or plot or collaboration to prevent public policy moving in a certain way or to push it in a certain way"[2]; the third is that Jews are greedy and acquisitive, and spend all their waking hours exploiting non-Jews. The libels share the premise that Jews hate and despise non-Jews. Sometimes they overlap, as when a young Englishwoman (an activist in the English version of the American Civil Liberties Union) told me at her London dinner table in 1962: "Jews suck the blood of the English working classes."

The "master trope" among these three in England, according to Julius, has been the blood libel, permeating all literary genres and making England's literary antisemitism more abundant and flagrant than that of any other country. "The master trope supposes a well-intentioned Christian placed in peril by a sinister Jew or Jews. The Christian is often a boy: . . . caught, the victim does not protest, and submits to the malevolent attentions of the Jew; if the victim escapes death, it is by a miracle; if he dies, the facts of the crime, and the location of his body, are revealed by a miracle; the Jew or Jews are often apprehended and punished. It is from within these variables that the first work of literary anti-Semitism, the ballad, 'Sir Hugh, or The Jew's Daughter' . . . and the three canonic works ['Prioress' Tale', *Merchant of Venice, Oliver Twist*] of literary anti-Semitism . . . are all written" (xxxviii). (One did not have to be an English *literary* artist to subscribe to the blood libel. Who, after reading Julius' book, will be able to gawk in admiration at London's Gothic Revival masterpiece called the Houses of Parliament, without recalling that its primary architect A. W. N. Pugin excoriated anyone who raised doubts about the truth of the Hugh of Lincoln story: "there are no reasonable grounds," said Pugin, "for disbelieving any portion of the history. The Jews are well known to have perpetrated similar atrocities at various periods, and . . . the body of the blessed Hugh . . . was found a few years since, adjacent to the place where the shrine formerly stood" (115). QED.

Of the blood libel, one may say *plus ça change, plus c'est la même chose.* Still today, drawing on the essential details of the ancient blood libel are England's "anti-Zionist" versions of the ancient hatred, such as the versified eruption of Oxford poetaster Tom Paulin about alleged child murder by Israeli soldiers and the ten-minute play by Caryl Churchill entitled *Seven Jewish Children—A Play for Gaza* (2009). In his critique of Paulin's 2001 poem, "Killed in Crossfire," about the (phony) story of the little Arab boy (Mohammed al-Dura) reported killed in Gaza by Israeli gunfire, Julius observes: "The most vulgar anti-Semitism speaks in 'Crossfire.' . . . The poem has several specifically *literary* anti-Semitic resonances. In its theme of the killing of Gentile children by perfidious Jews, and the miraculous disclosure of these crimes, the poem alludes to 'Little Sir Hugh' and *The Prioress's Tale*." But whereas Dickens had no programmatic intent to harm Jews when he wrote *Oliver Twist* and so might plausibly have expressed puzzlement about "what to make of him," Paulin, whose recommendation, discussed elsewhere in this book, that Jewish residents of the disputed territories of Judea and Samaria "should be shot dead" became for bashful Israelophobes the classic instance of what they deem "legitimate criticism of Israeli policies," cannot plead similar puzzlement. "Entirely voluntarily, but without any good reason whatever, Paulin has made himself a prisoner of anti-Semitic discourse" (236–40).

Of the Churchill playlet Bernard Harrison, whose carefully reasoned book about (mostly) contemporary English antisemitism (*The Resurgence of Antisemitism*, 2006) has by no means been supplanted by Julius' history, remarks: "Even the Blood Libel has recently been given new legs by Caryl Churchill: At one point one of the characters is made to say, 'Tell her we killed the babies by mistake,' with the clear implication . . . that in fact they were killed on purpose . . . singled out precisely with that end in view." One Zionist "elder" in the play says: "I wouldn't care if we wiped them out . . . tell her we're better haters, tell her we're chosen people, tell her I look at one of their [Arab] children covered in blood. . . ."[3]

Julius' insistence on the tenacity of these dominant tropes from the Middle Ages into contemporary England and also his stress upon the dismaying fact that England has "never," during all these centuries, "suffered any culture-guilt" (144) for its persecution of Jews do not mean that he scants the differences between the England of the Middle Ages and the England of the nineteenth or twentieth centuries. Neither does he fail to see that centering attention on the permanence of certain tropes and linking medieval or Renaissance writings with, for example, Gothic novels of the early nineteenth century, may work at cross purposes with his historical narrative. A centuries-old history of Jew-hatred "cannot quite be parceled into self-contained episodes" (341). Another cause of tension between permanence and progression in the book is that English literary antisemitism, paradoxically, so far from being a "response" to the actual presence of Jews in the country, a reflection of tense Jewish–Christian relations, was " a product of the absence of Jews, of their empirical invisibility" (170). They were absent from England, let us recall, for almost 400 years; and it was not until 1871, after decades of what seemed interminable national debate (and after the converted Jew Disraeli finally took up their cause) that all their civil disabilities were legally removed.

Julius' narrative tells the story of how England became the last European country to receive and the first to expel the Jews (in 1290), analyzes the differences between the savagery of its medieval antisemitism (in the late 1270s half the country's adult Jewish male population was executed, a barbaric act not repeated in any of the subsequent periods or even literary versions of English antisemitism), recounts the Jews' readmission to the country in the seventeenth century, the phenomenon of occasional philosemitism in Victorian England, and the "minor" nature of modern English antisemitism, which has usually been verbally aggressive without becoming physically violent. If, as Julius tersely observes, twentieth-century antisemitism is "a tale of two protocols," the Elders of Zion forgery and the Wannsee plan to murder European Jewry, England's antisemites opted for the former. But the picture may change with the now massive presence in the United Kingdom of Islamic fundamentalists, who have been largely responsible for the enormous increase of anti-Jewish violence there, already the subject of parliamentary investigation and report.

The largest part of this very large book (comprising a 58-page introduction followed by 783 pages of text and notes) is called "Versions" [of Antisemitism], and is permeated by what might be called Julius' taxonomic approach, which is surprisingly cool and detached given the fact that in his acknowledgements he likens the task of writing *Trials of the Diaspora* to "swimming long-distance through a sewer" (xi). These eight chapters (not logically parallel) are: Medieval English Anti-Semitism, English Literary Anti-Semitism, Modern English Anti-Semitism, The Mentality of Modern English Anti-Semitism, Contemporary Secular Anti-Zionisms, Contemporary Confessional Anti-Zionisms, and a Conclusion.

The inhabitants of this "sewer" include many unpleasant (if sometimes talented) people, but perhaps the most unpleasant among them are themselves Jews—that is to say, Jews who are antisemites. Antisemitism not being a genetically inherited disease, Jews can succumb to it as readily as anybody else. Such Jews are omnipresent in the book: "There have always," observes Julius, "been Jews ready to side with anti-Semites" (4). In the first of his numerous classification schemes, "Four Kinds of Enemy," the Jews enter the scene in the category of "opportunistic enemies." They make a return appearance, just a few pages later, in the category of "irrational enemies" or "oppositionist Jews," who are often mistaken for antisemites, but did not actually join up with antisemites until they became "scourges of the Jewish State" (30). In the Middle Ages Jewish converts to Christianity were prominent among those eager to give public testimony, often in coerced debates, against their still benighted former coreligionists, even if this meant revealing that, yes, Jewish males do menstruate, just as many Christian theologians alleged. But as late as the Victorian period Thackeray (in *Barry Lyndon* [1844]) could observe the huge role played by the Jewish convert in the public onslaught against Jews: "He [a minister of police] visited church every morning, confessed once a week, and hated Jews and Protestants as much as an inquisitor could do. He never lost an opportunity of proving his sincerity, of persecuting . . . whenever occasion fell his way" (33).

In later chapters, for example the one about the xenophobia unleashed against Jewish immigrants from Eastern Europe in the four decades before World War I, we learn of English Jews, a full decade earlier, "stealing a march" on self-proclaimed antisemites by denying to their coreligionists advantages they themselves enjoyed for fear that the advantages would be lost if too many arrived to claim them. And if we are shocked by the enormous role of English Jews in the current war of ideas (and agitprop) against Zionism and Israel's existence, Julius shows that, as late as 1928, eleven years after the Balfour Declaration and six after Britain was awarded the Mandate for Palestine by the League of Nations, English Jews were still the country's "most implacable enemies" (292) of Zionism. (Indeed, they provide a Jewish subdivision of the treasonous Englishman to whom British Foreign Secretary George Canning alluded when he said [early in the nineteenth century]: "A steady patriot of the world alone/The friend of every country but his own.")

But is anti-Zionism, a few willfully blind (and often highly contentious) people still ask, really a modern form of the ancient hatred, a replacement—as one of Philip Roth's characters says—of the Jew who in the past was perpetually on trial (in those Inquisitional debates, in *The Merchant of Venice*, in *Oliver Twist*, and in the Dreyfus Trial), by the Israeli who is now daily on trial, in the *Guardian*, *The*

New Statesman, The Independent, and the Oxford Union)? Julius' definition of the "new" antisemitism would seem to settle the matter: "[The new antisemitism] first emerged in the late 1960s and early 1970s in consequence of the Six Day War, but became hegemonic in the 1990s and 2000s in consequence of certain developments mostly unrelated to the Middle East [e.g., the collapse of the Soviet Union and—outside of university English departments—Marxism] It is to be distinguished from the 'old anti-Semitism' because it takes Israel and the Zionist project as its collective term for the Jews, because its geographic hub is Western Europe, because self-identified Jews are among its advocates, and because it comes from the Left—indeed, has become part of the common sense among people of a broadly progressive temper. It is taken to be continuous with the 'old anti-Semitism' in its principal stratagems and tropes, while novel in its specific focus upon the Jewish State—uniquely evil and without the right to exist. It demonizes Jewish nationalists in place of Jewish usurers, Jewish capitalists, and Jewish communists. [It displays] one-eyed refusal to find fault with any party other than Israel" (441). To put it more succinctly, whereas Jews were formerly denied "the right to live," now Israel is denied "the right to exist."

Where then do the Jews fit into the "new" antisemitism? Many Jews, as we have already noticed, opposed Zionism prior to the establishment of the state of Israel in 1948. But, as even the anti-Zionist Leonard Woolf could recognize: "I was against Zionism . . . but in politics and history once something has been done radically to change the past into a new present, you must not act upon a situation which no longer exists, but upon the facts that face one" (547). It was one thing for Jews to oppose Zionism in the 1920s, quite another to call for the annihilation of a living society of millions of people in the sixties or seventies or today.

In Julius' taxonomy of "Contemporary Confessional [i.e., religious] Anti-Zionisms" in England, Jews place second, right after "Muslim anti-Zionism," a dismal account of (mainly) theorists and practitioners of Jew-killing, and just before Christian anti-Zionism (in a country where the Established Church is often said to be the main impediment to religion). In several respects England's Jewish anti-Zionists resemble America's. They too raise "leftist" questions about the Jewish state, such as "Can Israel be both Jewish and democratic?" However plausible the question may seem when posed in the United States, it strikes one as blatantly hypocritical when put by subjects of Britain, a Christian state with an official Protestant church, a Protestant monarch, a Protestant educational system (and official forms that habitually ask for one's "Christian name"). The old slogan of assimilationist Jews was "Be a Jew at home and a man in the street." But the Jewish divisions of the anti-Israel struggle are led in England (as in America) by a new kind of assimilated Jew, an anti-Zionist who is very much a Jew in the street and a man (or woman) at home; and who expresses loathing of Israel less in leftist terms than in what purport to be Jewish ones; and—the ultimate paradox—whose Jewish "identity" is entirely dependent on the existence of the State of Israel, whose "right to exist" he ardently denies. "The new Jewish anti-Zionism," Julius wisely observes, "inaugurates a return for many Jews to some kind of Jewish identity. They no longer seek, as with previous generations, to relieve themselves of the burden of their Jewish origins; rather, they reassume the burden, in order further to burden their fellow-Jews" (548). Like their American counterparts mentioned in the introduction to this book, the Anglo-Jewish defamers of Israel exemplify a new reality: "When a man can no longer be a Jew, he becomes an anti-Zionist."

Julius names Jacqueline Rose, the London University English professor and literary critic who has psychoanalyzed Zionism and Israel and concluded that this movement, which was founded and is to this day led by secular Zionists, is "messianic" and therefore fanatical and dangerous. She is "ashamed" of Israel and would like to see the country "abolish itself." In the aftermath of Arab suicide bombings, she can always be relied on to urge "understanding" of the killers and to lash out against "those wishing to denigrate suicide bombers and their culture." She cannot tolerate the expression "Jewish suffering." She is so obsessed with the Israeli–Nazi equation beloved of modern antisemites (and so slovenly a scholar) that she alleged Hitler and Herzl both to have received the inspiration for their most famous books, *Mein Kampf* and *Der Judenstaat*, from attending the very same performance of Wagner in Paris. (Only London's "progressive" book reviewers and the readers paid by Princeton University Press to evaluate her book manuscript[4] failed to remind her that Hitler did not set foot in Paris until 1940, and Herzl died in 1904.) What, one wonders, would remain of the Judaism or even "Jewishness" of a Jacqueline Rose, whom Julius names as the typical representative of England's "Diaspora Jewish" anti-Zionists[5] if, as she ardently desires, the Jewish state were to vanish? Would her spiritual yearnings be satisfied with that peculiarly Jewish form of parochialism called "universalism"? I suspect not.

Notes

1. Not everyone will assent to Julius' assumption that this trio comprises *the* preeminent English writers. Is Dickens unquestionably a greater writer than Milton? Milton, moreover, unlike Julius' trio, was both learned in and respectful of rabbinic interpretation. He knew midrash very well and made use of many rabbinical glosses in *Paradise Lost*. See on this subject Harold Fisch, *The Biblical Presence in Shakespeare, Milton and Blake* (Oxford: Clarendon Press, 1999), 158–78; Golda S. Werman, "Midrash in *Paradise Lost*," *Milton Studies* 18 (1983): 145–71. Of course, like many other "Hebraists," Milton, as we shall see in the next chapter, detested Jews ("Judaizing beasts"), Judaism, and Mosaic law.
2. Anthony Julius, *Trials of the Diaspora: A History of Anti-Semitism in England* (Oxford: Oxford University Press, 2010), 557. Subsequent references to this work appear in parentheses in the text.
3. Bernard Harrison, "Supping with a Short Spoon: The 'New' Anti-Semitism and Its Defenders," Lecture of June 22, 2009, Hebrew University, Jerusalem. On the subject of the durability of the blood libel, see Raphael Israeli, *Blood Libel and Its Derivatives* (Piscataway, NJ: Transaction Publishers, 2011).
4. Her book *The Question of Zionism*, in which most of these utterances are to be found, was published by Princeton University Press in 2005.
5. This label distinguishes them from England's Israeli, or ex-Israeli, anti-Zionists, who interpret Hamas' call for Israel's annihilation as "an ethical cry to the world" and make even Rose and her comrades appear sweetly reasonable.

British Philosemitism: A Thing of the Past?

The two images farthest removed from each other which can be comprehended under one term, are, I think, Isaiah—'Hear, O heavens, and give ear, O earth!'—and Levi of Holywell Street—'Old Clothes!'—both of them Jews, you'll observe.
—Samuel Taylor Coleridge, *Table Talk*, August 14, 1833

Readers who find a steady diet of books about the antisemitism of England's learned (and also not so learned) classes more unpleasant than exploratory surgery will find a welcome antidote in Gertrude Himmelfarb's learned, scintillating, and (mostly) optimistic historical essay about the countertradition that she calls English "philosemitism." Professor Himmelfarb has been writing, with consummate mastery, about English intellectual life since 1952. Robert Nisbet once said of her that "Doubtless God could create a better interpreter" of this subject, "but doubtless God hasn't." In 2004, she received the National Humanities Medal awarded by the president. More recently, she has followed in the footsteps of the late Milton Himmelfarb, her very wise and learned brother, in writing about the Jewish dimension of English history and literature. In 2009, she published *The Jewish Odyssey of George Eliot*, and in 2011, *The People of the Book*.

Like the word "antisemitism," the term "people of the book" is steeped in ambiguity, tainted in its origin, and generally applied anachronistically. The term originated with Muhammad and appears first (and often) in the Koran to refer to both Jews and Christians. There it usually has pejorative overtones, as in "Ye People of the Book! Why reject ye the Signs of Allah." Similarly, "philosemitism" was originally pejorative, and it was invented, like its opposite, "antisemitism," by German Jew-haters. They used it to disparage people they deemed unduly sympathetic to Jews. The term "antisemitism" itself was a pseudoscientific euphemism for old-fashioned Jew-hatred, and to this day is often invoked by devotees of the Arab cause: "How can I be called an anti-semite [spelled thus] when I support the Semites called Arabs?" The answer to this dishonest question is that antisemites do not hate "Semites": they hate Jews.

Himmelfarb, without denying either the pioneering role of England's antisemites (the inventors of the blood libel, and the first to expel their country's Jewish population) or their recent resurgence (as, for example, inventors of the Boycott/Divest/Sanction onslaught against the Jewish state), tries to balance it with "another aspect of Jewish experience—the respect, even reverence, for Jews and Judaism displayed by non-Jews before and after the Holocaust."[1] Most of the English thinkers, writers, and politicians she discusses converted both "People of the Book" and "philosemitism" into positive terms. As she uses the word, philosemitism among the English may take the form of love of Jews as "God's ancient people," or toleration of them (as with liberal politicians like Macaulay), or admiration and worship of the Hebrew Bible, even when they call it "Old Testament," which for literate Jews is a calumny.

Himmelfarb knows that philosemitism is a cat that can jump in many directions. She admits that some formidable persecutors of the Jews have had far better Hebrew than their Jewish victims. (In America, Yale and Harvard combined excellent instruction in Hebrew with base discrimination against Jews.) John Milton, whose fluency in Hebrew, poetry permeated by the Hebrew Bible, and commentaries on Tanach and Maimonides, would seem to give the lie to Anthony Julius' claim (discussed earlier) that the greatest English writers have been its most flagrant antisemites, hated both Judaism and Jews. Only the fact that he was employed by Cromwell kept him from publicly opposing his master's decision to readmit Jews to England. He disparaged them as "Judaizing beasts," and argued that "the existence of God is proved ... by their dispersion ... throughout the whole world ... on account of their sins" (31).

Himmelfarb celebrates those philosemites like John Locke, an advocate of toleration, and Locke's friend Isaac Newton, who searched the Bible for evidence of "the restoration of the Jewish nation ... spoken of by the old Prophets" (39). Many of them developed the habit of imitating (perhaps appropriating) the historical Jewish experience and bringing it home, as Blake would later write, "to England's green and pleasant land." "Perhaps the highest compliment the English could pay the Jews," Himmelfarb observes, "was to refer to their own country as 'Israel' and to their own people as 'Israelites'" (41). (In 1968, former

Prime Minister Harold Macmillan actually said that "the future I hope for Britain is . . . like that of Israel," which in the Six Days' War had displayed "what any great people need—resolution, courage, determination").[2] At one point Himmelfarb calls Joseph Addison's admiration for real, living Jews the embodiment of "philosemitism in its purest form" (43) because the eighteenth-century essayist's Judeophilia was primarily "natural" rather than strongly religious or evangelical. Addison admired Jews for staunch adherence to their religion in spite of persecution, and did not aspire to convert them to his. But Jews rarely get what they desire in "pure" form, which may explain why they often resist taking "yes" for an answer where philosemites are concerned.

The book's most striking examples of philosemitism's mixture of blessing and curse both come from the Victorian period. The first is the book's only Jewish philosemite: Benjamin Disraeli. His story is well known. In March 1817, as young Benjamin was approaching bar mitzvah age, his father Isaac (already at odds with his synagogue) responded with alacrity to the suggestion of a Christian friend that he have his children baptized into the Church of England, so that they could have the chances available to other English children. Unlike his brothers Raphael and Jacobus, who were quickly baptized and renamed (Ralph and James), Benjamin was reluctant, but he eventually succumbed. For some time he showed little sign of his Jewish "background." When he traveled to the Holy Land as a young man, "of Jewish places of worship he saw nothing," and his glowing description of Jerusalem makes no mention of Jews whatsoever. Such facts would not surprise those of his latter-day critics who have alleged that his ideas of Jewishness were never hindered by any actual knowledge of the subject. Yet those ideas permeated not only his novels but also his parliamentary speeches. His chief idea was a bizarre, discomfiting mixture of sense and (mostly) nonsense called "racial Judaism." A typical example is his grotesque insistence that "half Christendom worships a Jewess, and the other half a Jew." His ignorance of Judaism was so vast that he knew nothing of Jewish dietary laws, and when a clergyman in his employ told him that the Sabbath for which he always expressed contempt was a Jewish invention, he fired the man. In *Tancred* (1847), the only Disraeli novel Himmelfarb discusses at length, the author's spokesman Sidonia sees crypto-Jews managing affairs everywhere, as professors, ambassadors, generals, and cabinet members; he also wonders whether Mozart, Haydn, and Beethoven were Jewish. Hannah Arendt, in a savage attack on Disraeli, pointed out that he "produced the entire set of theories about Jewish influence and organization that we usually find in the more vicious forms of antisemitism"[3] (and in Disraeli's contemporaries like Carlyle, who called him "a cursed old Jew, not worth his weight in cold bacon," and Lord Palmerston, who moaned that "we are all dreadfully disgusted at the prospect of having a Jew for our Prime Minister").

And yet, and yet—there is something genuine, honorable, even irresistible, in Disraeli's Jewish imaginings. In *Tancred*, he alludes to the "days of political justice when Jerusalem belonged to the Jews," and says that those days will return because the Jews in exile have diligently gone on pretending they were still living in their ancient homeland. In one of the few passages where he shows some awareness of Jewish religious practice, Disraeli describes Jews in Whitechapel or some other "icy clime" preparing once every year to live for a week in their *sukkah*. He concludes thus: "The vineyards of Israel have ceased to exist, but the eternal law enjoins the children of Israel still to celebrate the vintage. A race that persists in celebrating their vintage, although they have no fruits to gather, will regain their vineyards." When Himmelfarb calls Disraeli "the quintessential philosemite" (100), it is because he substantiated the witticism (to be coined by Haim Hazaz in 1942) that when a man can no longer be a Jew, he becomes a Zionist. England was the Israel of Disraeli's imagination, and he deserves the street named after him in modern Jerusalem.

And then there was Anthony Ashley Cooper, 7th earl of Shaftesbury (1801–1885). The paradox in his case was not the Miltonic tension between love for the Hebrew Bible and blind hatred for Judaism and Jews. Shaftesbury combined genuine love for both with unswerving loyalty to a Christian England. He was "an Evangelical of the Evangelicals," and also felt deep, almost idolatrous reverence for Jews, to whom he made a point of bowing when he passed them on the streets of Germany. He aspired to be a modern Cyrus, restoring God's people not merely to "Palestine" but to "Eretz Israel." He coined what would later become a Zionist slogan: "There is a country *without a nation*; and God now, in His wisdom and mercy, directs us to *a nation without a country*" (124–25). Yet he was a missionary not only *for* but *to* Jews, whom he aspired to convert to Christianity, and he opposed admitting them to Parliament or suspending, for their sake, the requirement that MPs pledge to serve "on the true faith of a Christian." England eventually did, after decades of debate, allow Jews to serve in Parliament without taking that oath. Yet even today, when British Israel-haters fulminate against a Jewish state, England remains a *Christian* state, with an official Protestant church, a Protestant monarch, and a Protestant educational system. Should English Jews have spurned or welcomed Shaftesbury's support? Would they have been better off under the atheist regimes of communism? More to the point (as Himmelfarb intimates): should Israeli and American Jews rejoice in the support of Shaftesbury's spiritual descendants, or be frightened by it? Menachem Begin, when asked this question, had no hesitation about answering: "Look, when the Messiah comes, we will simply ask him: 'Have you been here before?'"

In modern times, the most important British philosemites were the Liberal Prime Minister (1916–1922), Lloyd George, his Conservative Foreign Secretary Arthur Balfour, and Winston Churchill. George, as a child, was immersed "in the history of the Hebrews." Balfour, author of the 1917 endorsement of "a national home for the Jewish people" in Palestine, was a product of "the Old Testament training" that permeated Scottish culture before it became worm-eaten with leftism. Churchill, England's leader through World War II, was sui generis, a philosemite and a philo-Zionist without much religion but convinced of Disraeli's dictum that "The Lord deals with the nations as the nations deal with the Jews" (139). His great parliamentary speech of January 1949, urging laggard Britain to recognize Israel was the culminating moment of English philosemitism. The Jews' creation of Israel just a few years after the Holocaust, said Churchill, was an event of biblical magnitude, worthy of The People of the Book: "The coming into being of a Jewish state in Palestine is an event in world history to be viewed in the perspective, not of a generation or a century, but in the perspective of a thousand, two thousand or even three thousand years. . . . an event in world history" (145).

There are no Churchills (or Macmillans) in England today. As the astute young English writer Paul Bogdanor has said to me, "one would need the eyes of Argus to find any philosemitism in England now." Professor Himmelfarb is fully aware of the gloomy verdict rendered on contemporary England in the books by such keen observers as Anthony Julius, Robert Wistrich, and Melanie Phillips.[4] But she considers their conclusions "overly pessimistic" (4). She must have finished writing her own book at just about the time in the summer of 2011 that hundreds of people in London were being beaten and having their homes and businesses wrecked, and a smaller number were being murdered, by rampaging mobs, more barbaric than anything imagined by Dickens, whose fear of the London mob was boundless. Yet Himmelfarb believes that England—"modern England"—remains "a model of liberality and civility" (4). Let us hope that she proves right.

Notes

1. *The People of the Book: Philosemitism in England, from Cromwell to Churchill* (New York and London: Encounter Books, 2011), 3. Subsequent references to this work appear in parentheses in the text.
2. *Saturday Review of Literature* 51 (1968).
3. Hannah Arendt, *Antisemitism* (New York: Harcourt, Brace, 1951), 71.
4. Robert S. Wistrich, *A Lethal Obsession: Anti-Semitism from Antiquity to the Global Jihad* (New York: Random House, 2010); Anthony Julius, *Trials of the Diaspora* (Oxford: Oxford University Press, 2010); Melanie Phillips, *Londonistan* (New York: Encounter Books, 2006).

Medieval Zionism: Yehuda Halevi

In the final chapter of *Yehuda Halevi*, Hillel Halkin reveals that "This book began with another book."[1] That earlier book is entitled *Letters to an American Jewish Friend* (1977), a dazzling polemic in support of the thesis that Israel and Israel alone holds the Jewish future, so that it is now the only natural and justifiable place for a Jew to live. "Once again," Halkin had written, "we are a people speaking our own language and living in our own land. (You may be as skeptical as you wish about the specifically Jewish value of a country of the Bible that has been shoddily urbanized or of an Israeli Hebrew that is illiterate and ill-spoken. I tell you, they are still everything.... A land and a language! They are the ground beneath a people's feet and the air it breathes in and out. With them all things are possible ... you cannot even buy cigarettes in Hebrew without stirring up the Bible; you cannot walk the streets of Tel Aviv without treading on promised land.)"[2]

The idea for that book came in 1975 (just five years after Halkin and his wife had moved to Israel from New York, where he had worked as assistant editor at *Midstream*), from Maier Deshell, then the editor of the Jewish Publication Society (indeed, the very prince of editors). The aforementioned title was at first merely a provisional one, awaiting replacement by something flashier. The manuscript was well on its way through the publication process when Halkin, reading Yehuda Halevi's *The Kuzari*, a defense of Judaism written in the form of a dialogue between a Khazar king and the rabbi who converts him, came upon the king's accusation that Jews pray daily for their restoration to Zion yet do nothing to bring it about and the rabbi's acknowledgment that the king is correct: the Jews' talk about the Land of Israel is nothing more than "the starling's caw." Aha! thought Halkin, there is my title. Deshell, of course, thought otherwise: he did not wish JPS to seem in the business of publishing a guidebook to birdcalls. But that exchange between rabbi and king did become the epigraph to *Letters to an American Jewish Friend*, moved from Halevi's 1140 work of autobiographical fiction (written in Hebrew-lettered Arabic) to Halkin's polemic of 1977. The young writer knew that his reading of Halevi had involved him in a recognition scene in which study of the past became a discovery of his own buried life: over 800 years before Halkin had written of the holiness of Tel Aviv, Halevi had argued that it was incumbent upon Jews not only to *dream* of the restoration of Jewish independence but to settle in Palestine. That is why the great Hebrew poet and philosopher of Spain, who was also a prosperous medical doctor and recognized leader in the Jewish community, decided "to give up his way of life, family, friendships, and comforts for a voyage of no return to a country where nothing awaited him but danger, loneliness, and hardship" (128). Like Halkin, Halevi believed that there must be something in everyone's life that he is "willing to die for" (291).

Halkin's sense of affinity between Halevi and himself did not, and does not now, distort his sense of the many ways in which Halevi's world was very different from his own. In medieval Spain, some of the fiercest and even, on occasion, violent debates between Jews concerned such religio-poetic questions as whether Jewish poets were required to adhere to biblical rules of syllabic stress. Learned medieval Jews like Halevi believed and unabashedly declared that Judaism is *true*, a declaration that today might get one expelled from a Reform or Conservative synagogue. Palestine's largest Jewish community at the time—about 200 people—was in Acre (Akko), not Jerusalem; indeed, the Crusaders who then controlled the Holy Land toward which Halevi yearned had barred Jews from living in Jerusalem, where a Jewish pilgrim would in 1141 have been hard put to find a Jewish home to stay in, or a kosher meal to eat, or a synagogue in which to pray.

Nevertheless, as Herman Melville wrote in his essay on Hawthorne, "Genius, all over the world, stands hand in hand, and one shock of recognition runs the whole circle round." Halkin, reading in *The Kuzari* the rabbi's rationalizations for exile (for example, that God *wants* Jews to remain in exile so that they can plant the seed of Mosaic monotheism in post-Mosaic religions), at once recognized, just as Halevi did, the feebleness of standard Diaspora apologetics, little more than self-protective arguments (very like those of the "American friend" to whom Halkin wrote his letters of 1977). Who can doubt that similar arguments heard by Halevi from Egyptian Jews who, despite their proximity to the Holy Land, rarely ventured into Palestine, and also enjoyed all the luxuries (including saunas) of civilized Egyptian life, reminded Halkin of the anti-aliyah temptations of the fleshpots in America? Halkin also recognizes that modern variants of the rabbi's apologia for lingering in exile are now a standard part of what has come to be called "Diasporism," embraced by numerous Jews who insist that—apart from such minor exceptions as the expulsions from England and France and Spain and the destruction of European Jewry—Jews thrive and live safely only in the Diaspora. Unlike contemporary Diasporists, however, Halevi's fictional rabbi finally admits to himself that "he has been living a lie. Nothing he has taught the king has the slightest value unless he decides to live in the Land of Israel" (186).

One of the things the rabbi teaches the king is that Judaism is a universal religion. Although *The Kuzari* was not written for gentiles, who could not have read its Hebrew-lettered Arabic, it is about the conversion of a gentile to Judaism and therefore about what Judaism has to say to gentiles, especially to very intelligent ones like the Khazar king. As Halkin remarks, "a religion that can speak only to its own adherents diminishes them as well" (297). It is hardly necessary to add that Judaism's universalism means that everybody can become a Jew, but not that everybody *must* become a Jew.

A writer of Halkin's stature does not so much choose his subject as he is chosen by it, and the ghost of Halevi has chosen well. Halkin's imperial intellect has for decades ranged magisterially over literature, history, and politics. He is Israel's foremost translator from Hebrew and Yiddish, a skilled practitioner of the higher journalism, an astute commentator on politics, a scourge of Israeli leftists whose motto is "the other country, right or wrong." His eloquence is such that a prominent Israeli novelist once told me that he had been tempted to make Halkin his translator (from Hebrew into English) but feared that this translator "would be in competition with the author."

Halkin's new book is at once biography, history, literary criticism, and political argument. Here is his own bare outline of the story: "The young man, whose name was Yehuda ben Shmuel Halevi . . . was to become one of the great Hebrew poets of all time. He was also to write one of the most important works of religious philosophy in the Jewish canon [*The Kuzari*]; to make, late in life, a personal decision that was to resound in Jewish history; to then vanish mysteriously, leaving no record of whether this decision was carried out in full; to be turned subsequently into a legend, most of whose poetry was lost; to have, in modern times, first, his lost verse miraculously recovered, and then, his fate clarified with the help of an astonishing archival discovery [the Cairo *Geniza*]; and finally, to be implicated in our own age, more than any other medieval Jewish figure, in the great intellectual and political debates regarding Zionism and the state of Israel" (19). Halevi was adopted by nineteenth-century Jewish nationalism because he celebrated Jewish nationhood as a historical force in its own right, and by 1967 he had become the national, indeed the "nationalized" poet of Israel. Later, predictably, he became the arch-villain and (what else?) "racist" of the Israeli left, most notably Yeshayahu Leibowitz and other disseminators of the Israeli–Nazi equation. The fiercely leftist Sidra Ezrahi thinks it was lucky for Halevi that he was (probably) murdered by an Arab before he became (like herself) disillusioned with Zion (and Zionism). Halkin's book, in response to these detractors, now restores Halevi, gloriously, as the very Romantic yet also very Jewish poet who not only lamented "My heart in the East/But the rest of me far in the West" but answered "Yes" to this question: "Can I do what I've vowed to and must? . . . leave/All the best of grand Spain/For one glimpse of Jerusalem's dust" (115).

Much of Halevi's story is set in Spain, in what has been mistakenly (and today often propagandistically) called "the Golden Age" (a term invented by Heinrich Heine) of *convivencia* or a relative harmony among Muslims, Christians, and Jews, a "culture of tolerance" (25). Halkin is at great pains to clear away such cant. Yes, Halevi was trilingual; he learned Hebrew in school, and was fluent in Arabic, which was spoken at home, as well as in Spanish; he also wrote Hebrew poetry according to the rules of Arabic prosody. He belonged to several languages, but never to more than one people. For Halevi, as for Spanish Jews generally, tolerance was characteristic neither of Christians nor Muslims, who competed with each other for political and military dominance. In 1066, 3,000 Jews were killed in Grenada—by Muslims. The puritanical Almoravids required Jews to pay off their war debts to avoid forced conversion to Islam. In Aragon in 1109, Jews were robbed and murdered by rioting Muslims. The Almohad invasion and conquest of southern Spain in 1146 forced Jewish conversion to Islam. Maimonides (then a child of ten) and his family had been forced to flee from Cordoba in 1148 when "a new wave of Islamic intolerance swept in from North Africa" (21–24, 242). The mature Maimonides, often held up by "Golden Age" cheerleaders as an ecumenical foil to the "Zionist" Halevi, probably recalled this unpleasantness when he wrote, in his *Epistle to Yemen*: "Remember, my coreligionists, that on account of the vast number of our sins God has hurled us into the midst of these people, the Arabs, who have persecuted us severely, and passed baneful and discriminatory legislation against us. . . . Never did a nation molest, degrade, debase, and hate us as much as they" (295). Halkin also points out that the Christian quarrel with Judaism, although more bitter than Islam's, was also less demeaning to Jews because Christianity believed every word of the Hebrew Bible to be divinely given, and true, whereas Islam denied Jewish reality from its starting point in Abraham and rewrote, in the Koran, the life of every major figure in the Bible.[3]

The one deficiency of this otherwise splendid book reflects the slovenly editing that has marred several books in Schocken's Nextbook series. Although obviously a scholarly book, written by a man of scholarly conscience, *Yehuda Halevi* lacks notes, bibliography, and index. These are not just formal deficiencies: they lessen the staying power of a book eminently deserving of a long life.

Notes

1. Hillel Halkin, *Yehuda Halevi* (New York: Nextbook/Schocken, 2010), 282. (Subsequent references to this work appear in parentheses in the text.) Another book with which Halkin might have begun is Avi Erlich's *Ancient Zionism: The Biblical Origins of the National Idea* (New York: Free Press, 1995), which shows the extent to which the Jewish ethical system is linked to the Land of Israel.
2. *Letters to an American Jewish Friend: A Zionist's Polemic* (Philadelphia, PA: Jewish Publication Society, 1977), 182.
3. *Yehuda Halevi*, 110.

Hitler's American Professors

It is common knowledge that Hitler's professors (the title of Max Weinreich's famous book of 1946) were the first to make antisemitism both academically respectable and complicit in murder. Stephen Norwood's *The Third Reich in the Ivory Tower*[1] massively demonstrates how these professors and the universities and genocidal regime they served were themselves made respectable in America during the Nazi regime's formative years by the faculty and administrators of major American universities and colleges, among them Harvard, Columbia, Chicago, and the Seven Sisters women's colleges. They played a major role in legitimizing the Nazi regime, negatively by refusing to take a stand against it and positively by welcoming Nazi officials to their campuses and participating enthusiastically in student exchange programs with German institutions that had become travesties of universities. Norwood describes how, at the very time when many groups in America were, starting in 1933, demonstrating in the streets against the Hitler regime and boycotting its products, universities (widely, if mistakenly, assumed to be the home of the highly instructed—especially where Europe was the subject—and morally sensitive) were doing business as usual, refusing to attend, much less organize, anti-Nazi protests. When Robert Hutchins, president of the University of Chicago, was reproached for sailing across the Atlantic on a German ship flying the Nazi flag, he could not see what all the fuss was about and continued to make his frequent trans-Atlantic voyages on the *Europa*. (During the years from 1933 to 1938, Hutchins' university hired a grand total of ten German–Jewish refugee professors.)

Harvard's special contribution to making the antisemitic policies and actions of the Third Reich respectable among America's learned classes came mainly in its pattern of inviting prominent Nazis to lecture and receive honors in Cambridge. Harvard president James Conant invited and warmly welcomed Ernst Hanfstaengl, a Nazi leader and close friend (also look-alike) of Hitler, to attend his class' twenty-fifth reunion at the Harvard commencement of June 1934. One of the book's striking photos shows this worthy demonstrating the Hitler salute while standing in the reception line; apparently he had developed it during his cheerleader days back in 1909. Nor was Harvard lacking in its own, homegrown Nazis: Germanics professor John Walz spoke at Nazi rallies in Boston. (Those who think that the Modern Language Association sank to its lowest points when MIT professor Louis Kampf assumed its presidency in 1972 and Edward Said in 1999, should keep in mind that Walz became president of this dominant organization of scholars of literature and language long before.) So deeply entrenched was the belief that it was acceptable, indeed laudable, to welcome and honor spokesmen for the Nazi regime that university presidents reacted with fury against those who thought and publicly said otherwise. At Harvard, for example, seven protestors of Hanfstaengl's presence in Harvard Square were arrested for speaking without a permit and confined in prison for six months at hard labor. When Columbia president Nicholas Murray Butler sent a professorial delegate to Heidelberg's 550th anniversary celebration (a Nazi propaganda festival at which Josef Goebbels officially received delegates) a student named Robert Burke publicly criticized Butler. For this offense he was summarily forbidden to register for further classes at the college. He was being expelled for "deliver[ing] a speech in which he had referred to the President disrespectfully" and been brazenly contemptuous of "good manners" and "good taste" (97–99) in his language. Columbia, located in New York City, had more trouble than Harvard with student opposition to antisemitism because, despite its quota system, it had a large body of Jewish students; at Harvard, student opinion, for example, in the *Harvard Crimson* was decidedly welcoming to spokesmen for the new Germany.

The frequency with which "good manners" were invoked by these university presidents as a reason for welcoming Nazi spokesmen and cracking down on obstreperous Jews objecting to their presence raises the question of whether these academics were themselves motivated by a kind of antisemitism. Bernard Harrison distinguishes between social and political antisemitism. The former is a prejudice that would exclude Jews from country clubs or certain professions; the latter, far more lethal, is a prejudice of panic, which views Jews as an absolutely depraved people, whose aim is world domination, and who pursue that aim by incessant destructive activity aimed at the control of non-Jewish societies and destabilization of the world order. The latter, of course, was the type officially espoused by the Nazi regime. Most of the American university officials whose egregious actions and statements Norwood abundantly cites were social antisemites. But by no means all. Take, for example, Dean Virginia Gildersleeve of Barnard College in the thirties. She found time, amidst her efforts to reduce the number of Jews at Barnard, to wage a decades-long campaign against "International Zionism," the "Zionist control of the media of communication" in the United States, and politicians who out of "fear of the "Jewish vote," "bullied" Arabs into letting "alien foreigners" (130) into Palestine. In other words, she was a forerunner of such contemporary peddlers of Jewish conspiracy theory as Professors Stephen Walt, John Mearsheimer, and Noam Chomsky. Although he has elsewhere written forcefully on the subject, within the book itself Norwood refrains from linking the university-based antisemitism of the thirties with that of today, Harvard's invitation to Hanfstaengl with Columbia's invitation to Iranian dictator Ahmadinejad or English poetaster Tom Paulin or with the countless instances of Judeophobia that darken the current academic scene.[2]

Most contemporary instances of campus-based antisemitism (like the ones at University of California's Berkeley, Santa Cruz, and Irvine campuses which in 2011 led to investigations by the federal government for civil rights violations) derive from the left rather than the right. But even in 1938, some of academia's most liberal organizations were very reluctant to isolate or criticize Nazi Germany. When one of these organizations, the World Youth Congress, held its convention at Vassar College, it tried very hard to get the Nazis to send representatives to Poughkeepsie, promising to ban all criticism of the Hitler regime at the convention, to refuse representation to anti-Nazi refugee groups, and even to make German the official language of the convention! All to no avail—and why? Because these liberal idealists could not agree to the demand of the Hitler Youth that no communists be allowed to participate. Yet, even in the absence of the Nazis, many of the American delegation to the convention publicly declared their opposition to criticism of Nazi Germany because "a lasting peace" cannot be achieved "by a condemnatory attitude toward any nation" (229).

A more perfect realization of Matthew Arnold's Thucydidean image of "ignorant armies clash[ing] by night" could hardly be imagined.

Norwood's final chapter centers on the ways in which universities responded (or failed to respond) to the nationwide Nazi pogrom of November 10, 1938, carried out against the entire Jewish population of Germany. The National Socialist regime, its storm troopers acting in concert with many "ordinary Germans," destroyed over a thousand synagogues, smashed over 7,000 Jewish shops and businesses, ransacked Jewish homes, arrested 30,000 Jewish men and sent them to concentration camps, and then ordered the already impoverished Jews to pay for the damage that the Nazis had done to Jewish property. These events did disturb the equanimity of the professors and administrators, several of whom added their voices to the numerous public condemnations of what Thomas Dewey called "a dictatorship gone mad" (231). But, as historian Peter Gay, a young witness of Kristallnacht, recalled, their protests "sounded very good" yet proved hollow because "none of this verbal onslaught led to the action we needed: a place to go" (241). The universities imposed severe limits on refugee scholarships available to Jews in flight for their lives.

Perhaps the most poignant existential realization of the "ivory tower's" immoral thoughtlessness in opening its welcoming arms to Nazis was the University of Chicago's long, loving relationship with Mircea Eliade. Eliade had been a loyal servant of, and propaganda attaché for, the Nazi government of Romania from 1940 to 1945, an ardent supporter of the Iron Guard, whose barbaric massacres of Jews, acts that would have shamed animals, shocked even the Germans. Emigrating to the United States after the war, Eliade became a celebrated scholar of comparative religion, was hired by Chicago in 1956, and became chairman of its Department of the History of Religion. When his visa expired, the university persuaded the State Department to grant him a special waiver allowing him to stay in the United States forever because his work in Chicago was "indispensable to the security and welfare of the United States" (253). In 1981, Chicago's president Hannah Gray congratulated him on publication of the first volume of his autobiography: "You have had a fascinating life, and I'm delighted that you've put it down to inform and instruct all of us. It's a wonderful story." The only Chicago-based dissenter from this orgy of oily sycophancy was Saul Bellow, the protagonist of whose novel *Ravelstein* (2000) says of one Grielescu (based on Eliade):

"Grielescu is making use of you. In the old country he was a fascist. He needs to live that down. The man was a Hitlerite. . . . Do you have any memory of the massacre in Bucharest when they hung people alive on meat hooks in the slaughterhouse and . . . skinned them alive? Just give a thought now and then to those people on the meat hooks."[3] And just what is the lesson Eliade's "wonderful story" and others like it in Norwood's book teach us? It is that knowledge is one thing, virtue another. If you expect moral nourishment from professors, you should try getting warmth from the moon.

Notes

1. Stephen H. Norwood, *The Third Reich in the Ivory Tower: Complicity and Conflict* (New York: Cambridge University Press, 2009). References to this book will appear in parentheses in the text.
2. On this subject, see Eunice G. Pollack, ed., *Anti-Semitism on the Campus: Past and Present* (Brighton, MA: Academic Studies Press, 2011).
3. This grisly episode of the Holocaust appears elsewhere in the present book, in the essay on Cynthia Ozick's *Foreign Bodies*.

Hitler's (Palestinian) Arabs

The equation of Israelis with Nazis seems to have originated in British official circles in 1941. Years before there was a modern Jewish state, the Foreign Office was using the epithet "Jewish Nazi state" to refer to Jewish Palestine. Ironically, it was precisely the leadership of Arab Palestine that in 1941 was deeply entwined with the actual Nazis, not the metaphorical ones of febrile British imaginations. Haj Amin el-Husseini, the universally recognized leader ("Grand Mufti," as he called himself) of Palestinian Arabs and, in the eyes of Hitler, who called him "the Moslem Pope," of the whole Muslim world, was negotiating amiably with the Nazi leadership. He offered, with typical bravado, to destroy the 30,000–40,000 British soldiers stationed in Palestine. In return, he wanted Hitler's commitment to "solve" the problem of Jewish minorities in all Arab countries by applying the same racial ideology and methods being used to "solve" the problem in the territories controlled by the Nazis.

In her formidable and meticulously researched book about the Mufti,[1] Jennie Lebel, a historian living in Tel Aviv, traces the career of this international criminal who rose to power in Palestine largely by the traditional regional expedient of murdering his political opponents. Foreshadowing the globalization of later Palestinian leaders, he conceived of his struggle against the Jews—whom he deemed "the lowest race among the nations" (158)—as one of worldwide scope. In April of 1936, he asked the Italians for help in poisoning the drinking water of Tel Aviv. In the same year he received assistance from the German government in organizing anti-Jewish riots in Jaffa and Jerusalem. These riots and their successors eventually caused the British government, headed by Neville Chamberlain, to abrogate the Balfour Declaration and renounce the obligations it had assumed under the terms of the Mandate in the famous "White Paper" of 1939. This act of

British appeasement, like many others, failed to achieve its goal; during World War II the Arab population of Palestine was overwhelmingly on the side of the Axis. The riots also proved to be a perfect example of the axiom that violent actions against Jews presage the torching of many others as well.

In October 1941, the Mufti was welcomed to Rome by Mussolini, to whom he offered Muslim collaboration in exchange for the Duce's recognition of an Arab state run on fascist principles. A month later he arrived in Berlin, where he looked forward not only to meeting (on November 28) with Hitler and Ribbentrop but also to moving into—so he specified—"a large Jewish apartment" (107). What he wanted from Hitler was a declaration of commitment to a four-point plan: (1) the Axis would give material support to Arab countries seeking liberation from British occupation; (2) the Axis would recognize the sovereignty and independence of the Arab countries in the Middle East; (3) the Axis would cancel the decision regarding a "Jewish national Home" (108) in Palestine; and (4) the details of this declaration would be the foundation of a formal alliance between the Axis powers and the Arab people.

What the Mufti offered in return was a commitment to win the support, both military and political, of European Muslims for the Nazi cause. The photo (one of about a hundred that illustrate Lebel's book) taken of el-Husseini and Hitler chatting with each other on sofas a few feet apart was not only the prize souvenir in the Mufti's family scrapbook, but a recruiting device. It was subsequently distributed to millions of Muslims in the occupied Soviet Union, in Bosnia, in Kosovo, and also to Soviet Muslim POWs in German prison camps. It helped greatly in the formation, organized by Himmler and the Mufti, of Muslim divisions in the Waffen SS. In January 1944, Haj Amin blessed the newly formed Muslim SS divisions as follows: "As you know, the world is today divided into two camps: one is the camp of the Allies, led by world Jewry, which means by forces that were always enemies of Islam and oppressed Moslems, conquered our lands, fought against our religion . . . " (221). The other, Germany, was not only friendly to Islam, but headed by a man whom the Mufti had often proclaimed a descendant of the Prophet and savior of Islam: Adolf Hitler (139).

Although the Mufti was an oily sycophant who craved Nazi flattery and was delighted when Hitler pronounced him an "honorary Aryan" (241), he was not entirely wrong in sensing in Hitler and Himmler a certain sympathy with Islam. Hitler was reported to have said that he liked Islam so much that he would like to proclaim it as the SS religion. Islam, unlike Christianity, impressed him as a "male religion" (242). Himmler thought Islam the only religion that did not find fault with warfare, and whereas the typical Christian soldier went to war fearing death, the Muslims believed that a place in paradise awaited them after death.

Lebel suggests that the relations between the Arab and Nazi leaders were based on something more than a quid pro quo, i.e., Arab help in the Nazi war effort in exchange for Nazi help in the struggle against the Jews and British. They also shared certain values, if bloodthirstiness and all-consuming Jew-hatred can be called "values." Leo Strauss, the great University of Chicago political philosopher, once wrote that the Nazi regime was the only regime he knew of "based on no principle other than the negation of Jews."[2] But Haj Amin and the Palestinian political culture derived from him challenge the Nazis' claim to uniqueness in this respect. Like the Nazis with whom he conspired, the Mufti seems to have devoted most of his working hours to devising ways of destroying Jews.

In more than one instance, in fact, Haj Amin outdid the Germans in the single-mindedness of his hatred. In 1942, for example, Dieter Wisliceny, Eichmann's assistant for Slovakia and Hungary, agreed to an exchange of 10,000 Jewish children, mostly orphans, for German citizens who were being held in Allied prison camps. The Jewish children were to be transferred to Palestine. Suddenly, Eichmann called to tell Wisliceny that the deal was off; the Mufti had heard of these preparations from his agents in Palestine, and protested them to Himmler, who promptly ordered that no plans should ever again be made to rescue Jewish children from the German death machine and send them to Palestine. That the Mufti knew perfectly well what would be the fate of Jewish children who remained in German hands is made clear by Lebel: he was among the few members of the inner circle who knew from an early stage of Hitler's intention to eradicate European Jewry.

Indeed, el-Husseini was so enamored of Hitler and his program for the "final solution" that he was on occasion willing to sacrifice the cause of Arab independence in order to keep the Arabs loyal to the Nazis. At the same time (1943–1944) that he was calling for North African Arab soldiers to defect from the Allied armies, he obscured the fact that the Allies had openly guaranteed future Arab independence while the Germans kept silent about the matter. Instead, he kept telling his fellow Arabs that the Allies planned to turn North Africa into "a second Jewish homeland" to which they would bring not only the remainder of European Jewry but also "some of the Jews and Negroes from America" (142).

At war's end, Haj Amin escaped from Germany, and was neither arrested nor prosecuted by the Allies, though he was a war criminal and the inciter of other war criminals. After his arrival in Egypt in 1946, he organized the murder of political opponents, including the president of Lebanon and King Abdullah of Jordan. He died in his Beirut home on July 4, 1974. Among his mourning relatives was one Yasser Arafat, who emulated his mother's cousin in international terrorism and the conviction that destroying a Jewish nation took precedence over building a Palestinian one. But Arafat added to these proclivities a nimble persuasiveness that enabled the Palestinian Arabs to win victories in their war against the Jews that they had been unable to win on the battlefield.

Lebel has provided us with a full portrait of the political career of one of the vilest scoundrels of the scoundrel-rich twentieth century. Her narrative gives the lie, on a massive scale, to the claim that Palestinian Arabs had nothing whatever to do with the Holocaust. It also shrewdly interprets those parts of the Mufti's story that shed light on present developments, in the Palestinian movement, in the Arab world, in the Muslim populations of Europe (especially the former Yugoslavia), and in the unceasing campaign to expel Israel from the family of nations.

Notes

1. *The Mufti of Jerusalem: Haj Amin el-Husseini and National Socialism* [in Serbian], trans. Paul Munch (Belgrade: Cigoja Stampa, 2007). Subsequent references to this work appear in parentheses in the text.
2. Leo Strauss, "Why We Remain Jews," in *Jewish Philosophy and the Crisis of Modernity*, ed. Kenneth H. Green (Albany, NY: SUNY Press, 1997), 321.

Beethoven and the Holocaust in Hungary

The incredibility of the Holocaust has been a central theme of Holocaust literature and scholarship from their inception. In 1951, Hannah Arendt stressed the extent to which the Nazis relied on the likelihood that the wild improbability of the scale of their crimes would guarantee that, should they lose the war, they and their preposterous lies would be believed, whereas their victims would be derided as fantasists. "The Nazis did not even consider it necessary to keep this discovery to themselves. Hitler circulated millions of copies of his book in which he stated that to be successful, a lie must be enormous—which did not prevent people from believing him as, similarly, the Nazis' proclamations, repeated *ad nauseam*, that the Jews would be exterminated like bedbugs (i.e., with poison gas) prevented anybody from *not* believing them."[1] Abba Kovner, the commander of the Jewish underground in Vilna, wrote: "That they could all be murdered, the Jews of Vilna, Kovno, Bialystok, Warsaw, the millions with their wives and children—hardly a single one wanted to believe that. What was the meaning of this? Was it just blindness?"[2] To which question Arendt offered an answer: "There is a great temptation to explain away the intrinsically incredible by means of liberal rationalizations. In each one of us, there lurks such a liberal, wheedling us with the voice of common sense."[3]

Nowhere was the incredibility of Germany's campaign to destroy Jewry more extreme than in Hungary. In *Night*, the "non-fictional novel" that has long been considered the classic personal account by a Hungarian survivor of the Holocaust, Elie Wiesel records the following conversation in Auschwitz between a veteran prisoner and a newly arrived one: "You'd have done better to have hanged yourselves where you were than to come here. Didn't you know what was in store for you at Auschwitz? Haven't you heard about it? In 1944?" No, we had not heard. No one had told us. He could not believe his ears.

As historians Raul Hilberg and Randolph Braham have observed, by 1944, Hungary, with its 750,000 Jews, was the only important area of Europe still untouched by deportations to the killing centers. But in March the Germans overran the country, the only one in which the organizers of mass murder knew that the war was lost when they began their operations. The Hungarian Jews were almost the only Jews in Europe who had full warning and knowledge of what was to come while their community was still unharmed. The mass deportation of Hungary's Jews was also unique because it was carried out openly, in full view of the whole world. Rudolf Kastner, associate president of the Zionist Organization in Hungary, wrote: "In Budapest we had a unique opportunity to follow the fate of European Jewry. We had seen how they had been disappearing one after the other from the map of Europe. At the moment of the occupation of Hungary, the number of dead Jews amounted to over five million. We knew very well about the work of the *Einsatzgruppen*. We knew more than was . . . necessary about Auschwitz. . . . We had, as early as 1942, a complete picture of what had been happening in the East with the Jews deported to Auschwitz and the other extermination camps."[4] Nevertheless, Eichmann had only to set up a *Judenrat* to publish all German orders to the Jews, and to assure them they had nothing to fear if they cooperated. In a period of just seven weeks (May 15–July 9), 430,000 Hungarian Jews were deported to Auschwitz. Did they repress the detailed knowledge they already had about the five million already murdered, and deliberately fool themselves, or is Yehuda Bauer correct in arguing that information and knowledge are not the same thing? "The information was there all the time, including information regarding the ways in which the Nazis were misleading and fooling their victims. The point is that this information was rejected, people did not *want* to know, because knowledge would have caused pain and suffering, and there was seemingly no way out."[5]

Little Zsuzsi Abonyi (who is now Zsuzsanna Ozsvath, professor of literature and the history of ideas at the University of Texas) received a child's version of this information in 1940, when she was in the third grade. At a birthday party in the Hungarian town of Bekescsaba, while standing in line for a slice of the cake, she met a girl named Hanna, who had arrived in Hungary after escaping from Poland with her mother. In fluent Hungarian, she told Zsuzsi about German roundups of Polish Jews, separation of children from parents, old from young,

Nazi sadism in all its infinite variety, and raw murder, including the shooting of Hanna's father and grandfather in the marketplace. Could this happen in Hungary too? "We don't live in a ghetto! . . . Are there ghettos in Hungary? Will the Germans build some for us?"[6] That marketplace would haunt Zsuzsi's imagination, like fate in a Greek tragedy, from this time through the terrible year of 1944. Her father, whom she loved and trusted, told her that "What the Germans did in Poland could never happen in Hungary! Never! Hungarians wouldn't allow it" (8). But this assurance could not make her forget his unguarded reaction to a radio news broadcast of March 12, 1938, announcing the *Anschluss* (Germany's occupation of Austria): "Everything is over" (6). No parental denial of Hanna's report from Poland could have the force of those three words.

Young Zsuzsi may have been protected from the truth of Hungarian Jewry's plight by her parents, but very little of the truth was protected from *her*. Overhearing their discussions of ways to escape the Germans' net (eagerly spread by their very willing Hungarian Arrow Cross accomplices)—flight to Palestine via Romania, going into hiding at a Hungarian resort, splitting the family—she proposed an alternative: suicide. "With wide eyes, my mother looked at me. 'I had to live for forty-six years to hear my twelve-year-old say this,' she sighed bitterly." "How," the mature Ozsvath asks herself, "did I know about gas chambers on March 19, 1944? I cannot answer the question" (65).

One escape route that the Ozsvath parents did try, in June of 1944, was quick conversion to Roman Catholicism. The reason why it failed them may be evident from the morally bankrupt language in which it was offered. On May 15, 1944, when deportations of Hungarian Jewry had already begun in the Carpathians, the Church declared: "The Apostolic Nunciature considers it to be its duty to protest against such measures. Not from a false sense of compassion, but on behalf of thousands of Christians, it once again appeals to the Hungarian government not to continue this war against the Jews beyond the limits prescribed by . . . the commandments of God."[7] Certainly, no "false sense of compassion" protected Zsuzsi's father from being arrested in October of 1944 and marched off to a camp: "that was worse than any of my nightmares, worse than my fears of Hanna's marketplace, worse than my decision to take my life . . ." (118–19). Later, Laszlo Abonyi was sent on a death march to Austria, but managed to escape and rejoin his family in Hungary.

This powerful and astute memoir, written by a mature woman many years after the events narrated, gives a child's eye view of the Holocaust in Hungary. Such a narrative must strike a balance between self-criticism and self-respect. The criticism sometimes comes from a more knowledgeable adult: how could a twelve-year-old understand that the Germans, having already lost the war, were hell-bent on destroying the Jews, or that their Arrow Cross allies, fully aware that Jews made up half the country's doctors, nearly half its lawyers, a third of its trading population, thought that letting Hungary go to rack and ruin was a cheap price to pay for a free hand in murder. At other times, the grown-up Ozsvath criticizes young Zsuzsi for making the rescue mission of her heroic gentile nanny Erzsi, more difficult, as when she gets expelled from a convent for revealing her Jewish identity (while posing as a Lutheran).

But the self-respect that Zsuzsanna Ozsvath shows toward young Zsuzsi Abonyi is more important, and well deserved. Throughout the book she paints a masterly picture of the intellectual culture of young Zsuzsi and of her sector of Hungarian Jewry that is remarkable both in itself and in its revelation of what the Holocaust does *not* teach. Here, for example, is the description of the activities of children ages nine to eighteen in the grossly overcrowded Abonyi "yellow-star" or "Ghetto" House. "We invented new roles and new characters, placing them next to Romeo and Juliet or Lear and Ophelia, echoing these characters' pain or happiness or counteracting them, using a text that was similar to Shakespeare's style. Besides Shakespeare, we studied parts of, and participated in, plays of Molière, Racine, Ibsen, and Goethe. . . . We recited Rilke's lyrics and his *Tales about God*, . . . we recited poems by . . . Shakespeare, Milton, and Oscar Wilde. We also wrote about and discussed books, politics, ethics, and religion, with a passion that made us inseparable from one another, a passion that . . . defined our notions of play and friendship . . . for the rest of our days" (99). Zsuzsi had to absent herself from some of these activities to practice the piano several times a day because she was already an accomplished classical pianist. At a later and grimmer stage of the Nazi occupation, when life hung only by "a slender thread," Zsuzsi "started to practice again, still learning more Bach preludes and studying several Beethoven sonatas," reading (for the first time without parental supervision) Dickens, Hugo, Balzac, Thomas Mann, and "writing a diary" (122). A century and a half after Matthew Arnold defined poetry and imaginative literature generally as "a criticism of life," we learn from this stunning memoir what he really meant: not that literature says explicitly what is "wrong" with life, but that by its coherence, brightness, and energy, it implies what life *might* be, but all too often is not. She now understood why "my mother always wanted me to learn poetry by heart."

Even at the height of the Soviet siege late in 1944, when she finds herself abandoned, hiding in the closet of a house under artillery bombardment and watching Jews being shot into the Danube by Arrow Cross Nazis, Zsuzsi practices the piano, but (of course) without a piano, and creates the golden world of music in opposition to the brazen world of Budapest. It is one of the book's great passages:

> Trembling for a while and crying, I decided to 'practice the piano in my head.' I went back to the closet and started to imagine I was playing Beethoven's f-minor sonata, op. 3, from the first measure to the last. Some passages went very well, some, not at all. While my right hand's fingers were really singing in the second part, my left hand's were too slow playing the triplets in the fourth part. 'I need to practice this more,' I thought. But I did not go back . . . rather, I started to play the second sonata in A major; and again, I thought through every single note. In the meantime, the bombing started anew (153–54).
>
> Lonely and frightened, she lived for three days in that closet while the bombing continued, "practicing" piano pieces she knew by heart and also praying: " I knew very little Hebrew, so I mixed my personal prayer in Hungarian with such Hebrew prayers as the 'Shema' and the Passover questions I had recited at our family's Seder in my grandfather's house . . .: *Manishtana halylo ha zeh* [Why is this night different . . .] (154).

One wonders whether, in the vast body of Holocaust literature, there is a more striking example of the Hebraic-Hellenic synthesis in the life of cultivated European Jews. At the very least, it sharply contradicts what the Holocaust "teaches" people like George Steiner, who writes that "By killing the Jew, Western culture would eradicate those who had 'invented' God . . ." and notes that Beethoven concerts were being held in Munich while people were being tortured in nearby Dachau. "What immortal poem," asks Steiner (with feigned innocence) "has ever stopped or mitigated political terror?"[8] From Ozsvath's memoir we learn that the heritage of Western culture is not to be abandoned just because we have rediscovered what sensible people have always known: that culture is not the highest value of human existence, that works of culture are defenseless against their misuse by scoundrels, that cultural achievements of the past are not merely conditioned and tainted by historical circumstances but also ultimately capable of transcending those circumstances. Let us therefore be thankful that twelve-year-old Zsuzsi could practice Beethoven and Bach while hiding from shells and murderers, and that—unlike Steiner—she knew that Jews were being murdered by Nazis, not "Western culture."

The passage that gives this book its title is Ozsvath's description of what she saw from her hiding place: "I tried to look outside through the shattered blinds. But what did I see? My God! It was an image I will not forget for as long as I live: a bunch of children, men, and women were standing on the bank of the Danube, on their chests the palm-sized yellow star. They were bound together by ropes. At least four or five Nyilas [Hungarian Nazis] aimed their guns at them, shooting them into the river, which flowed red like blood" (152). History makes metaphor. In October 2010, newspapers all over the world featured front-page reports that "Red Sludge hits blue Danube," apparently the result of toxic mud flowing into the river. Ancient prophets believed that moral gloom was an accurate predictor of physical gloom: "The light shall be darkened in the heavens thereof, and the stars shall withdraw their shining" (Joel 2:10). Many Nyilas who shot Jews into the Danube were "boys" at the time they committed their crimes. One wonders—if not for long—whether those still alive recognized some connection between the red Danube of 1944 and the red Danube of 2010. Certainly Zsuzsanna Ozsvath does.

Notes

1. Hannah Arendt, *The Origins of Totalitarianism* (New York: Harcourt, Brace & World, 1951), III, 137.
2. Abba Kovner, "The Mission of the Survivors," a speech delivered in 1945 to soldiers of the Jewish Brigade in Italy. The speech was taken down by Meir Argov, later a member of the Knesset.
3. Arendt, *Origins of Totalitarianism*, III, 138.
4. Raul Hilberg, *The Destruction of the European Jews* (Chicago, IL: Quadrangle Books, 1961), 529.
5. Yehuda Bauer, *The Holocaust in Historical Perspective* (Seattle, WA: University of Washington Press, 1978), 106.
6. Zsuzsanna Ozsvath, *When the Danube Ran Red* (Syracuse, NY: Syracuse University Press, 2010), 3. (Subsequent references to this book will appear in parentheses in the text.)
7. Hilberg, *Destruction of the European Jews*, 539.
8. *In Bluebeard's Castle: Some Notes toward the Redefinition of Culture* (New Haven, CT: Yale University Press, 1971), 41, 63, 86.

Israel's "Original Sin": The Refugees of 1948

There is only one country in the world whose "right to exist"—though recognized by the League of Nations nearly a century ago and realized in the United Nations by an internationally recognized act of self-determination in 1948—is considered a legitimate subject of discussion and debate, in books, in journals, in churches, in classrooms, and even in synagogues. The reason why Israel has this unenviable distinction has little to do with the history of the Middle East "conflict" and much to do with the history of antisemitism. For example, a widely publicized 2007 BBC poll of 28,000 people in 27 countries showed Israel as "least-liked" country in the entire world, and, among Europeans polled, most disliked in Germany; yes, in the very country where the Jews' "right to live" was also once a popular topic, Israel-haters outnumbered Israel-admirers by 77 percent to 10 percent.

Nevertheless, it is still important to recognize that those people for whom public denial of Israel's "right to exist" constitutes a ticket of admission to "progressive" circles allege that Israel's "original sin" consists of having come into existence as a result of ethnic cleansing of Palestine's Arab population in 1947–1948, as the British Mandate was coming to an end. Efraim Karsh's *Palestine Betrayed* massively and irrefutably destroys this particular slander, showing that the flight of a large segment of Palestinian Arabs (somewhere between 538,000 and 609,000 refugees) was a self-inflicted calamity. It resulted from the disunity, corruption, abominable leadership, and half-hearted followership among the Palestinian Arabs, and of territorial greed and imperial ambition among the Arab nations, who had no interest whatever in establishing a Palestinian state but only in grabbing some part of Palestine for themselves. If the invading Arab armies had succeeded in defeating the Jews and destroying the newly created state, its territory would not have been handed over to the Palestinian

Arabs but divided among the invading forces. Iraq and Transjordan, for example, declared their intention to occupy "the whole, repeat the whole, of Palestine" when the British withdrew. It was the Zionists and not the Arab states (which had been rejecting partition since 1937) who accepted a two-state solution.[1]

Karsh's book is less an act of discovery than of recovery. He takes us back to what was clear to everyone at the time, but in the intervening decades (starting in the early 1950s at the instigation of the Nazi collaborator Haj Amin el-Husseini) has been obscured by layers of obfuscation, distortion, historical amnesia, and outright lies. All have served to cast Israel as the main culprit in the Palestinian "catastrophe" and transform the aggressors into helpless victims of, in the words of one Islamist leader: "an organized . . . cunning, devious, and evil people that . . . buried Hitler and defeated Japan . . . that has Truman in its pay, enslaves Churchill . . . and colonizes London, New York, and Washington" (3). Even Ben-Gurion's insistence in October 1937 that "We do not wish and do not need to expel Arabs and take their place. All our aspiration is built on the assumption—proven throughout all our activity in the Land [of Israel] . . . that there is enough room in the country for ourselves and the Arabs" (26) has been distorted to say exactly the opposite.

Palestine Betrayed is primarily a history of the five and a half month period between the passing of the UN resolution (November 29, 1947) to partition Palestine into two independent states: one Arab, one Jewish, with Jerusalem under an international regime (its residents free to choose citizenship in either state) and the end of the British Mandate. During that time the Palestinian forces of Husseini, assisted by a large pan-Arab irregular army, launched thousands of attacks on their Jewish neighbors to prevent the establishment of Israel. But by May 14, 1948, when the state was proclaimed, 300,000–340,000 Arabs had fled their homes to other parts of Palestine and to the neighboring Arab states; eventually the number would swell to about 600,000.

Karsh, exploiting more fully and fruitfully than anyone ever has, the archival resources pertaining to the Arab "evacuation frenzy" (184), describes it in vast detail, takes account, in separate chapters, of local variations in Haifa (assigned to the Jewish state), Jaffa (assigned, as the most important Arab town in Palestine, to the Arab state), and Jerusalem, and analyzes their causes. Why did Palestinian Arab society collapse during those five and a half months of fighting? Why did huge numbers of Arabs, even while Jewish forces were on the defensive and in no position to drive them out, take flight while their Jewish neighbors, facing similar challenges and dislocations of war, and suffering a higher casualty rate, stay put and fight? Why, when the Jewish mayor of Haifa pleaded with them to remain where they were and promised to maintain harmonious relations, did the city's Arabs listen to the Arab Higher Command that told them, in effect, to "get out so we can get in"? Many Arab leaders believed that "the absence of the women and children from Palestine would free the men for fighting." As one of them put it: "Let the blood flow in the streets. Our goal is to destroy everything. We're emptying all mixed-population localities—suburbs, villages, and cities—so that when the blow comes, it will be powerful and sustained" (239). Instead, the opposite happened: it was the Arab leaders themselves who proved most eager to get out of Palestine and stay out. In Haifa, for example, the Arabs were deserted by their military commanders. The American vice-consul reported that "Arab Higher Command all left Haifa some hours before the battle took place" (134). This failure of leadership was a leading cause of the more general flight. Ironically, it was Haifa's Jewish authorities who made valiant attempts to convince Haifa's Arabs to remain in the city; it was the Zionists and not the Arabs who wanted a two-state solution. "The mass departure of women and children," Karsh observes, "led to the total depopulation of cities and villages as the men chose to join their families rather than to stay behind and fight" (239).

But there were still more grievous failures. In a striking prefigurement of today's Middle East impasse, the Arabs gave much higher priority to destroying someone else's society than to building their own. The commander of Jaffa's Arab forces declared in February 1948: "I do not mind [the] destruction of Jaffa if we secure [the] destruction of Tel Aviv." Arab leaders took it for granted that Arab departure would be a defeat not for them, but for the Jews because their remaining would constitute tacit acknowledgment of acceptance of a Jewish state. Karsh suggests yet another explanation of the Arab flight: namely, that Palestinian Arabs lacked a strong sense of national identity, cohesion, and shared destiny. "Cities and towns acted as if they were self-contained units, eschewing the smallest sacrifice on behalf of other localities" (240).

Atrocity stories invented by Arab leaders exacerbated panic; intended to incite hatred of the Jews, they created fear of them instead. The Deir Yassin killings, by Irgun and Lehi fighters, took place on April 9, 1948, but could hardly explain the enormous flight of Arabs—a third from Haifa, still more from Jaffa—before that. Moreover, the specter of (conjectural) Jewish atrocities also had a deep psychological dimension, what Christopher Sykes called the Palestinians' "bad conscience" about their own actual atrocities against Jews. In 1921, they had murdered ninety Jews in Jaffa; in 1929, they had butchered 133 Jews in several locations, most hideously in Hebron, where, in Sykes's words, they committed "deeds which would have been revolting among animals"[2]; and in April 1948, they murdered seventy-seven doctors, nurses, and scientists en route to Hadassah Hospital. They thought Jewish forces, given the upper hand, would behave as they themselves had done.

Will Karsh's book explode the big lie about Israel's origins? Probably not. In May of 2011, Mahmoud Abbas, the supposedly moderate head of the Palestinian Authority, took to the op-ed pages of the *New York Times* to make the case for return of the Arab refugees of 1948 to Israel by recounting his own tale of (alleged) expulsion by the Zionists. "Sixty-three years ago," he wrote, "a 13-year-old Palestinian boy was forced to leave his home in the Galilean city of Safed and flee with his family to Syria. . . . He took up shelter in a canvas tent . . . Though he and his family wished for decades to return to their homes and homeland, they were denied that most basic of human rights. That child's story, like that of so many other Palestinians, is mine." In fact, Abbas and family had not been expelled. In an Arab-language interview a few years earlier, he had revealed that they had *not* been expelled by Jewish forces; neither (since Abbas' father was wealthy) had they lived in a tent of any kind. Huge numbers of these refugees were ordered or bullied into leaving Safed by the Arab Higher Command. The British departure from the town on April 16 brought an Arab attack on its tiny Jewish community. One Arab fighter later recalled: "We were the majority, and the feeling among us was that we would defeat the Jews with sticks and rocks." British Intelligence reported that "the Arabs were beginning to evacuate Safed although the Jews have not yet attacked them." Following the pattern of larger cities like Haifa (fully described in Karsh's book) and for the very same reason, Safed's Arabs were in full flight by May 9. There was no act of Jewish expulsion. Apparently the fact-checkers of the *New York Times*, insofar as they operate at all, do not operate on the op-ed pages. Karsh, like numerous other readers of Abbas' self-serving fable, pointed out its fantastic nature, but with a sense of weary futility.[3] "Lies," according to the old adage, "have long legs" and get halfway around the globe before truth even begins to catch up with them." Still, we ought to know what the truth really is.

Notes

1. Efraim Karsh, *Palestine Betrayed* (New Haven, CT: Yale University Press, 2010), 89. Subsequent references will be included in parentheses within the text.
2. Christopher Sykes, *Cross Roads to Israel: Palestine from Balfour to Bevin* (London: Collins, 1965), 118.
3. "Abbas' Fable," *Jerusalem Post*, May 20, 2011.

"If I Am Not for Myself, Who Will Be for Me?" The History of *Commentary* Magazine

Running Commentary[1] is the story of a magazine and also of the people who created it, nurtured it, quarreled about it, shaped or (according to detractors) misshaped it, sometimes abandoned and attacked it, during its long history. Benjamin Balint, the author, calls these New York (mostly Jewish) intellectuals by the name Norman Podhoretz invented: "[They] resembled nothing so much as a loosely knit, self-formed Family . . . bound by a common language and frame of reference, a shared ordering of values, and an intense crisscrossing alertness to one another's judgments. They were kinsmen of a common cause, a common past, and a common set of ancestors" (6).

The title of Balint's critical history derives from Elliot Cohen's "Act of Affirmation" in the inaugural issue of November 1945. "Commentary means a 'running comment.' We will keep abreast of the march of events. Commentary also means 'interpretation.' . . . But there is also a traditional Jewish meaning of commentary . . . which we as editors cherish. Our ancient scribes and sages . . . only wrote commentaries on the revelation which was the Law. But we know that these everchanging interpretations of the past by the men of wisdom and men of insight of each generation, became for that generation more than merely commentaries. [They] became the truth that men lived by."

The year 1945 marked "an epoch in world history" because World War II had just ended, the age of nuclear destruction had (in August) just begun, and the destruction of European Jewry ("slaughtered like cattle") was now common knowledge. Although Cohen believed that "the great Nazi secret weapon of World War II" had been an antisemitism (a word he never actually uses) that few European voices protested, few European hands opposed, his hopes were as great as his fears, in large part because the center of gravity of the Jewish world was now America, and not the European graveyard. (He did not mention the *yishuv* in Palestine, and nobody on his staff could speak Hebrew.) "*Commentary*," he declared, "is an act of faith in our possibilities in America." This belief in one crucial aspect of American exceptionalism—its resistance to political antisemitism—eased the movement of Cohen and his main writers from Marxism to an Americanism that has characterized the magazine throughout its history with the exception of the years 1960–1968, when Podhoretz pushed it far to the Left. As Balint, with characteristic precision, says: "By teaching that there need be no contradiction between Jewish particularism and full participation in the larger culture, *Commentary* showed Jews how to weave the strands of Jewishness into the texture of American life" (210).

Although Cohen understood that for Jews survival would long remain more crucial than self-definition (an American–Jewish obsession), he nevertheless believed that, as *Commentary* stalwart Ruth Wisse would later say, it was the duty of American Jews to judge *The New York Times* by the standards of Judaism, not Judaism by the standards of the *Times*: "We suffer our own special questionings, which . . . we believe humanity should share with us, possibly for the common good." He also raised, at least by implication, the question that (so Balint believes) besets the magazine to this day: how to realize in its contents the moral poise of "the two perfectly balanced parts" of Rabbi Hillel's teaching: "If I am not for myself, who will be for me? And if I am for myself alone, what am I?" (133).

As managing editor of the *Menorah Journal*, a forerunner of *Commentary*, Cohen expressed the view that the intellect of American Jews had failed to keep pace with their economic and political progress. "Judaism cannot survive if intelligent Jews come to despise it" (14). Among the writers he drew to that magazine was Lionel Trilling (1905–1975), who said that he had never before seen a Jewish publication "that was not shoddy and disgusting," yet by 1929 had come to believe that "the whole purpose of practical Jewish endeavor is to create a community that can read the *Menorah Journal*" (14–15). Trilling wrote essays, reviews, and stories for the journal, whose editor he considered a master of English prose, "a man of genius" (15) and the greatest teacher he had ever known. Nevertheless, when Cohen was appointed by the American Jewish Committee as *Commentary*'s editor and invited Trilling (an abiding presence in Balint's book) to join its board of contributing editors, Trilling interpreted it as Cohen's "impulse to 'degrade' me by involving me in [a] Jewish venture" and had "little hesitation or regret" in saying no (26). Despite Trilling's praise of his writing, Cohen was a "blocked" writer who (exactly like *Commentary*'s skilled third editor, Neal Kozodoy) preferred ventriloquism to publishing under his own name and established *Commentary*'s tradition of heavy editing. "Listen," Harold Rosenberg said to him: "If you want to write, write under your own name!" (19).

Under Cohen's direction, the new magazine virtually invented the history and sociology of American Jews. It showed new intellectual openness to Jewish religion, publishing Martin Buber, Abraham Joshua Heschel, Emil Fackenheim, Will Herberg, and Jacob Neusner. It was far ahead of the American Jewish community in confronting the Holocaust, publishing the work of historians like Cecil Roth, Fritz Stern, Hannah Arendt, and Lucy Dawidowicz, war veterans like Irving Kristol, diarists like Emanuel Ringelblum and Elie Wiesel. In 1952, Cohen purchased (for $250) rights to the diary of Anne Frank, which first appeared in America in two *Commentary* installments; they were crucial in making the girl deported from Amsterdam to be murdered in Nazi camps the most famous child of the twentieth century. (Prior to *Commentary*, it was not the *Partisan Review* Jews of the Family, such as Trilling, Irving Howe, and Philip Rahv, who agonized over the murder of their brethren in Europe, but less celebrated figures like Marie Syrkin, Ben Halpern, and Maurice Samuel.)

Cohen died, by his own hand, in 1960 and was replaced (after Kristol declined the job) by Podhoretz, whom Trilling considered his star undergraduate, destined for a literary career that might make him America's new Edmund Wilson. He began his long tenure, so Jacob Neusner remarked, by "remov[ing] all the mezuzahs from the doors" (84). This acerbity alluded to Podhoretz's shrinkage of the magazine's Jewish content (he dropped the "Cedars of Lebanon" column, where scholars like Neusner and Erich Isaac wrote about Jewish sources), rejection of Cohen's unswerving anticommunism, and resurrection of the Family's double alienation, from Judaism and from America. According to former managing editor Clement Greenberg, Podhoretz "didn't give a shit about the Jews" at that time (84).

Despite Podhoretz's undisguised desire to become the Family's great literary star, he grew more and more political, displaying some of the dogmatism and dictatorialness that he would subsequently allege to be characteristic of liberals. Podhoretz's *Commentary* strongly opposed the Vietnam war and disparaged American society in general. His first issues serialized Paul Goodman's *Growing Up Absurd,* which set forth pacifist/anarchist ideas that Howe had earlier, in *Commentary* itself, derided as "exuberantly reckless and irresponsible" (88). He also invited his then friend Norman Mailer, the Esau of American literature, to write (almost incomprehensibly) in 1963 about Buber's *Tales of the Hasidim.* The journal's Leftist lurch proved very popular with those who could afford subscriptions and advertisements: the former quickly tripled, and the latter increased tenfold. But when the verbal bomb-throwers joined forces with the actual bomb-throwers of the New Left, and Black Power advocates allied with what Trilling called "the adversary culture" (and Howe much harsher names) assaulted the universities, the Jews, America itself, and, after the 1967 war, the state of Israel, Podhoretz's Dionysian/Leftist phase was at an end. Subsequently the magazine would be a staunch defender of Israel in the war of ideas launched by her leftist and liberal enemies, sick with what Balint deftly calls "the political anorexia from which some Jews suffered, the will to cease to exist as a body" (112).

Podhoretz has said that "the most consequential thing I had ever done or ever would do in my entire professional life" (100–101) was to hire Neal Kozodoy, who became executive editor in 1968. When I wrote for the magazine in the eighties and nineties, I dealt almost exclusively with Kozodoy and had the sense that he was his own boss and did not need to have decisions approved by Podhoretz. He too had a strong literary background, and seems to have been primarily responsible for encouraging Robert Alter, a key contributor to *Commentary* since 1961, to undertake critical studies of the art of biblical narrative that endowed a whole generation with new eyes for reading the Hebrew Bible.

Under the joint leadership of Podhoretz and Kozodoy, *Commentary* now reverted to the Americanism of Cohen, but with a new definition that tied the defense of America, the one country in the world that was Israel's faithful ally, to that of the whole Jewish people. Contributing editors Alter and Milton Himmelfarb mocked the parochialism of Jewish universalism and xenophilia. Sanguine as Cohen had been that a Jewish magazine could influence the larger world, it is unlikely that—as Senator Daniel Patrick Moynihan observed in the magazine's fortieth-anniversary issue (1985)—Cohen "could have hoped for the influence *Commentary* has had on democratic thought these four long decades" (162). Moynihan knew whereof he spoke: he had in 1975 been catapulted by his *Commentary* article "The United States in Opposition" into the post of American ambassador to the UN, where he was an articulate defender of Israel. In the seventies, Podhoretz recruited Jeane Kirkpatrick to write for the magazine, and she too, in 1979, had the same good fortune plus the nickname "the ambassador from *Commentary*." Gone, for better or worse, were the days when the virtue of powerlessness was celebrated at E. 56th Street.

Part of the story of *Commentary*'s Family is what Joseph Epstein has likened to "the internecine viciousness of a Mafia family."[2] When I was working on my biography of Howe in the mid-nineties I received a great deal of help from Howe's longtime friend, the sociologist Dennis Wrong. After we had corresponded for months, he offered to send me his old letters from Howe. But when I expressed eagerness to see them, a long silence ensued—broken by his apologetic letter reporting that Howe's son forbade this, for two reasons. One was that I had published the remark made to me by I. B. Singer in 1981: "a wonderful man, Irving Howe. He's done so much for Yiddish literature, and for me. But he's not a youngster anymore, and still, still with this socialist *meshugas*." The other offense imputed to me was that "Alexander has written for *Commentary*." My rejoinder was that Howe himself had contributed no fewer than thirty-five pieces to the magazine (his last in 1974). At the time of this exchange with Wrong I was guilty of having contributed twenty-six (although Balint's narrative exonerates me entirely of that offense), and Wrong himself an equal number.

Whole journals have come into existence as anti-*Commentaries*. As early as 1954, Howe (convinced that Cohen's magazine was perpetuating the dogmatic intolerance of 1930s Marxism in the form of 1950s anti-Marxism) founded the socialist magazine *Dissent* (and made Lewis Coser, another frequent *Commentary* contributor, coeditor). "When intellectuals can do nothing else," Howe self-mockingly observed, "they start a magazine." Not surprisingly, Nathan Glazer, in *Commentary*, called *Dissent* "an unmitigated disaster" (73) and reminded readers of Howe's Achilles heel: his neutrality in the conflict between Nazism and the "bourgeois democracies." *Dissent*'s adversary position toward America's foreign policy, said Glazer, called to mind Orwell's remark that "if the radical intellectuals in England had had their way in the 20s and 30s, the Gestapo would have been walking the streets of London in 1940." Many years later, in 1986, Berkeley-trained New Leftist Michael Lerner founded *Tikkun* as "a liberal alternative to *Commentary*." Lerner had built his reputation on promotion of the Palestinian cause within the Jewish community. Intellectually, he was hardly a Howe and was never a *Commentary* contributor, but he managed to attract to his magazine's board (albeit briefly) not only Elie Wiesel but Robert Alter.

Balint describes these earlier convulsions fully and adroitly. But when faced with a more recent one, whose protagonists are still very active, he is diplomatic to the point of silence. In 1993, two of the magazine's most elegant minds, Alter and Wisse, squared off against each other. In 1992, Wisse published *If I Am Not for Myself . . . the Liberal Betrayal of the Jews*, in which she argued that "The defense of Israel against the Arabs, as against earlier anti-Semites, would require of liberals the kind of sustained exertion in the realm of ideas and political action that Israelis have had to manifest in the military defense of their country. Instead, many liberals sacrifice the Jews to liberal pieties and find that Israel is no longer a worthy cause." Alter, reviewing the book for the *New Republic* (November 30, 1992), could not find in it a single redeeming sentence. He excoriated it as "scurrilous," "perverse," "tendentious," "strident," "unpleasant," and (this with hammering insistence) "paranoid." He charged Wisse with failing to distinguish between leftists and liberals, anti-Zionist fanatics like Chomsky and "staunch friends" like Glazer, and falsely indicting Israeli novelists on the basis of a few texts. "Wisse is convinced that every day is Masada." This last imputation reminded many of an earlier episode in Alter's career as occasional writer on Jewish politics—his July 1973 *Commentary* article called "The Masada Complex," which accused Golda Meir of having had her political thinking muddled by poetry, and urged upon Israel "greater flexibility and . . . risk-taking." No article in *Commentary*'s history was more unfortunately timed: three months after Alter proposed that Israel jettison its "Masada" myth, the Arabs, showing no evidence of dispensing with *their* myths, launched the Yom Kippur War and nearly overran the state. This unhappy episode (which I, at that point a friend of both combatants) had the unhappy task of assessing in *Commentary*, also goes unrecorded in Balint's history.

Balint's avoidance of this particular Family feud seems all the odder in view of his insistence that a crucial element in *Commentary*'s (alleged) decline during the reign of Kozodoy (1995–2008), whom he nevertheless calls a "brilliant editor," was the sacrifice of its literary to its political instincts, politicizing its literary judgments and preferring supposed certainties over imaginative freedom. He does not date that decline from the accession of John Podhoretz, whom he calls "the dauphin," to the editorship; but his accession, even though it was probably not his father's idea, certainly continues what Balint mischievously calls the Family's "reticulum of consanguinity" (175).

Balint, who was an assistant editor of *Commentary* from 2001 to 2004, is a prodigiously talented, learned, and articulate young man, with a marvelous flair for anecdote and a chameleon-like capacity to express antithetical points of view as if he sympathized with both. In calling his book a critical history, I do not mean to label him *Commentary*'s detractor; "a questioner," as John Stuart Mill liked to say, "needs not be an enemy."

Notes

1. Benjamin Balint, *Running Commentary: The Contentious Magazine that Transformed the Jewish Left into the Neoconservative Right* (New York: Public Affairs Books, 2010). Subsequent references to this work appear in parentheses in the text.
2. "The Jewish Encyclopedia," *Weekly Standard*, July 5, 2010: 32.

End of the Holocaust?

I am in Norway on business for my product and written on a wall I read, 'Down with Israel.' I think, 'What did Israel ever do to Norway?' I know Israel is a terrible country, but after all, there are countries even more terrible. There are so many terrible countries—why is this country the most terrible? Why don't you read on Norwegian walls, 'Down with Russia,' 'Down with Chile,' 'Down with Libya'? Because Hitler didn't murder six million Libyans? I am walking in Norway and I am thinking, 'If only he had.' Because then they would write on Norwegian walls, 'Down with Libya' and leave Israel alone.
—Philip Roth, *The Counterlife*, 1986

Alvin Rosenfeld, professor of English and Jewish studies at Indiana University, member of the Executive Committee of the U.S. Holocaust Memorial Museum, author or editor of several important books about the Holocaust and its literature, has now added to his list of achievements a book that fills one with gloom and rage, in nearly equal measure. *The End of the Holocaust*[1] is not a history book (like Jon Bridgman's of the same title[2] about the liberation of the camps), but a critical survey of the vast array of assaults on Holocaust memory. Nearly all brazenly and flagrantly violate Cynthia Ozick's famous rule that "Jews are not metaphors—not for poets, not for novelists, not for theologians, not for murderers, and never for antisemites...."[3] She warned that the liberal habit of turning Jews in general and Auschwitz in particular into metaphors was both pernicious in itself and would result in mischief of every sort. Rosenfeld's book surveys the ideological and political wreckage Ozick predicted in 1975. The heart sinks and the mind reels in contemplating the perversions that Rosenfeld describes and exposes. They come from minor poets likening their divorce proceedings to Auschwitz, or Sylvia Plath her recurrent suicide attempts to the Holocaust; from scribblers of "the Holocaust and me" school like Anne Roiphe, for whom "God became the God of the Holocaust" in "the year of my puberty"; from venomous "progressives" like Philip Lopate (author of *Portrait of My Body*), who thinks the Holocaust a Jewish conspiracy whereby "one ethnic group tries to compel the rest of the world" to follow its political program and monopolizes all that beautiful Holocaust suffering which other groups would very much like, ex post facto, to share. (Ever short of decency in the Jewish direction—he even alleges that his own [Jewish] mother became "erotically excited" by the blue numbers on the arms of survivors—Lopate praised President Reagan's ill-conceived laying of a wreath at the Waffen SS cemetery in Bitburg in 1985 as a gesture of "old-fashioned Homeric nobility."[4])

The "end of the Holocaust" was foretold by survivor-writers like Jean Améry, Elie Wiesel, Imre Kertesz, and Primo Levi. It has also received the attention of scholars like Lucy Dawidowicz, Yehuda Bauer, Emil Fackenheim, and the author of this essay.[5] They feared that forgetting, inevitable with time, would be exacerbated by deliberate distortions, flabby sentimentality, the wheedling voice of "common sense" that Hannah Arendt found lurking inside the "liberal" cells of every mind,[6] ruthless politicization, and do-gooderism, i.e., confusing doing good with feeling good about what you are doing. Survivors themselves are now the targets of polemical desperadoes like Norman Finkelstein, Peter Novick, David Stannard, Marc Ellis, Karen Armstrong, and Avishai Margalit. They castigate Holocaust memory and scholarship as instruments of a vast diabolical plot, and allege that Jews grieve over their dead only for political purposes. They demand, in the words of Ellis, "ending Auschwitz" (261). Indeed, they speak of the Jews murdered in the twelve-year war against them in a way that fully justifies Rosenfeld in remarking that "in an age of resurgent antisemitism, respect for even the Jewish dead has become a dwindling commodity" (154).[7] Margalit, an Israeli whose motto appears to be "the other country, right or wrong," alleged in a November 1988 piece called "The Kitsch of Israel" that "Against the weapons of the Holocaust, the Palestinians are amateurs . . . as soon as operation 'Holocaust Memory' is put into high gear . . . the Palestinians cannot compete" (261). Still, Margalit does what he can to help. In this essay, recommended by the aforementioned Lopate as ultimate wisdom on memorializing the victims of the Holocaust, Margalit heaped scorn on the "children's room" at Yad Vashem with its "tape-recorded voices of children crying out in Yiddish, 'Mame, Tate.'" It was promptly pointed out by Reuven Dafni of Yad Vashem that Margalit was lying, that there was neither "children's room" nor tape of children's voices at Yad Vashem. There was, and is (as anyone who actually visits the place would know) a memorial to the 1.5 million murdered children and a tape-recorded voice that reads out those names that are known, along with ages and countries of origin. Such palpable fraud as Margalit's was perhaps not as audacious as the Mohammed al-Dura masquerade or the "Jeningrad" hoax or a dozen others generated in later years by Palestinophiles, but it was more than adequate to satisfy the appetite of readers of the *New York Review of Books*, which is the *Women's Wear Daily* for literary leftists, including Lopate, who had read it there.[8]

Rosenfeld shows how a large number of the 250 organizations around the world that now conduct Holocaust-related programs are as likely to abet the theft of the Holocaust as to oppose it. Mark Steyn, similarly, observed that "The people who run liberal Jewish groups are too blinkered to have grasped a basic point, which is that the principal beneficiaries of the Holocaust have been Muslims. Our parents and grandparents' generation, continental Europeans of the 1930s—they would never have entertained for a moment the erection of mosques in Brussels and Amsterdam and . . . all over the map it if hadn't been for official Holocaust guilt post-1945. So we have a situation where the people who have most successfully leveraged Holocaust guilt are the Muslims."[9] They have proved the most artful of the metaphor-makers against whom Ozick (prophetically) warned.

The nimbleness of apologists for Palestinian irredentism in latching onto the mournful coattails of Jewish history and exploiting Holocaust guilt by reinventing Palestinian Arabs as the shadow selves of Jews is by now an old story. In 1982, Conor Cruise O'Brien observed that "If your interlocutor can't keep Hitler out of the conversation . . . feverishly turning Jews into Nazis and Arabs into Jews—why then, I think you may well be talking to an anti-Jewist." Twenty years later Pierre-André Taguieff, in his admirable book on "the new Judeophobia," observed: "No one thought it a sign of mental disorder when Farouk Kaddoumi, a high PLO official, stated that "Israeli practices against Palestinians exceed the Holocaust in horror."[10] Neither had Edward Said's sanity (or probity) been questioned when, in 1989, he alleged that Zionists "were in touch with the Nazis in hopes of emulating their Reich in Palestine"; that Israeli "soldiers and politicians . . . are now engaged in visiting upon non-Jews many of the same evil practices anti-Semites waged against Holocaust victims"; and that "Israel's occupation increased in severity and outright cruelty, more than rivaling all other military occupations in modern history."[11] Said also encouraged the now widely accepted falsehood that Israel came into being because of Western guilt (expressed by the UN vote for partition in November 1947) over the Holocaust, asserting that it had served to "protect" Palestinian Jews "with the world's compassion."[12] Nothing could be farther from the truth, which is very nearly the exact opposite: Israel was created in spite, not because, of the Holocaust, which destroyed the most Zionist segment of the Jewish world—the Jews of Eastern Europe; and it was not the world's "compassion" but their own will and heroism that gave the Jews a state of their own.[13] Rosenfeld traces the distortion and degradation of the Holocaust "story" since World War II ended. He shows how popular representations have usually worked to dull rather than sharpen moral sensibility about the Jewish debacle. He documents the baneful influence of the cult of victimization, especially the intense competition for the mantle of victimhood, and how it has diverted attention away from the actual victims of Nazism. The meaning of Raul Hilberg's categories—perpetrators, victims, bystanders[14]—has been radically transformed by (mostly American) sentimentality and mindless optimism, by (mostly leftist) political machinations, and by (broadly ecumenical) religious obsessions.

Specifically American distortions include the need to teach cheerful and positive "lessons," which become lessons in what the Holocaust does *not* teach because they blow out of all sane proportion the actions of rescuers, or "righteous Gentiles." Forgotten in this orgy of Pollyannaism is Aharon Appelfeld's sober reflection: "During the Holocaust there were brave Germans, Ukrainians, and Poles who risked their lives to save Jews. But the Holocaust is not epitomized by the greatness of these marvelous individuals' hearts ... I say this because survivors sometimes feel deep gratitude to their rescuers and forget that the saviors were few, and those who betrayed Jews to the Nazis were many and evil."[15]

Rosenfeld recounts the shocking story of how Anne Frank's diary was first travestied by Broadway and Hollywood, then bowdlerized by German translators. In America, the spiritual anemia of Broadway and the rank dishonesty of people like director Garson Kanin created a bogus image of a young woman who was cheerfully optimistic, believed above all that "people are good at heart," was "happy" in the concentration camp of Bergen-Belsen (where in fact she died a horrible death). The manipulations of the Anne Frank story also obliterated her Jewish identity and gave Germans in particular a convenient "formula for easy forgiveness" of the crimes of their countrymen. Rosenfeld has been following this sorry tale, as it unfolded in America and Europe, especially Germany, for decades, and he has produced a searing indictment of its principal charlatans. He predicts that "If these trends continue unchecked, the Holocaust's most famous victim will still be remembered, but in ways that may put at risk an historically accurate and morally responsible memory of the Holocaust itself" (158).

Later chapters of the book deal with survivors of the Holocaust who became major literary figures permanently bound to their horrific experience of the camps. Some of them, most notably Améry and Levi, became victims of Auschwitz long after they appeared to have survived it: they took their own lives. Perhaps they had concluded that the full truth of Auschwitz might never be known (maybe because they themselves had failed as witnesses); or, if half-known, would be distorted. They were particularly disappointed by the refusal of Germans to confront their past honestly, and they despaired over the resurgence of Jew-hatred in Europe, especially on the political Left, which turned Holocaust images into the tool-kit of the "new" antisemitism, the pariah people into the pariah state. They knew there would be virtually no retribution; they feared there would be no memory; but few foresaw the possibility of a second Holocaust. One was the Hungarian Kertesz: "The antisemite of our age no longer loathes Jews; he wants Auschwitz" (278–79). Another was the Israeli poet Abba Kovner, who thought only Israel's acquisition of nuclear weapons could prevent it happening again. By now, however, a decade into the twenty-first century, that possibility is what Goethe would have called an open secret: visible to all, yet recognized by few, like the courageous German scholar Matthias Kuntzel. An astute observer of Holocaust deniers and their genocidal rhetoric, in Europe as well as Iran, Kuntzel insists that "Every denial of the Holocaust contains an appeal to repeat it" (243).

Rosenfeld's culminating chapter engages in combat with the ever-expanding divisions of warriors against Holocaust memory—almost in its entirety. They blame it for everything they deem inimical to the furtherance of their own (usually progressive) agendas; no matter the social or religious or ethnic problem, they find Jewish Holocaust memory responsible for it. Although they have no qualms about universities offering courses on American slavery or the fate of Native Americans that omit comparative reference to the Jewish catastrophe, they stridently oppose courses that deal exclusively with the destruction of European Jewry. Their all-consuming political obsession is with tightening the noose around Israel's throat.

Therefore, Rosenfeld charges, they link their appeal to Jews "to disengage from the Holocaust with an appeal for Jews to disengage from the exercise of political power by disconnecting from the state of Israel" (260). That most of these enemies of memory are professors will surprise nobody who recalls Victor Klemperer's acerbic remark, in a 1936 diary entry about Hitler's professors: "If one day the situation were reversed and the fate of the vanquished lay in my hands, then I would let all the ordinary folk go . . . but I would have all the intellectuals strung up, and the professors three feet higher than the rest; they would be left hanging from the lampposts for as long as was compatible with hygiene."[16]

Rosenfeld is never shrill and often eloquent. But his book, now the indispensable study of its subject, cannot be read with pleasure, even by people who believe that "in the destruction of the wicked, there is joy."[17] Rather, one is tempted to apply to it the words Rosenfeld uses about Améry: "There is, it is true, a price to be paid for reading a book like *At the Mind's Limits*, which is nothing if not distressing, but there is a far higher price to be paid by foregoing [such] an author, and that is the diminution of historical and moral consciousness itself."

Notes

1. *The End of the Holocaust* (Bloomington, IN: Indiana University Press, 2011). Subsequent references to the book appear in parentheses in the text.
2. Jon Bridgman, *The End of the Holocaust: The Liberation of the Camps* (Portland, OR: Areopagitica Press, 1990).
3. "A Liberal's Auschwitz," *Confrontation* (Spring 1975): 128.
4. *Testimony: Contemporary Writers Make the Holocaust Personal* (New York: Random House, 1989), 135, 287–307.
5. See, e.g., Lucy S. Dawidowicz, *What Is the Use of Jewish History* (New York: Schocken, 1992); Yehuda Bauer, *The Holocaust in Historical Perspective* (Seattle: University of Washington Press, 1978); Emil L. Fackenheim, *The Jewish Return into History* (New York: Schocken, 1978); Edward Alexander, *The Holocaust and the War of Ideas* (New Brunswick, NJ: Transaction Publishers, 1994).
6. Hannah Arendt, *Totalitarianism*, Part III of *The Origins of Totalitarianism* (New York: Harcourt Brace, 1951), 138.
7. On this matter of (dis)respect for the dead, see elsewhere in this volume "The New Mormons," about Jewish anti-Zionists converting their deceased grandparents.
8. See Margalit's comment on this "wrong information" he had received from "an employee at Yad Vashem itself" in his book *Views in Review* (New York: Farrar, Straus, Giroux, 1998), 217.

9. Mark Steyn, Interview on Canadian Radio with Michael Coren, November 2, 2010.
10. Pierre-André Taguieff, *Rising from the Muck: The New Anti-Semitism in Europe*, trans. Patrick Camiller [from French] (Chicago, IL: Ivan R. Dee, 2004), 72.
11. "An Exchange on Edward Said and Difference," *Critical Inquiry* 15 (Spring 1989): 636–41.
12. *The Question of Palestine* (New York: Times Books, 1979).
13. As Fouad Ajami has observed: "Jewish statehood was a fait accompli perhaps a decade before that vote. All the ingredients had been secured by Labor Zionism. . . . The hard work had been done in the three decades between the Balfour Declaration of 1917 and the vote on partition. Realism had guided the Zionist project. We will take a state even if it is the size of a tablecloth, said Chaim Weizmann . . ."—"The U.N. Can't Deliver a Palestinian State," *Wall Street Journal*, June 1, 2011.
14. *Perpetrators, Victims, Bystanders: The Jewish Catastrophe 1933–1945* (New York: Harper Collins, 1992).
15. Aharon Appelfeld, *Beyond Despair* (New York: Fromm Publishers, 1994), xiii.
16. Victor Klemperer, *I Will Bear Witness: A Diary of the Nazi Years, 1933–41* (New York: Modern Library, 1999).
17. *Proverbs* xi, 10.

III
Politics

Survival Precedes Definition: Ruth Wisse's Moral Imperative

"Clear your *mind* of cant." Has anyone who writes about the political dimension of Jewish experience ever taken this motto of Samuel Johnson's to heart more than Ruth Wisse? Has any voice ever laid siege more effectively to the barricades of stale cliché and bad logic that obscure "the Jewish problem?" Have you heard that Jews are an intransigent minority responsible for communism in capitalist countries, capitalism in communist countries, cosmopolitanism in nationalistic countries, and, in the minds of "realist" foreign-policy experts, every evil on the globe except avian flu? In fact, Wisse shows, the Jewish problem is really the problem of nations that must blame their dysfunction on Jews. Have you been told that Jews are too powerful ("98% control," according to Noam Chomsky)? On the contrary, "in the real world, Jews have too little power and influence [and] too little self-confidence about defending themselves."[1] Do you believe, as did isolationist foes of American entry into World War II or the current war against terror, that Franklin D. Roosevelt and George W. Bush caved in to Jewish demands that damaged genuine American interests? On the contrary, these leaders went to war not to save Jews but to defeat Nazism and Islamic fascism, which also (not accidentally) were anti-Jewish. Do you believe that the creation of Israel solved the problem of the Jews' relation to political power? You are mistaken: the permanent state of siege in which the Jewish state exists reproduces the constant burden of peril and political imbalance of the Diaspora. Do you think that Israel normalized "the most mythologized people in human history"?[2] Alas, that people has now acquired "international reputation greater than Jehovah's" (178). Do you think that moral superiority over their enemies is the chief desideratum for Jews, as when Golda Meir told Sadat she could forgive him for killing "our sons" but not for "making us kill yours" (156)? Think again, urges Wisse, remember that survival precedes definition, and that your enemies' designs upon you are a more compelling concern than your children's decency. To be decent, you need to be alive.

Although Wisse has spent her professional life as a teacher and scholar of Yiddish literature and language, she approaches these questions without the prejudices common among her colleagues. In 1954, Irving Howe praised Yiddish literature and the culture it reflected for the very characteristics that made the opposing camp of secular Jews, the Zionists, spurn it: "The virtue of powerlessness, the power of helplessness, the company of the dispossessed, the sanctity of the insulted and the injured . . ."[3] In later years Howe and Wisse became friends and literary collaborators. But he strongly disapproved of her forays into political writing, telling her she did not do them well and ought not to do them at all. He thought Wisse's view of Jewish history and politics incompatible with Yiddish tradition.

Wisse has always taken a very different view. In *Jews and Power*, she argues that when Jews were vanquished and sent into exile from their homeland they decided (unlike other conquered peoples of the ancient Near East—Jebusites, Hittites, and Girgashites) to remain faithful to their God and covenant; they were convinced that they had been exiled because of their sins and not because their God had proved powerless to protect them. Jews recognized that the price of such loyalty might be poverty and powerlessness, yet this was a price they were willing to pay. "But," insists Wisse, "when Jews then take that a step further and say that to be a Jew is to be weak and powerless—this is . . . romanticization, because Jews never wanted to be weak or poor. And until recently they certainly never made a virtue of it." In fact, she contends, glorification of powerlessness is "as antithetical to Judaism as belief in the divinity of Jesus" (175–76).

If power tends to corrupt, then powerlessness does worse than corrupt: it eliminates. Prior to Constantine's establishment of Christianity as the religion of the Roman Empire in the fourth century, Christianity and Judaism had almost equal numbers in Europe. The tendency to romanticize powerlessness and an abnormal political existence ought, Wisse believes, to have come to an end during World War I, when "an estimated half million Jews fought in the uniforms of the vying armies of Europe with no one to prevent the violence directed at *them*" (120). For Wisse, the crucial link between the study of Yiddish literature (the center of her academic career) and the study of Jewish politics is that "The Yiddish language, developed by European Jews over almost a thousand years, was practically erased along with them in a mere six, 1939–45. So studying Yiddish literature . . . concentrates the mind on Jewish political disabilities."[4]

Jews and Power is a short but ambitious book, a critical history of the Jews' problematic relation to power from 70 CE through the Oslo accords and their catastrophic aftermath. The prologue rivets attention with the book's foundational anecdote, an incident in occupied Warsaw in 1939. After Nazi soldiers harassed a Jewish child, his mother picked up her bruised little boy, and said: "Come inside the courtyard and *za a mentsh*" (ix). The mother was telling her son—in a well-known Yiddish expression—to become a decent human being.

Although that term conveyed to many Yiddish-speaking Jews the essence of "Jewishness," and Wisse herself was taught to revere it in her Montreal Jewish school, she now calls it into question. For she had also learned from the school's principal what had happened to Jewish children in Europe. "If each of you," he told the children, "was to take a notebook and write on every line of every page the name of a different child, and if we collected all your notebooks, it still would not equal the number of Jewish boys and girls who were murdered by the Germans." The little boy in Warsaw could not have done as his mother urged "because becoming fully human presupposed staying alive" (xi–xii). An injunction to behave decently that disregards your enemy's intention to remove you from the world is "moral solipsism," a peculiarly Jewish affliction that Wisse in an earlier book defined as "the Jewish moral strut."[5]

Part One: The Great Experiment" disputes the commonplace that Jewish politics came to an end when the Jews left their ancient homeland. In fact, Wisse argues, they were just as politically active outside Eretz Yisrael despite the fact that in Diaspora they were a nation without nationhood, land, central government, or means of self-defense, a people denied the dignity of being people. But the continued centrality of Jerusalem and of Hebrew in Jewish worship made them (as Abba Kovner and Emil Fackenheim also recognized) a dispersed rather than a dismembered people.

Jews in Diaspora tried to retain control over their national destiny by accepting responsibility for political failure. They devised a strategy of accommodation to defeat and to dependency on local rulers for protection. Jewish life outside of the ancient homeland would be determined by the best bargain that Jews could strike with Gentile rulers. With equality out of reach, Jews worked out a "politics of complementarity" (57). It afforded them temporary advantages, but the greater the benefits Jews derived from those in power, the greater the power rulers had over them. When necessary, their erstwhile protectors would sacrifice them to mob violence. The longer Jews remained in exile, the more they acquired the reputation of being easy prey.

The great set piece of this section of the book is Wisse's description of the "disputation" of 1263 in Barcelona between the Jewish apostate Pablo (Paul) Christiani and Nachmanides about the rival claims of Judaism and Christianity to the truth. Nachmanides was prohibited from attacking—as Christiani did abundantly—the "lies" of his opponent's religion, and restricted to proving that rabbinic sources did *not* bear witness to Christian truth. Christiani also argued that the failure of Jews to maintain their sovereignty confirmed the failure of their religion. Were there any *Jewish* officers in the courtroom? Employing her characteristic antithetical structure that contrasts the meaning of contiguous clauses or phrases while giving them parallel grammatical structure, Wisse sums up: "As the Christian he became, Pablo Christiani manifested the corrupting potential of power, but as the Jew he was, the corrupting temptations of powerlessness" (73). Despite the king's prior assurance of immunity from punishment, Nachmanides was charged with blasphemy and expelled from Spain.

Part Two of *Jews and Power* deals with the unanticipated bad consequences of emancipation. In France the Count of Clermont-Tonnerre declared that "Jews should be denied everything as a nation, but granted everything as individuals."

Frenchmen, Germans, and Englishmen were, of course, not expected to give up *their* national identities; in a pattern that exists among continuators of the Enlightenment up to the present day, only Jews were singled out for this second-class version of emancipation. Since traditional Jews pursued a way of life that fused religion with nationality, they were far less tempted by this offer than were their secularized brethren.

In the event, the latter were disappointed to find that replacement of one-man autocracies and systems of state-censorship by elected assemblies, the popular press, and other democratic institutions actually reduced Jewish influence and left Jews in many respects worse off than before. With kings toppled from their thrones, the new Hamans appealed to the citizenry, often with great success. Old-fashioned religious Jew-hatred evolved into the newly named (by Wilhelm Marr) "antisemitism," which, in Jonathan Sacks' definition, "exists whenever two contradictory factors appear in combination: the belief that Jews are so powerful that they are responsible for the evils of the world, and the knowledge that they are so powerless that they can be attacked with impunity."[6]

This combination of an enormous image (Christ-killers, bloated plutocrats, and Zionist imperialists,) with almost no political power proved irresistible to a new legion of predators. Antisemites called the Jews' talent for successful accommodation to unfavorable political circumstances a desire for conquest, a quest for domination. "The diabolical element in this accusation," observes Wisse, "was to have charged Jews with seizing the political power they were unwilling to wield. Marr's attack on the Jews would succeed precisely because they lacked the will to political power of which he accused them" (91).

By the end of the nineteenth century the new antisemitism, culminating in the Dreyfus affair, the dress rehearsal for the Nazi movement, had become "the most effective political ideology in Europe" (96). It provided European politicians with a simple explanation for whatever was going wrong: revolution, psychoanalysis, pornography, and moral turpitude. This pan-European campaign against the Jews as the cause of all misfortunes foreshadowed in several ways today's "new" antisemitism that centers on Israel, not least in its use of the scam which claims that Jewish responses to the campaign of defamation are proof of just how much power Jews do wield and how they use it to stifle all "criticism" of Israel—such as the call to remove it from the family of nations.

Although Wisse does not explicitly reproach Jews for the political strategy they adopted during centuries of exile, she insists that by the end of the nineteenth century it was clear that they needed an alternative to a failing strategy. Ideologically this alternative was Zionism, which even the sour Hannah Arendt called "the only political answer Jews have ever found to antisemitism and the only ideology in which they have ever taken seriously a hostility that would place them in the center of world events."[7]

Part Three of *Jews and Power* discusses the extent to which the "Return to Zion" has represented both a break with the old politics of adaptation and a continuation of it; a belated recognition of the need for self-defense and a persisting Jewish inability to see themselves through the eyes of their enemies; a rescue of the Jews from their status as a pariah people and a discovery that the pariah people have become the pariah nation. "Not until Jabotinsky thought of organizing Jewish military units in the British army did Zionist leadership begin to consider the possibility of a Jewish armed force that would fight under its own insignia and flag." Again the repudiation of "Yiddish" wisdom was required to see the obvious. Jabotinsky wrote that "this very normal idea [self-defense] would have occurred . . . to any normal person," which is rendered in Jewish colloquial usage by the Yiddish expression "*goyishe kop*" (122). Jabotinsky was saying that he wishes Jews, forever preening themselves on their supposed cleverness, could become as simpleminded as Gentiles.

But even those Zionist leaders who managed to acquire something of a *goyishe kop*— including Jabotinsky and Ben-Gurion—could not foresee that the Arab and Muslim countries would make anti-Zionism into a way of life, and the Palestinian Arabs into a kind of antination deriving their entire meaning and purpose from the goal of destroying Israel. Nor did they foresee that the Diaspora strategy of accommodation could take its deadliest form in Zion itself, in the Chelm-like strategy of yielding contiguous territory to enemies dedicated to Israel's destruction, financing and arming their forces in the hope of conciliating them and gaining security. No *goyishe kop* in the history of nations had ever come up with such a clever idea, the ultimate expression of "moral solipsism" (166–68). Obviously, the creation of Israel has not solved the problem of the Jews' relation to political power. Truly to be moral, Wisse argues, modern Jews, who are largely without faith in the power of the Almighty, must themselves supply the missing dimension of power; otherwise, they are signing a suicide pact with each new enemy that comes along.

Wisse's concluding section returns to a theme adumbrated in her introduction: the question of why Jews have figured and still figure so prominently in the politics of regimes that also threaten the rest of the world: Nazi Germany, the Soviet Union, Iran, and the multitudinous troops of Islamic fascism. Although this is more bad news, it does have a positive dimension: namely, that the Jews' new political status, achieved by the existence of a Jewish state, has given them a new role as an ally, with something to offer America and the other democracies. Wisse believes that at least America is learning the lesson that "Thugs who get away with harassing Jewish citizens go on to torch the rest of the citizenry" (183).

Jews and Power is a powerful salvo in the war of ideas over the Jewish state, a war that Israel has been losing almost as steadily as she has (until recently) been winning on the battlefield. It is a crucial war too, because, as John Stuart Mill wrote in his 1838 essay on Jeremy Bentham, "philosophy, which to the superficial appears a thing so remote from the business of life and the outward interests of men, is in reality the thing on earth which most influences them, and in the long run overbears every other influence save those which it must itself obey."

Notes

1. "Are American Jews Too Powerful? Not Even Close," *Washington Post*, November 4, 2007.
2. Ruth R. Wisse, *Jews and Power* (New York: Schocken, 2007), 92. (Subsequent references to this work appear in parentheses in the text.)
3. Introduction to *A Treasury of Yiddish Stories* (New York: Viking, 1954), 38.
4. "Are American Jews Too Powerful?"
5. *If I Am Not for Myself . . . The Liberal Betrayal of the Jews* (New York: Free Press, 1992), 77–80.
6. Jonathan Sacks, "Lecture to Inter-Parliamentary Committee Against Antisemitism on February 28, 2002," *A New Antisemitism* (London: Profile Books, 2003), 40.
7. *Antisemitism* (New York: Harcourt, Brace & World, 1951), 120.

"Pharaoh Who Knew Not Joseph": Obama Demotes the Jews

The Keynote Address, July 2004

Barack Obama first came to national prominence in July 2004 when he delivered the keynote address at the Democratic National Convention in Boston. He had been an Illinois state senator since 1997 and was now a candidate for the United States Senate. He delivered, very skillfully, a well-written speech in which his personal history played a role as important as what he said about policy matters and the two wonderful nominees (John Kerry for president and John Edwards for vice president). He presented his own unusual story, as the offspring of a marriage between a black African (who had given him what he called the "African name" Barack) of humble social position and a white woman from Kansas, as a tale possible only in America: "in no other country on earth is my story even possible." In those days he expressed no qualms and indulged in no sarcasm about American "exceptionalism." He laid stress upon the peculiarly American "belief that we are all connected as one people."

Nevertheless, he went out of his way to pay tribute to several subdivisions that inform the slogan: "e pluribus unum." He did not mention any religious group—neither Muslim nor Christian nor Jew—except perhaps by implication when he said that "John Kerry . . . will never . . . use faith as a wedge to divide us." But he did allude respectfully to Latino, Black, Asian, and gay Americans. He did not mention Jews at all—unless we count his inclusion, among the serious problems still besetting this unique and wonderful country, the following: "If there's an Arab-American family being rounded up without benefit of an attorney or due process, that threatens my civil liberties." How many Jews felt a twinge of uneasiness at that reference to families "being rounded up"? If one "Googles" the phrase, one quickly comes up with allusions to the classic instance of it in modern memory: the "rounding up of Jewish families in Nazi Germany." Were Arab-American families, in the summer of 2004, really being "rounded up" en masse in government-ordered ethnic cleansing? How many Jews among Obama's multitudinous listeners heard in this little verbal sleight of hand by Obama, this artful theft of the Jews' sad history, this single instance in his entire speech of the flagrant anti-American exaggerativeness of his leftist friends in Chicago, an alarm bell?

Europhilia versus American Exceptionalism

After he himself received the Democratic nomination for the presidency four years later, Barack Obama became the first American president who campaigned for the office in Europe as well as the United States, as if his popularity there would redound to his credit here. In July of 2008, before a huge Berlin crowd of 200,000 people, he called himself "a citizen of the world" (though, he prudentially added, also "a proud citizen of the United States") and an ardent advocate of "global citizenship." He even told the Germans that his Kenyan father had been inspired by the "dream" of freedom and opportunity in "the West" (almost as if Barack Hussein Obama Sr. had aspired to Germany rather than America).

What was one to make of candidate Obama's tremendous popularity on a continent where, unless we made an exception for one undersecretary in France at the time (2008), not a single high government position was held by a black person? Was it that he kept offering "apologies" for many instances of American misbehavior? Or that he promised, for example at the G-20 summit (March 30, 2009), that he would be more respectful of Europe than George W. Bush, and that Americans would no longer be "dictating solutions" to other countries? Did it have something to do with the fact that, unlike President Bush in London in November 2003, he did *not* express open and unmannerly disapproval of Europe's resurgent antisemitism to European political leaders?[1] Or was it that, in sharp contradiction to his own exceptional story, by now a thousand times magnified by his presidential nomination, he kept sneering at the notion of "American exceptionalism"? As Shelby Steele has pointed out, Obama "represents a truly inspiring American exceptionalism: He is the first black in the entire history of Western civilization to lead a Western nation—and the most powerful black man in recorded history, but he reached this apex only through the good offices of the great American democracy."[2]

Just what is this American exceptionalism about which so much ink has been spilled by Obama interpreters? The idea that American democracy made this country "the first new nation" goes back to Alexis de Tocqueville's great book *Democracy in America*, published in 1835 and 1840. How much Obama really knows of the "exceptionalism" doctrine when he disaparages it (for example, in response to questions from journalists) by saying it is merely the American version of parochial nationalism found all over the globe, it is difficult to say. On more than one occasion, he has displayed what William Hazlitt used to call "the ignorance of the learned." How much the journalists themselves, who usually display the ignorance of the unlearned, know it is even more difficult to say. (*Democracy in America* itself is so complex, undulating, and diverse that it was invoked by both sides of the debate in the British Parliament about the 1867 Reform Bill, which finally committed laggard England irrevocably to democracy.)

Despite his uneasiness about its "tyranny of the majority," Tocqueville extolled America for its liberty, its egalitarianism, its reliance upon individual initiative rather than government direction, and its *laissez-faire values.* He tried to define America's greatness at the end of the first volume of *Democracy in America* by contrasting it with that of Russia; they seemed to him the two nations "marked out by the will of Heaven to sway the destinies of half the globe." "The Anglo-American relies upon personal interest to accomplish his ends and gives free scope to the unguided strength and common sense of the people; the Russian centers all the authority of society in a single arm. The principal instrument of the former is freedom; of the latter, servitude."

In the twentieth century, Tocqueville's idea of American uniqueness was often used to argue that socialism had failed in America from cultural, "subjective" causes far more than objective economic and material ones. Werner Sombart asserted, in a famously pithy and vivid observation in his 1906 book *Why is There No Socialism in the United States?* that America is "the promised land of capitalism," where "on the reefs of roast beef and apple pie socialist Utopias ... are sent to their doom."

Although Sombart assigned Jews a large role in the development of capitalism, for most Jews American exceptionalism has primarily meant something else: refuge from Europe's endemic and apparently incurable addiction to political antisemitism. As William Buckley once remarked, antisemitism exists in America as a social prejudice; but in England (and Europe generally) it is a way of life. Nazism, promulgated in Germany, had conquered most of Europe, destroyed the continent's Jewish civilization, and, in a profound sense, its own. As Irving Howe observed in 1953: "If God didn't choose us, went the Yiddish proverb, then the world chose us. How bitter was the irony of this remark no one could know until the world of the East European Jews came to its end in the ashes of Maidenek and Auschwitz—at the time and place, that is, when Western civilization collapsed."[3] The founders of *Commentary* Magazine, as noted elsewhere in this book, began their journal in 1945 by declaring that the Jewish future lay in America, not in the European charnel house.

Why then, in 2008, was Obama's enormous European popularity being held up by his supporters, including (if not especially) the "progressive" Jewish ones, as an important reason why Americans should vote for him in the November election? Why should America, a nation that was built up by immigrants, many of whom had fled from Europe's religious and political persecution, grinding poverty, and fiercely competitive nationalisms, now look to Europe as a model of wisdom in facing up to the major crises of our time, especially when it was not doing at all well in facing up to them itself? Why should Jewish Americans, at a time when the resurgence of Europe's antisemitism was already the subject of numerous books and hundreds of articles, have failed to find fault with Obama's puzzling Europhilia?

The Inaugural Address and After

In his inaugural address of January 20, 2009, President Barack Hussein Obama jettisoned the long-established locution that embodies the generally accepted notion of "the Judeo-Christian tradition." That tradition, in America, mandates the phrase "Christians and Jews," with Christians in first place for the good reason that the roots of this country and most of those who founded it are Christian. Obama, however, said in his first presidential speech to America that "We are a nation of Christians and Muslims," and then, after a slight pause, "Jews and Hindus," another slight pause, "and unbelievers." Later, in his first full presidential interview, with *Al-Arabiya* on January 26, he demoted the Jews still further, calling America a country of "Muslims, Christians, Jews." Since then Obama's actions (and inactions) with respect to Jewish concerns suggest that this demotion is real and not merely verbal, that the verbal demotion was a reliable predictor of, among other things, the contempt with which Obama would treat Israel's prime minister Benjamin Netanyahu on his official visits to the United States in March 2010 and May 2011.[4]

The first appointments to Obama's Middle East "team" were mostly leftovers from the Clinton administration—peace processors like George Mitchell and Dennis Ross, trotting out (for about the fifteenth time) the stale formulas of peace conferences and the "two-state solution." But the new faces in positions that are crucial to formulation of Middle East policy were people notable for a distinct lack of charity in the Israeli direction, like Susan Rice at the UN and Samantha Power as Director of Multilateral Affairs at the National Security Council. Power had in the past advocated ending all aid to Israel and even invading it to protect Palestinians from Israeli "genocide." (One of her newly assigned tasks was to look over the shoulder of Hillary Clinton, whom she had called "a monster" in 2008.)

The Obama administration also chose Charles Freeman to serve as chairman of the National Intelligence Council. Freeman had blamed Israel not only for 9/11 and world terrorism but for nearly every evil on the globe. But when his close ties to Saudi Arabia and China (and his approval of the Tiananmen Square massacre) became public knowledge, he withdrew.

Late in 2009, by which time several critics of the administration had begun to affix to Obama the label "the first anti-Israel president," he appointed a Director of the Office to Monitor and Combat Antisemitism. Despite her impressive title, Hannah Rosenthal's first public pronouncements on the subject prompted many to remark that hiring her to monitor antisemitism was like hiring a deaf person to tune your piano. Not only had she been a board member of the anti-Israel "J Street" organization (largely funded by George Soros), but she harshly attacked Israeli ambassador to the United States Michael Oren for declining an invitation to address that unsavory group, from which "he could have learned a lot." She was also making speeches (in Kazakhstan, for example!) equating antisemitism with that evanescent phenomenon called "Islamophobia."[5] Far more disturbing than Obama's appointments, however, was his own obsession with appeasing the forces of militant Islam through flattery and oily sycophancy, embodied in his now famous bow from the waist before Saudi Arabia's King Abdullah in April of 2009. (There were also unconfirmed reports of his having told Jewish leaders at a July 2009 White House meeting that he wanted to "change the way the Arabs see us" by putting "space" between the U. S. and Israel.) His public utterances have been characterized by a hammering insistence on the need to "respect" Islam. He urged this no fewer than seven times in his *Al-Arabiya* interview, as if he were emulating George Galloway's far left and pro-Hamas "Respect Party" in England.

At least as crucial for understanding Obama's icy indifference to Jewish fears has been what he has *not* said, especially during his first presidential grand tour of Europe, the continent that in his mind represents the high moral standards America must strive to satisfy. His visit took place a week or so after the Religion of Perpetual Outrage had been expressing its outrage over Israeli actions in Gaza by staging virulent, often violent pro-Hamas demonstrations throughout the old (and increasingly post-Christian) continent. Muslim Brotherhood members and their sympathizers took to the streets of European cities screaming, "Death to Israel! Death to the Jews!" In several cities they were joined by members of parliament. And shortly after Muslim mobs had intimidated policemen in London and Malmo, smashed up the Place de l'Opera in Paris, burned Israeli and American flags while chanting *Allahu Akbar*, Obama was busily apologizing to Europe in general for "our past arrogance." All this happened while Europe was once again in full retreat, as the French-American writer Nidra Poller, reporting the latest conflagration from Paris, observed, from "enraged [Muslim] mobs bearing down on helpless victims."[6]

Nowhere in Europe was this more blatant than in Turkey, chosen by Obama for the culmination of his European Grand Tour. In the three months prior to Obama's speeches there in early April, Turkey had been the scene of the fiercest anti-Israel and antisemitic agitation in all of Europe, extending from the streets to schools, newspapers, and TV stations—for the very good reason that it was encouraged by prime minister Erdogan, who declared that "Israelis know very well how to kill" and that "Jews control the media." (All this, let us recall, happened over a year before the infamous Turkish "flotilla" attempt to break Israel's blockade of Gaza at the end of May 2010 and Erdogan's emergence as Europe's most bellicose national leader.) But nary a word about this little unpleasantness crept into Obama's speeches to Turkish parliamentarians and students. Rather, it was full of his usual calls for "respect" plus assurances that America is not and "never will be" at war with Islam. He also said, cryptically, that Islam had made great contributions to America's development—by which he did not mean the impetus that Muslim piracy had given to the founding of the United

"Pharaoh Who Knew Not Joseph": Obama Demotes the Jews

States Navy two centuries earlier. He did indicate, in one of his Turkish addresses, that the Muslim world was perhaps overly inclined to blame all its problems on Israel, but "balanced" this by saying that "some of my Jewish friends" (he did not name names) do the same in reverse. Listening to him, a new arrival from Mars might well have gotten the impression that it is Muslims and not Jews who are the constant target of physical and verbal aggression throughout Europe.

Obama resumed the oratorical thrust of his program of "outreach" to and "engagement" with Islam with an ambitious address to "the Muslim world" called "A New Beginning." It was given on June 4, 2009, under the joint auspices of Al-Azhar and Cairo Universities. (Egypt, it should be remembered, was at that point still very much an American ally and the most powerful nation in the Arab world.)

The speech emphasized both the size and importance of America's Muslim population, vowed Obama's personal commitment to "fight against negative stereotypes" of Muslims, and (once again) pledged that "America is not—and never will be—at war with Islam." He repeated his standard assurance that America (in the new age of Obama) would no longer dictate solutions. He did, however, make one exception to that pledge: "The United States does not accept the legitimacy of continued Israeli settlements. . . . It is time for those settlements to stop." By paying obeisance to the favorite theater idol (to use Francis Bacon's category) of the peace-processors of the State Department, he was reiterating the shopworn absurdity which holds that the Arabs repeatedly rejected the two-state solution (in 1937, 1947, 2000, and 2008) because of "settlements" and now wanted only to return to the lines that existed between 1948 and 1967, the nineteen years during which the disputed territories had been entirely in their possession. (This was hardly surprising, especially since rumor had it that the speech had been written for him by a notorious peace-processor named [like several others] Stephen Cohen.)

Far more troubling than this recitation of old formulas was Obama's flattery (was it unwitting or deliberate?) of the well-known prejudices of his Egyptian audience about how and why the state of Israel came into existence. Obama of course knows that a very large majority of Muslims believe that Jews have no rights in the land which they inhabited for 3,300 years and ruled for 1,900. They harbor the delusion that Israel was foisted upon the Arabs in the UN General Assembly partition vote of 1947 by Western nations afflicted by guilty conscience over the Holocaust, a crime for which the Arabs themselves bear (or so they believe) no responsibility whatever. He also licentiously implied a false equivalence between the Jewish experience of the Holocaust and the "more than sixty years" of Palestinian suffering "in pursuit of a homeland." Although he said nothing of the responsibility borne by the Palestinians themselves and the Arab nations in general for that suffering, he did indicate that blowing up buses and firing rockets at children were not the best stepping-stones to statehood. Instead, and with commendable courage given the audience he was addressing, he invoked the counter example of how black people had peacefully fought slavery and segregation in America and South Africa. What he did not invoke, however, was the counterexample of the Zionist movement, which had devoted itself for decades before the UN vote of 1947 to building up its own society rather than destroying that of its neighbor. As Fouad Ajami would later (in May 2011) observe of the Palestinian move to gain statehood via a UN General Assembly vote: "The [November 29, 1947] vote at the General Assembly was of immense help, but it wasn't the decisive factor in the founding of the Jewish state. The hard work had been done in the three decades between the Balfour Declaration of 1917 and the vote on partition. Realism had guided the Zionist project. We will take a state even if it is the size of a tablecloth, said Chaim Weizmann...."[7]

Conclusion

In May of 2011, Obama (not for the first time) showed his supercilious contempt for Benjamin Netanyahu, his official guest in Washington, by becoming the first American president explicitly and publicly to endorse, prior to any negotiations on other issues (such as Jerusalem and refugees), the June 1967 armistice lines of the Six-Day War launched by the Arabs as the basis for negotiating a final border. He did this shortly after the Palestinian Authority had announced its alliance with Hamas (and therefore its return to the ways of Yasser Arafat). Many observers expressed surprise that Obama would risk alienating "the Jewish vote" and Jewish financial support, both of which he had received abundantly in the 2008 election campaign. But when, at the annual AIPAC conference in Washington on May 22, Obama made the ritual gestures in favor of a "non-militarized" Palestine and of Israel as "a Jewish state," his (largely Jewish) audience of Israel supporters rose, just like trained seals, to applaud him.

By autumn of 2011, leaders of two major Jewish organizations of liberal but also Zionist proclivities decided to deal with the Jews'

Obama problem in an extraordinary way. The American Jewish Committee and the Anti-Defamation League announced "a national pledge for unity on Israel." It was based on a (hitherto unheard of) axiom that "America's friendship with Israel . . . has always transcended politics" and "U.S.-Israel friendship should never be used as a political wedge issue." A naïve observer might assume that the executive directors of these organizations (David Harris and Abraham Foxman) had never heard of Jewish political opposition to such prominent Israel-haters as Charles Percy or Cynthia McKinney or Patrick Buchanan or Ernest Hollings. Of course they had; but the risk of appearing historically ignorant was a far less serious matter than their need to protect President Obama from (well-earned) censure.[8]

The inability of Jews to recognize political realities is one of the marvels of human nature. James Baker once, with typical nastiness, alluded to it when he responded to expressions of American–Jewish unhappiness with his Middle East policies as follows: "Fuck the Jews, they don't vote for us anyway." Now Barack Obama seemed to be saying: "Fuck the Jews, they always vote for us anyway."

Notes

1. Bush, speaking at Whitehall Palace on November 19, 2003, had said: "Europe's leaders—and all leaders—should strongly oppose antisemitism, which poisons public debates over the future of the Middle East." A personal note: when, at a reception in the White House in December 2003, I commended Bush for his criticism of European leaders for their indifference to the resurgent antisemitism, he replied, with alacrity: "It's worse than indifference."
2. Shelby Steele, "Obama's Unspoken Re-Election Edge," *Wall Street Journal*, May 25, 2011.
3. Introduction to *A Treasury of Yiddish Stories* (New York: The Viking Press, 1954), 12.
4. See on this subject Bret Stephens, "An Anti-Israel President," *Wall Street Journal*, May 24, 2011.
5. See Edward Rothstein's trenchant critique of Rosenthal in "A Hatred that Resists Exorcism," *New York Times*, July 5, 2010.
6. Nidra Poller, "Baked on the Premises—[French] TOAST," posted March 16, 2009, on *Atlas Shrugged* and *Outpost* websites.
7. Fouad Ajami, "The U.N. Can't Deliver a Palestinian State," *Wall Street Journal*, June 1, 2011.
8. See Douglas J. Feith, "Israel Should Be a U.S. Campaign Issue," *Wall Street Journal*, November 2, 2011.

The Meaning of Criticism

"Critics of Israeli Policy" or Apologists for Ahmadinejad?

A 2009 addition[1] to the ever-burgeoning genre of books instructing Israel on the most suitable method (one-state solution, no-state solution, final solution) of ceasing to exist was adorned by a blurb from Noam Chomsky: "Constance Hilliard raises very critical issues... and unless those who call themselves 'supporters of Israel' are willing to face these moral and geopolitical realities, they may in reality be supporters of Israel's moral degeneration and ultimate destruction." It is a commonplace that the moral passions are far more imperious and impatient than the self-seeking ones, and who could have a stronger sense of his moral rectitude than a man who has been an apologist for Pol Pot in Cambodia, a collaborator with neo-Nazi Holocaust-deniers in France, and with antisemitism-deniers everywhere? "Antisemitism," Chomsky has declared, "is no longer a problem, fortunately. It's raised, but it's raised because privileged people want to make sure they have total control, not just 98% control; That's why anti-Semitism is becoming an issue..."[2] Beautiful and touching words, but words by no means unusual in the parlance of those who deem Israel uniquely evil and, with help from its "supporters," responsible for the unredeemed state of mankind, perhaps even for global warming. (Clare Short, a member of Tony Blair's cabinet until 2003, charged that Israel is "much worse than the original apartheid state" because it "undermines the international community's reaction to global warming.")

Chomsky is generally (and mistakenly) identified as "a critic of Israel." But he is by no means the only beneficiary of the flagrantly euphemistic redefinition of "criticism" where Israel and its numerous enemies are concerned. Examples abound. A Vassar professor (writing in *Judaism* Magazine, no less) refers to Intifada II, in the course of which Palestinian Arab suicide bombers, pogromists, and lynch mobs slaughtered over a thousand people (most of them Israeli Jews) and wounded thousands more, as "a critique of Zionism."³ A Panglossian writer in the *Chronicle of Higher Education* assures readers that "calls to destroy Israel, or to throw it into the Mediterranean Sea . . . are not evidence of hatred of Jews," but merely "reflect a quarrel with the State of Israel."⁴ Some critique, some quarrel! When questions were raised in November 2003 about the indecency of Harvard and Columbia honoring and playing host to Oxford poetaster, blood libel subscriber, and *London Review of Books* regular Tom Paulin after he had urged that Jews living in Judea/Samaria "should be shot dead" and announced that he "never believed that Israel had the right to exist at all," his apologists in Cambridge and Morningside Heights defended his right "to criticize Israeli policy."⁵ But the prize for redefinition of the term "criticism" where Israel and Jews are its object should probably go to the Swedish Chancellor of Justice (Goran Lambertz) who in 2006 ruled that repeated calls from the Grand Mosque of Stockholm to "Kill the Jews" by dispatching suicide bombers to Israel and other Jewish population centers were not unlawful racial incitement to murder. Rather, ruled this Swedish Solomon, they "should be judged differently and therefore be regarded as permissible because, although highly critical of the Jews, they were used by one side in an ongoing and far-reaching conflict where calls to arms and insults are part of the everyday climate in the rhetoric that surrounds it."⁶

Just what, then, does "criticism" mean? The Victorian poet and critic Matthew Arnold defined criticism (by which term he did not mean merely literary criticism) as "the attempt to see the object as in itself it really is."⁷ Writing in 1865, he believed he was still living in the shadow of the French Revolution and the Reign of Terror, but also in the new age of science. He wanted criticism to model itself on the disinterested observation of science and not the fierce political partisanship that derived from the Revolution: like science, criticism should espouse no party and no cause, except the cause of truth. Its proper aim is to see the object as it really is, not to destroy the object. Dickens, a few years earlier in *Tale of Two Cities* (1859) had encapsulated the murderous aspect of French politicide by mocking its two favorite slogans: "Liberty, Equality, Fraternity—or Death" and (Chamfort's version) "Sois Mon Frère, ou Je Te Tue." (Be my brother, or I'll kill you.)

The "critics of Israel" who deny its "right to exist" and threaten it with destruction if it fails to dance to their tune may be dishonest, despicable, consumed with bloodlust, but let us not deny them their triumph. In the war of ideas, they have beaten us at almost every turn, and by "us" I mean those for whom the foundation of Israel was one of the (few) redeeming acts of a blood-soaked and shameful century. A widely publicized 2007 BBC poll of 28,000 people in 27 countries shows Israel as "least-liked" country in the entire world, and, among Europeans polled, most disliked in Germany; yes, in the very country where the Jews' "right to live" was once a popular topic, Israel-haters outpolled Israel-admirers by 77 percent to 10 percent. And still greater triumphs than those in the war for public opinion may yet await these "critics." Their threats to Israel are not idle ones. On their own, the Chomskys and Paulins and Norman Finkelsteins and Tony Judts and Alexander Cockburns cannot visit upon Israel the terrible fate they think it deserves; but they know they have a powerful ally named Iran, under the leadership of someone bent not merely, like the "critics," on politicide but on genocide; someone who daily promises to "remove Israel from the map" with nuclear weapons and watches with glee as the international noose tightens around Israel's throat and the umbrellas go up in Europe and Washington.

Should Liberals be Exempt from Criticism?

Linked, however absurdly, with the question of whether "criticism" comprises not merely the effort to see an object as it really is but also the exhortation to destroy it, has, for several decades, been another question. Should liberals or "progressives" themselves be exempt from criticism when they "criticize" Israel (and its supporters) in a manner that draws heavily upon the centuries-old canards of antisemitism, flagrant and blatant calumnies, licentious equations, and the premise that the world's only Jewish state is also the only state in the world guilty by its very existence.

As long ago as 1950, in *The Liberal Imagination*, Lionel Trilling had called attention to what he called the "conformity of dissent" among liberals, a conformity bolstered by the quaint premise that liberals should not only have the right to go their own way, but to do so without any questions ever being asked of them. This premise, insofar as it pertained to the relentless assault on Israel by self-styled "progressives," became the subject of heated dispute in 2006 following publication of a booklet by Alvin Rosenfeld called "'Progressive' Jewish Thought and the New Anti-Semitism."[8] It recounted the varied attempts by Jewish progressives (Rosenfeld studiously avoided the term "liberal") to depict Israel as the epitome of apartheid, the one genuine inheritor of Nazism, evil incarnate. The booklet was widely and furiously attacked, by Jews and Gentiles, for trying to "silence critics of Israel by calling them antisemitic." These critics (defamers might be a better word) were soon repeating, as if by rote, the charge that Rosenfeld was trying to "silence" them by pointing out the licentious character of their equations between Israel and apartheid South Africa or Nazi Germany. But how was his criticism a threat to free speech or a strategy for closing down debate on the Middle East conflict? So pervasive was the bizarre notion that entering a debate is equivalent to trying to shut it down—Rosenfeld called it a "scam"—that I myself, offering to reply to a *Jerusalem Post* broadside against Rosenfeld by a Columbia University journalism professor named Freedman, was scolded by the *Post*'s opinion editor, Elliot Jager, as follows: "Why would you want to argue in favor of censorship?"

Bernard Harrison, whose study of the resurgence of antisemitism is discussed elsewhere in this book, then took up the cudgels in a defense of Rosenfeld which he entitled "Israel, Anti-Semitism, and Free Speech." He asks how, exactly, does the "forensic sophism, the dialectical scam," whereby people like John Judis, Stephen Walt and John Mearsheimer, Jimmy Carter, Tony Judt, and George Soros turn a debate about Israel into one about free speech work? In reply, he offers a classic definition:

> One advances some 'anti-Zionist' thesis out of the 'Nazi analogy' box—some defamatory thesis, call it Td, which would be hard to make stick by normal processes of argument—while at the same time suggesting in an undertone that more people would be prepared to say 'these things' if they were not so afraid of the Israel Lobby. Up pops some Jew, preferably a distinguished one, right on schedule, to point out... that Td is defamatory and stinks of anti-Semitism. This gives the author of the proposition exactly what he was after in the first place: namely, empirical evidence that there is indeed a Jewish Conspiracy to suppress 'the truth' about Israel. The press raises a hue and cry and, like a pack of hounds diverted from the scent by a trailed sack of aniseed, hares off on this new tack. The debate is turned from one about Israel into one about free speech, and Td, the original bit of defamation that started it all, doesn't have to be defended after all. Game, set, and match to the 'anti-Zionist.'[9]

Just how, asks Harrison, does the "silencing," if it existed at all, of such (very audible) figures as George Soros, Jimmy Carter, and the Walt-Mearsheimer duo work? Would the *London Review of Books*, *The New York Review of Books*, CNN, BBC, and National Public Radio suddenly fold their hitherto welcoming arms to Israel's manifold accusers? The question has only to be asked for the absurdity of its premise to be revealed. To put the absurdity in its proper perspective, let us conclude with a statement about being "silenced" by a writer who understand what that meant. In 1932, Isaac Babel published his *Red Cavalry* stories to considerable acclaim; but he soon came under attack by the Soviet literary bureaucracy and stopped writing. In 1934, he spoke at the first Soviet Writer's Congress, where he announced that he was practicing a new literary genre, of which he proclaimed himself the master: "I am the master of the genre of silence." In 1937, Babel was arrested; he died in a concentration camp in 1939 or 1940. That is what it really means for a writer to be silenced.

Notes

1. Constance B. Hilliard, *Does Israel Have a Future? The Case for a Post-Zionist State* (Washington, DC: Potomac Books, 2009).
2. Noam Chomsky, Speech to the Scottish Palestine Solidarity Campaign, delivered by live video from MIT (October 11, 2002); published as "Anti-Semitism, Zionism and the Palestinians," *Variant* (a Scottish arts magazine) 2, no. 16 (Winter 2002): 12–14.
3. Andrew Bush, "Postzionism and Its Neighbors," *Judaism* 52 (Winter/Spring 2003): 111.
4. Amitai Etzioni, "Harsh Lessons in Incivility," *Chronicle of Higher Education*, November 1, 2002.
5. See the essay "Poetaster" in this book.
6. Lambertz's ruling was widely reported in the Swedish press.
7. "The Function of Criticism at the Present Time," in *Essays in Criticism* (London: Macmillan, 1865).
8. Alvin Rosenfeld, *"Progressive" Jewish Thought and the New Anti-Semitism* (New York: American Jewish Committee, 2006).
9. Bernard Harrison, *Israel, Anti-Semitism, and Free Speech* (New York: American Jewish Committee, 2007), 37.

Professors for Suicide Bombing: The Explosive Power of Boredom

Of the variegated forms of murderous assault that the Palestinian Arabs unleashed against Israel during the Al-Aqsa Intifada—often called the Oslo War—starting in September 2000, none proved so cruel or lethal, or so perfectly embodied absolute evil, as suicide bombings, which killed a large percentage of the 1,100 Israelis and 64 foreigners murdered during the war. Yet none exercised so hypnotic a spell upon, or elicited so much fawning admiration from, the "learned classes" in England and America. In July of 2004, when the second Intifada had nearly run its course (Arafat died in November), the British press reported that London mayor Ken Livingstone had given a "warm welcome" to the Muslim cleric Dr. al-Qaradawi, who ardently defended Palestinian suicide bombers on the grounds that they were carrying out "martyrdom operations," which he pronounced definitely permissible "within the rules of Islam." This prompted the *Sunday Telegraph* to remark that Qaradawi held many views "that might raise even more eyebrows around an Islington dinner table: after all, there are now so many British people who seem depressingly ready to defend the deliberate targeting and blowing to pieces of Jewish grandmothers and small children that it is almost de rigueur."[1] The novelist Kurt Vonnegut weighed in with praise for the killers because "they are dying for their own self-respect."[2]

In the course of Arafat's campaign to "soften up" Israel up for concessions even more far-reaching than those of the Oslo accords, well over 300 suicide bombers succeeded in detonating themselves—in crowded buses and cafes, in university cafeterias, at a Passover seder, and almost any place where children could be found in sizable numbers.

They killed hundreds of people and maimed thousands. These human bombs, most of them teenagers inculcated from kindergarten with Jew-hatred, but also mothers and grandmothers, generally acted out of a superabundance of hope: hope of driving the Jews out of Israel; hope of making their families wealthy with the enormous bonuses at first guaranteed by Iraq and Arafat, then by other Arab (and Iranian) benefactors; and above all, hope of heaven. And so, of course, professors imprisoned in Marxist clichés of socioeconomic determinism concluded—on the basis of no evidence whatever—that the suicide bombers, mostly products of upper middle class families, had acted out of poverty, hopelessness, and despair. Princeton historian Sean Wilentz observed in *The New Republic* in 2002 that the "root cause" of suicide bombings appeared to be "money, education and privilege."[3] Indeed, Islamic Jihad had itself declared: "We do not take depressed people [to become suicide bombers]."[4]

Beyond this, liberalism's angelic sociology was invoked to "explain" suicide bombing as the inevitable result and measure of Israeli oppression: "Each new act of murder and suicide," wrote Paul Berman in *Terror and Liberalism*, "testified to how oppressive were the Israelis. Palestinian terror, in this view, was the measure of Israeli guilt. The more grotesque the terror, the deeper the guilt. . . . And even Nazism struck many of Israel's critics as much too pale an explanation for the horrific nature of Israeli action. For the pathos of suicide terror is limitless, and if Palestinian teenagers were blowing themselves up in acts of random murder, a rational explanation was going to require ever more extreme tropes, beyond even Nazism."[5]

This particular form of atrocity not only failed to disturb the equanimity of our heavily petted professors, but elicited from many of them a steady stream of rhapsodic admiration, sympathetic identification (with the murderers, not their victims), and high-toned apologia. The stream eventually became a torrent so huge as to suggest that what Irving Howe liked to call "the explosive power of boredom" is a distinct occupational hazard of academia. A few examples from among many—a philosopher, a literary theorist, a theologian, and a psychoanalytic critic—may serve to illustrate the pattern.

1. Ted Honderich, a Canadian-born philosopher who became a British subject and spent his career in England, has long been a popular speaker on North American campuses, where he seems to appeal powerfully to bloodlust among the learned—especially where it is Jewish blood that is in question. Although his speciality is "Mind and

Logic," Honderich's itch to be clever has often led him to stentorian pronouncements about politics, especially violent politics. In 1980, he published an "ethical" defense of violence and mass murder called *Violence for Equality*, a title that calls to mind Dickens's encapsulation (in *A Tale of Two Cities*) of revolutionary France's Reign of Terror: "Liberty, Equality, Fraternity, or Death."

Not long after 9/11, Honderich decided to shine the light of pure reason and moral philosophy upon that day's horrific massacres in a book called *After the Terror*. The essence of his argument is that there is no moral distinction between acts of omission and acts of commission. The West, having failed to eliminate the poverty that its capitalist system introduced to the world, was collectively responsible for 9/11. "Is it possible," Honderich asked, "to suppose that the September 11 attacks had nothing at all to do with . . . Malawi, Mozambique, Zambia and Sierra Leone?" He stopped a hair short of saying that Osama bin Laden and his fellow idealists were justified in murdering thousands of people in order to feed millions.

But the philosopher was far less cautious about the "moral right" of Palestinian Arabs to blow up Jews, a right he defended vigorously (and piously): "Those Palestinians who have resorted to violence have been right . . . and those who have killed themselves in the cause of their people have indeed sanctified themselves." In an interview, the eminent logician explained the distinction between suicide bombings in Manhattan and in Jerusalem: "The likely justification depends importantly on the fact that the suffering that is caused does have a probability of success." In other words, if Palestinian terrorists should succeed in their goal of destroying Israel, mass murder will have been justified; if they fail, it will not.

Upon finishing *After the Terror*, Honderich—a socialist millionaire—offered to donate 5,000 British pounds from his advance on royalties to Oxfam. But to his astonishment—and indeed that of many who have observed England's moral debacle of recent years—the charity refused the money, which it viewed as morally tainted by what old-fashioned people call incitement to murder. "Oxfam's purpose," said a spokesman, "is to overcome poverty and suffering. We believe that the lives of all human beings are of equal value. We do not endorse acts of violence."[6]

But Honderich's North American audiences proved far less squeamish. Palestinian Arabs, he told a receptive crowd in Toronto in September 2002, have a "moral right" to blow up Jews, and he very much wanted to encourage them to exercise that right, i.e., to do still more abundantly that which, one might have thought, they were already doing adequately. "To claim a moral right on behalf of the Palestinians to their terrorism is to say that they are right to engage in it, that it is permissible if not obligatory."[7] He expatiated further on the "moral right" to murder in *The Independent,* one of his favorite venues, on November 2, 2006. More recently, he has given his thirst for Jewish blood full rein from such platforms as Alexander Cockburn's *Counterpunch* (October 25, 2011) and Iranian TV (October 10, 2011). In both places he reiterated the first principle of Honderichian ethics: "The Palestinians have a *moral* right to their terrorism . . . no less to be reverenced than the fact of Jewish lives now rooted in Israel." For his Iranian audience, he did make some concession to pity, but of the self-regarding sort: "I happen to believe this and it's gotten me into trouble." By "trouble" he meant that someone had had the temerity to call him an antisemite. But this was a logical impossibility since "I happen to be married to a Jewish woman."[8]

Honderich spent his academic career at the University College in London, where he was professor of mind and logic. Those familiar with that institution know that it houses the nicely dressed skeleton (and Madame Tussaud wax head) of Jeremy Bentham, the philosopher who measured morality by the quantity of pleasure delivered: if the greatest happiness of the greatest number of citizens could be arrived at by twenty-nine of them deciding, because they had the power to do so, to feast upon citizen number thirty, then it was right and proper for them to do so. If Dostoevsky's idealistic utilitarian Raskolnikov was Bentham with an axe in his hand, then Honderich is Bentham with a bomb in his brain.

2. Nor is he the only academic luminary whose lucubrations on suicide bombing demonstrate Raskolnikov tendencies. There is also Columbia University's Gayatri Chakravorty Spivak. What philosophy has become in the hands of Honderich, the opaque pseudojargon of literary postmodernism has become in the hands of Spivak. George Orwell wrote in 1946 ("Politics and the English Language") that in our time "political language is designed to make lies sound truthful and murder respectable, and to give an appearance of solidity to pure wind." Orwell's crowning example was "a comfortable English professor" defending Soviet totalitarianism and mass murder with polysyllabic gibberish and Latinized euphemism. Already in 1989, Spivak had "explained" Edward Said's call for the murder of Palestinian

Arab "collaborators" as "words for Palestinian solidarity."[9] But in June of 2002, at the height (or depths) of the Oslo War, speaking at Leeds University, this celebrated tribune of "international feminism" outdid even herself: "Suicide bombing—and the planes of 9/11 were living bombs—is a purposive self-annihilation, a confrontation between oneself and oneself, the extreme end of autoeroticism, killing oneself as other, in the process killing others. . . . Suicidal resistance is a message inscribed on the body when no other means will get through. It is both execution and mourning . . . you die with me for the same cause, no matter which side you are on. Because no matter who you are there are no designated killees [sic] in suicide bombing . . . It is a response . . . to the state terrorism practiced outside of its own ambit by the United States and in the Palestinian case additionally to an absolute failure of hospitality."[10]

This is what Lionel Trilling called the language of nonthought, employed to blur the distinction between suicide and murder, to obliterate the victims—"no designated killees" here!—metaphysically as well as physically. By bringing America into the range of her devastating intellect, Spivak goes beyond Honderich. Although he blamed America itself for the Arab massacres of 9/11, he stopped short of moral justification for that attack; like many other English academics he is hesitant about biting the hand he hopes will feed him. But Spivak, already comfortably ensconced (in a "chair") and amply nourished at Morningside Heights, had no such compunction.

Since no apologist for suicide bombing rhapsodizes so lyrically about it as Spivak, it is at this point worth recalling just what happens when a conventional bomb is exploded in a contained space, such as a city bus traveling through downtown Jerusalem, where the intifada massacres often took place. I quote from Dr. Pekka Sinervo, the University of Toronto physicist: "A person sitting nearby would feel, momentarily, a shock wave slamming into his or her body, with an 'overpressure' of 300,000 pounds. Such a blast would crush the chest, rupture liver, spleen, heart and lungs, melt eyes, pull organs away from surrounding tissue, separate hands from arms and feet from legs. Bodies would fly through the air or be impaled on the jagged edges of crumpled metal and broken glass."[11]

3. The third member of my quartet of academic apologists for suicide bombing is Karen Armstrong, a former Catholic nun who specializes in comparative religion. Born near Birmingham, England, she spent seven years in the Society of the Holy Child Jesus

convent during the sixties but rebelled against what she derided as the "regimented way of life," and (not one to leave quietly) wrote a book called *Through the Narrow Gate*, in which she derided the convent's religious discipline. She recounts how she was "suicidal" at that point in her life. English Catholics, so she claims, hate her as "the runaway nun," and send her "excrement in the mail." Perhaps they are not aware that, since she habitually attaches the label "fundamentalist" to any religious person who does not share her politics, her likening of Pope John Paul II to a Muslim fundamentalist was not necessarily an anti-Catholic gesture.[12]

Armstrong has written a best-selling book called *Understanding Islam*, and she played a key role in the (scandalously uncritical) Public Broadcasting System's program of December 2002 called "Legacy of a Prophet," which celebrated the life of Muhammed and was widely described as "a film for [Islamic] missionaries." In a lengthy interview with *Al-Ahram Weekly* in July 2002, Armstrong recounted how, during her time in Israel in the mideighties working on a documentary about the revelations of St. Paul, she herself had a revelation: she heard some Israelis refer to "dirty Arabs" and instantly recognized that today's Israelis are to today's Arabs what Nazis were to Jews in the thirties and forties, and that "the Israelis can do what they want because America will always support them." Vigorously insisting that there is "nothing . . . anti-Western" about Islam, she has called for a reinvigorated jihad by her Muslim friends, whom she advises to "march down the street at Ground Zero in New York." Palestinian suicide bombers are motivated not by religion, because "this is not how religion works"—QED—but by "absolute hopelessness." Armstrong's justification for suicide bombing grows out of her fine sense of equity in military struggle. These poor people, she complains, "don't have F-16s, and they don't have tanks. They don't have anything to match Israel's arsenal. They only have their own bodies." In other words, murdering innocent people is a permissible, indeed praiseworthy grab for equality by an "occupied" people.[13]

It goes without saying that Armstrong, like all of Arafat's professorial apologists over the years, overlooks the troublesome fact that it was Arab hatred and aggression—in 1967 as in 2003—that led to "occupation" and not occupation to hatred and aggression (or indeed, that Israeli withdrawal from the disputed territories has invariably led to greater Arab violence and extremism). She also has failed to notice that Arafat, Abu-Mazen, and their acolytes have been backed militarily, financially, and politically by 1.2 billion Muslims, by 21 Arab nations (as well as the non-Arab nation of Iran), and by the European Union. Not to mention just how powerful and "equalizing" a weapon in the hands of radical Muslim Arabs is the total disregard for the sanctity of human life, as a result of which nineteen technically competent barbarians could attack two American cities, killing thousands of people and causing billions of dollars of property damage. But for Armstrong the only thing 9/11 revealed was the "intolerance" of Western society, and perhaps the need to create strategic equity for disadvantaged Muslims by giving them nuclear bombs.

Armstrong has in recent years been promulgating an ecumenical scheme that she calls "The Charter for Compassion." Theatrically "unveiled" by her in 2009 and modestly touted as "the best idea humanity ever had," it is a treacly eclectic compound of Unitarianism, the positivists' "religion of humanity," and such dubious saints as Desmond Tutu. Alas (and very much like Tutu himself) Armstrong is notably short of civility towards living Jews and much inclined to scold Jews who kick up a fuss over the resurgence of antisemitism in Europe for being "emotionally stuck in the horrors of the Nazi era." Ironically, before blossoming forth as a global savior, she for years taught Christianity and comparative religion at London's Leo Baeck College. Mindful of the irony that she should be employed by a school named after a scholarly, mild-mannered Jew who was forced into a tragic leadership role during the Nazi period, she has bared her teeth in such gestures of mean spite towards her occasional employers, who have been learning the wisdom of the old adage that "if you don't want people to dislike you, don't do them favors." Armstrong's only qualm about suicide bombings is that they may tarnish the glorious image that Palestinian Arabs currently enjoy in England. As she may perhaps remember from her Catholic period, Cardinal Newman wrote (in *The Idea of a University*) that for ethical temperaments like hers, "it is detection, not the sin, which is the crime."

4. Finally, and as if to prove William Buckley's allegation that in England antisemitism is not just a hobby but a way of life, we have Jacqueline Rose, another professor of English literature (though of psychoanalytic bent) and also a purveyor of that special brand of antisemitism that comes with an artificial "Jewish" flavor—in her case strong enough to have earned her a prominent place in Howard Jacobson's novelistic satire of "the Jews of Shame," *The Finkler Question*. Rose too is in love with mournful death, especially of the Jewish

sort, and still more with its purveyors. In 2004, just three days after a Palestinian suicide bomber had killed three people and wounded thirty-two others in Tel Aviv's open-air market, she rushed forward to spill ink on behalf of those who had spilled blood, publishing an article urging everybody to understand suicide bombers "without condescension" and to recognize their deeds as acts of passionate identification with Israelis. She not only regurgitated the standard clichés about Palestinian mass murderers as "people driven to extremes," but (in the manner of Spivak) waxed eloquent about bonding with Islamic fanatics, lashed out, with all the fury of an anthropological egalitarian, against "those wishing to denigrate suicide bombers and their culture," and (in less egalitarian manner) finally declared that "culture" vastly superior to the Jewish culture of a butchered Israeli teenager—Malki Roth—who had addressed a Rosh Hashanah letter to God expressing the hope (never to be realized) that she would live another year, and that the Messiah would arrive. "In the lowest deep," as Milton's Satan astutely observed, "a lower deep."[14]

Honderich, Spivak, Armstrong, and Rose proffer variations on a single theme. But they all treat the dead and mangled bodies of innocent people as if they were so much fertilizer to feed diseased imaginations. If these professors of terror looked upon the victims as human beings they could not possibly justify the mass murder of Israelis and others using speculative arguments and licentious moral equations, based upon political and historical ignorance so vast that they would shock an ordinarily attentive sixth-grader.

Hitler's professors were the first to make antisemitism both academically respectable and complicit in crime. They have now found their successors in the professors of Arafat, of bin Laden, of Hamas, and of Ahmadinejad. Their grotesque apologetics serve as another reminder (as if we needed one) that knowledge is one thing, sanctity another.

Notes

1. *Sunday Telegraph*, July 11, 2004.
2. *The Australian*, November 19, 2005.
3. See also in the online edition of the *New Republic* for June 20, 2002, the review essay "Does Poverty Cause Terrorism?"
4. See on this subject "What Cherie [Blair] Really Thinks," *Daily Telegraph*, June 19, 2002.
5. Paul Berman, *Terror and Liberalism* (New York: W. W. Norton, 2003), 134, 137.

6. *The Guardian*, October 9, 2002.
7. *National Post* (Canada), September 25, 2002.
8. *Counterpunch*, October 25, 2011; Iranian TV, October 20, 2011.
9. Letter in *Commentary*, December 1989.
10. Professor Michael Weingrad's transcription of this lecture appeared in the July 29, 2002 online edition of the *New Republic*: http://tnr.com/doc.mhtml?i=20020729&s=notebook072902bush
11. Quoted in Rosie DiManno, "Unlike Victims, Bomber Died without Pain," *Toronto Star*, June 19, 2002. (The *Toronto Star* is owned by Honderich's family.) Bruce Hoffman, author of *Inside Terrorism* (1999), pointed out that although Spivak and her friends call suicidal bus-bombings erotic acts, they are carefully scheduled: "Winter and summer are the better seasons for bombing buses in Jerusalem, because the closed windows (for heat or air-conditioning) intensify the force of the blast, maximizing the bombs' killing potential."—"The Logic of Suicide Terrorism," *Atlantic Monthly*, June 2003, 42.
12. Interview with Mary Rourke, *Los Angeles Times*, October 9, 2000.
13. *Al-Ahram Weekly, 4–10 July 2002*. The full text of the interview appears at: http://www.ahram.org.eg/weekly/2002/593/intrvw.htm. See also Michael Freund, "British Lecturer Justifies Suicide Bombings," *Jerusalem Post Internet Edition*, July 10, 2002.
14. "Deadly Embrace," *London Review of Books*, November 4, 2004.

Back to 1933: How the Academic Boycott of Israel Began

On April 6, 2002, 123 university academics and researchers (their number would later rise to 250) from across Europe signed an open letter, published in Britain's *Guardian* newspaper, calling for a moratorium on all cultural and research links with Israel until the Israeli government abided by (unspecified) UN resolutions and returned yet again to negotiations with Yasser Arafat to be conducted in accordance with the principles laid down in the latest Saudi peace plan. The petition was organized and published at the very time Israelis were being butchered on a daily basis, mainly by brainwashed teenage suicide bombers, Arab versions of the Hitler Youth. It declared, in high Pecksniffian style, that since the Israeli government was "impervious to moral appeals from world leaders" Israel's cultural and research institutions should be denied further funding from the European Union and the European Science Foundation. It neglected to recommend that the European Union suspend its very generous financing of Yasser Arafat or that Chinese scholars be boycotted until China withdraws from Tibet. The petition was the brainchild of Steven Rose, director of the Brain and Behavior Research Group at Gresham College, London, and the great majority of its signatories were British. Indeed, the whole BDS (Boycott, Divest, Sanction) movement completes England's trilogy of antisemitic pioneering, along with the medieval blood libel and expulsion of its Jewish residents.

Nevertheless, the boycott assault on Israel included academics from a host of European countries, a number sufficient to give it the appearance of a pan-European campaign against the Jews. It even had the obligatory display Israeli, one Eva Jablonka of Tel Aviv University. (Nine other Israeli leftists added their names as soon as they found out about this easy new opportunity for international renown.)

In June, Mona Baker, director of the Center for Translation and Intercultural Studies at the University of Manchester Institute of Science and Technology (UMIST) decided to practice what the all-European petitioners had preached: she dismissed from the boards of the two journals she owns and edits two Israelis, Miriam Shlesinger of Bar-Ilan University and Gideon Toury of Tel Aviv University. She also added that she would no longer accept articles from Israeli researchers, and it was later revealed that she would not "allow" books originating from her private publishing house (St. Jerome) to be purchased by Israeli institutions. One paradox of the firing, which would be repeated often in later stages of the boycott, was that Shlesinger was a member in good standing of the Israeli Left, former chairman of Amnesty International's Israeli chapter, and ever at the ready with "criticism of Israeli policies in the West Bank . . ." Toury, for his part, opposed taking any retaliatory action against Baker—this had been proposed by an American teaching fellow at Leeds named Michael Weingrad—because "a boycott is a boycott is a boycott." A small contingent of Toury's (mostly British) friends in linguistics issued a statement objecting to his dismissal because: "We agree with Noam Chomsky's view that one does not boycott people or their cultural institutions as an expression of political protest."

It was hard to say whether this document was more notable for its lack of Jewish self-respect or for sheer ignorance (of the fact that Chomsky was leading the American campaign for disinvestment from Israel, the economic phalanx of the professorial campaign to demonize and isolate Israel). A few (non-British) members of Baker's boards resigned because they objected to the dismissal of people solely "on the basis of [their] passport," especially by a journal entitled *The Translator: Studies in Intercultural Communication.* But, for the most part, the dismissals raised no public opposition from within the British university system, just as almost none had been raised back in April when Tom Paulin, stalwart of the IRA school of poetics and lecturer at Oxford, had urged that American Jews living in the disputed territories of Judea and Samaria "should be shot dead."

The situation changed only when a prominent American scholar, Professor Stephen Greenblatt of Harvard, intervened. After arriving in

England in early July 2002 to receive an honorary degree from London University, Greenblatt called Baker's actions "repellent," "dangerous," and "intellectually and morally bankrupt." "Excluding scholars because of the passports that they carry or because of their skin color, religion or political party, corrupts the integrity of intellectual work," he said. Greenblatt's statement forced the British public to pay attention to Baker's boycott. Even a writer for the venomously anti-Israel *Guardian* was emboldened to criticize the way in which the European boycotters' petition was being carried to extreme and radical form in Britain: a British lecturer working at Tel Aviv University applied for a post back home in the United Kingdom and was told by the head of the first department to which he applied: "No, we don't accept any applicants from a Nazi state."

Greenblatt was still treating the boycott mainly as a violation of academic freedom—plausibly enough, since Rose had declared that "Academic freedom I find a completely spurious argument . . ." But the real issue was an antisemitic campaign to transform the pariah people into the pariah state, as became evident in the rhetorically violent reactions to Greenblatt's criticism. Baker herself quickly announced that she repented of nothing. She was "not against Israeli nationals per se; only Israeli institutions as part of the Israeli state which I absolutely deplore." She was acting on behalf of good Europeans everywhere, and refused to reveal where she herself was born—Egypt, as it happens.

Greenblatt was also assaulted by another inhabitant of the academic fever swamps of Manchester, Baker's colleague Michael Sinnott, a professor of "paper science." Springing chivalrously to Baker's defense, he called Greenblatt's open letter to her "sanctimonious claptrap," decried Israel as "the mirror-image of Nazism," and asserted that what made Israel a unique menace to the world was "the breathtaking power of the American Jewish lobby." In a seven-year sojourn at the University of Illinois in Chicago (UIC), he had felt the power of the insatiable Jews on his own pulses. First, "the Israeli atrocities for which my tax dollars were paying were never reported in the American news media, which were either controlled by Jews, or browbeaten by them in the way you have just exemplified"; second, his "pay raises at UIC never really recovered" from his defiantly scheduling a graduate class on the Jewish Sabbath. The UMIST administration, already busy distancing itself from Baker, now had a still greater embarrassment on its hands when the *Sunday Telegraph* (September 29) reported Sinnott's letter. It "launched an investigation" into the abstruse question of whether Sinnott might be an antisemite. Sinnott, ever mindful of his "pay raises," issued a weasely statement of regret, not over his slander but over its detection.

As the boycott campaign intensified, its guiding lights were plagued by problems of definition bearing a ghoulish resemblance to those that once beset the Nazis in deciding just which people were to be considered fitting victims of discrimination, oppression, and (eventually) murder. Perhaps this is why Baker struck up an acquaintance with David Irving, who in December reported on his website that she had kindly taken the trouble to alert him to an ad placed by Amazon.com in the Israeli press which might be considered supportive of that terrible country. The Hitler-loving historian could have supplied Baker with information about problems the Nazis faced in implementing their boycott: Should the targeted group be people with four Jewish grandparents or perhaps just three or two? Some Baker defenders had chastised Greenblatt for suggesting that it was their Israeli nationality that led to the sacking of the two Israelis. By no means! It was just the fact that they worked for Israeli universities. But what of Arabs who worked for Israeli universities? If the Hebrew University employee whose mass murder of the people in the Mount Scopus cafeteria was the perfect existential realization of the boycotters' ideas had survived his exploit, would he have been banned from joining Baker's janitorial staff in Manchester?

There was also the problem of ideology. Could the professors who organized the boycott have been so ignorant of the Israeli political scene as not to know that the Israeli professoriat is the center of anti-Zionist polemic and political activity in the country? Many of the targets of the boycott would inevitably be people with political views similar to those of the boycotters themselves, especially the assumption that it is "occupation" that leads to Arab hatred of Israel, and not Arab hatred of Israel that leads to occupation.

The most paradoxical example of the boycott's effect was Oren Yiftachel, a political geographer from Ben-Gurion University, described by *Ha'aretz* as "hold[ing] extreme leftist political views." Yiftachel had coauthored a paper with an Arab Israeli political scientist from Haifa University named As'ad Ghanem, dealing with the attitude of Israeli authorities to Arabs within Israel proper and the disputed territories.

They submitted it to the English periodical *Political Geography*, whose editor, David Slater, returned it with a note saying it had been rejected because its authors were Israelis.

Here was a case to test the mettle of a boycotter! A *mischling* article, half-Jewish, half-Arab, wholly the product of people carrying Israeli passports and working for Israeli institutions, yet expressing opinions on Israel as Satan's laboratory indistinguishable from Slater's. Poor Slater, apparently unable to amputate the Jewish part of the article from the Arab part and (to quote him) "not sure to what extent [the authors] had been critical of Israel," rejected the submission in its entirety. Or so it seemed—for after half a year of wrangling, it emerged that Slater might accept the paper if only its authors would insert some more paragraphs likening Israel to apartheid South Africa. In other words, the Englishman might relax his boycotting principles if his ideological prejudices could be more amply satisfied.

Exactly what happened at this point is not easy to discover. Since Yiftachel is one of those Israeli academics who adheres to the motto "the other country, right or wrong," it is hard to believe he would balk at describing Israel as an apartheid state. He had in the past denounced Israeli governments as racist or dictatorial and had coauthored with Ghanem a piece in *Ha'aretz* urging Jews to participate in "Land Day." But now he had become the classic instance of somebody "hoist with his own petard," caught in his own trap. At one point he complained to Slater "that rejecting a person because of his [national] origin, from an academic point of view, is very problematic." Not only did it interfere with the progress of Yiftachel's career, it hurt the anti-Israel cause. "From a political and practical point of view, the boycott actually weakens the sources of opposition to the Israeli occupation in universities," he fretted. Poor Yiftachel found that when he and his colleague carried their message about Israeli wickedness to America, audiences would constantly pester them about—the boycott. Nor was this the only instance in which the boycott threatened to backfire. Susan Greenfield, neurobiologist and director of the Royal Institution, England's oldest independent research body, published a warning on December 14 that the boycott, "if it continues . . . will harm people in every sphere, but in medical research lives are potentially at risk." In 1941, Otto Warburg, one of Germany's preeminent cancer researchers, was facing dismissal from his post at the Kaiser Wilhelm Society because of his "half-Jewish" origins. Hitler, aware of the value of Warburg's research to the health of German citizens, alerted Goering, who promptly turned Warburg into a "quarter Jew." Would the boycotters emulate the (occasional) pragmatism of their predecessors, or stick firmly to their principles in order to reduce Israel to pariah status? More importantly, will the European Union, many of whose prominent members either participated or acquiesced in the destruction of European Jewry in the years 1933–1945, put a stop to the conspiracy of these spiritual descendants of those Max Weinreich famously called "Hitler's Professors," to expel the Jews (once again) from the family of nations? The question remains open.

Afrocentrism, Liberal Dogmatism, and Antisemitism at Wellesley College

Truth exists and can be known. This once unremarkable conviction is at the core of Mary Lefkowitz's compelling first-person narrative of her decade-long struggle, beginning at Wellesley College in the early nineties but extending well beyond the bucolic shores of Lake Waban, against a cadre of Afrocentrists, postmodernists, antisemites, devotees of "compensatory politics," and litigious race racketeers. It is a conviction that gives her a distinct advantage over her opponents because it prompts the obvious rhetorical question: which of two combatants in a dispute is more likely to be telling the truth, the one who believes that truth exists, or the one who does not and claims there are only "competing narratives"?

Lefkowitz is a distinguished classical scholar whose research has been mostly on "the ways in which myth and empirical reasoning intersect in ancient Greek historical writing, and this is probably why . . . it seemed only natural to want to find out why some people firmly believed that Greek philosophy was stolen from Egypt, even when it so obviously was not."[1] Among the believers in and propagators of the "Stolen Legacy" myth was an Africana [sic] Studies professor at Wellesley named Anthony Martin, who was telling the young women in his classes that Aristotle was a thief who pilfered books out of the great library of Alexandria and then presented their ideas as his own. The slight difficulty with this myth is that the Alexandria library was not built until after Aristotle's death. But when Lefkowitz took it upon herself to point this out, she was accused (by Martin and other

Afrocentrists) of being a racist, a conservative, a Jew, among other crimes.

Martin is the protagonist of *History Lesson's* foundational incident, which took place in a dormitory in October 1991 and provides a nearly perfect existential realization of his belief that any dispute involving a black person must be viewed as a racial incident. Martin, one of a group of faculty and students gathered to read *Twelfth Night*, left the reading to go to the men's room. As he left it, he was asked by a student dorm officer whose job it was to pose the question to unescorted males: "Excuse me, sir, who [sic] are you with?" Martin would not stoop to explain but instead berated the student for being "a fucking bitch, a racist, and a bigot." The student, Michelle Plantec, later recalled: "Martin's reaction was very violent. I don't know how to express how violent his reaction was. Plus, he is a very tall man and he was towering over me, pointing down into my face, and he wasn't saying very nice things. I was very scared and shaking" (16–17).

Martin, for his part, claimed that her question was typical of the "bigotry" that pervaded the Wellesley campus. To combat this "racist" assault, he marshaled his acolytes among the play readers, "the black community," and the head of the black student organization Ethos to retaliate against Plantec. His zeal appears to have intensified when he learned that she was a Jew. Plantec had a nervous breakdown and, after receiving psychiatric treatment (a fact widely advertised by Martin when he learned of it), dropped out of school. Particulars of the incident did not appear until May of 1993, by which time Lefkowitz had become aware of the lurid myths about the origins of Greek philosophy and (the one dearer to Martin's heart) the responsibility of Jews for the African slave trade, a myth that Martin was teaching in his classes with the help of a text published by the Nation of Islam. In December 1993, Martin initiated a frivolous lawsuit against Lefkowitz (which dragged on for five years before being tossed out) for her article about the "racist" incident and for damaging his reputation—by showing him ignorant of history.

How, Lefkowitz asks, with startling innocence, could such things have happened at Wellesley, "where we pride ourselves on being a multicultural community, with all the values of tolerance and understanding that the term implies" (25). But she has already answered this question in describing the political movement, which she had supported, to give black students privileges granted to no other ethnic group through "affirmative action and equal [i.e., unequal] opportunity programs." At Wellesley, these include the right to appoint one black person to serve on any college committee, and to exclude from the black student organization and the Africana Studies Department anyone not of African descent (6–7).

But inequality is not the best school in which to inculcate equality. It should not have come as a surprise to Lefkowitz that institutionalized affirmative action bred (as she herself admits) "an affirmative action program for the rewriting of history" (31). One Wellesley history professor actually came under attack for "hindering diversity" by saying the Holocaust was unique. Why should the Jews hoard all that suffering for themselves alone?

One question about Martin that Lefkowitz does not answer: how did the author of, among other masterpieces, *The Jewish Onslaught: Despatches from the Wellesley Battlefront*, come to be hired by Wellesley in the first place? The answer, according to a reliable informant of mine there, is this: "several Jewish women in English and History were behind his appointment in the sixties—white liberal guilt." One wonders (though not for long) whether these progressive types felt any misgivings about what they had done when Martin showed himself a tooth-baring Jew-hater and bullier of little women, who demonstrated that, in the world of identity politics, race trumps "gender."

In 1991, *The New Republic* suggested that Lefkowitz review a whole slew of books, including the second volume of Martin Bernal's *Black Athena*, which argued not merely that Greek culture was heavily dependent on earlier cultures in Egypt and the Near East, but had been stolen from Egypt, and that the inhabitants of ancient Egypt were Africans. In her review essay (1992), the forerunner of her book *Not Out of Africa* (1996), she demonstrated conclusively that there was no historical evidence that the Greeks ever stole anything from Egypt, including their philosophy. Bernal had gained undeserved authority for his espousal of "the Stolen Legacy" because he flew the flag of the academic left, depicted European civilization as a pod of muck, and claimed to be attacking racial and religious prejudice, as if this were the only possible explanation for the classicists' "pro-Greek" position.

It was not long before all the Afrocentrists, several of them deep-dyed antisemites, trained their guns on Lefkowitz, and only a woman of remarkable courage—she was receiving chemotherapy for breast cancer at the time—could have withstood and thrown back the assault. The level of discourse among her attackers is epitomized in the sputtering of one Wilson J. Moses, who called her "an obscure drudge in the academic backwaters of a classics department" (127). In the world of faculty time-servers and timid administrators ("the most sensitive region of an academic administration's anatomy," Lefkowitz remarks, "is the institutional pocketbook" [67]) bravery is a rare commodity; and coming to the defense of the Jews has never been an exercise for the faint-hearted. Lefkowitz's attackers espoused the (fascist) idea that physiology determines culture, so that knowledge of Africa is something you have to be born into (by African descent). It was a curious revival of the once-powerful WASP resistance to hiring Jews in English departments: how could a Jew understand or interpret the literature of Christendom? In the course of endless disputes with her adversaries, Lefkowitz challenged the multiculturalist dogma that members of minority groups (always with the exception of the Jews) cannot be racists, pointing out that race professionals like Martin and Wilson had turned themselves into professional racists.

Why, Lefkowitz often asks, did she feel compelled to get at the truth about the relations between the Greeks and the Egyptians? Who would be harmed by being taught what is not true? Her question reminds me of an exchange that once took place over my dinner table between a physician friend of mine and the eminent literary scholar, the late Robert Heilman. The physician had a Ph.D. in English and had published a highly regarded book about Shakespeare when he gave up a desirable tenure-line position to start medical school (at an advanced age). "Why did you do it?" asked Heilman. "Because I wanted to go into a field where mistakes have consequences and can be fatal." "Well," replied Heilman, "they can be fatal in the humanities too, only it takes a longer time for the harm to make itself felt." That is essentially Lefkowitz's answer, and it is a very good one.

History Lesson at its best reminds one of Matthew Arnold. Arnold too defended the Greek classics, not against racist yahoos but against positivism and science, and on visiting America was delighted to find that "in colleges like Smith College in Massachusetts, and Vassar College in the state of New York," young women ("the fair host of the Amazons") were studying Greek. Arnold also defined himself as "a Liberal, yet ... a Liberal tempered by experience, reflection, and renouncement." That is almost true of Lefkowitz, except (perhaps) for the renouncement. She shows very powerfully the horrendous effects of liberal shibboleths and nostrums—affirmative action, compensatory politics, "diversity," academic freedom to indoctrinate, multiculturalism, hate speech codes, condescension toward blacks—and yet she can never quite renounce them.

Take, for example, the last of these. From Henry James' *The Princess Casamassima* (1886) to Lionel Trilling's "The Other Margaret" (1945) American literature has given us scathing exposes of the liberal condescension which imputes all bad behavior by the poor and by members of minority groups to their inability to escape the influence of their environment and circumstances. These show that if you really believe in the equality of all members of the human family, you should accord them the same degree of responsibility for their actions that you give to people who read Greek and Latin. Trilling commented acidly on how "liberal and progressive people know that the poor are our equals in every sense except that of being equal to us."[2] At one point in her book, Lefkowitz derives satisfaction from the decision of Wellesley's History Department not to count courses in "Africana Studies" toward a history major. But what about the (black) students who are being taught nonsense? Does Wellesley have no obligation to them?

Late in the book, Lefkowitz expresses some misgiving about her evisceration of the ideology of Afrocentrism because she had not realized that "the myth of the Stolen Legacy had great symbolic value for those who believed in it." But what about "Creationism"—the (conjectural) teaching of which she often likens to the teaching of Afrocentrism? Does not it have, has it not long had, symbolic value for people who found Milton's biblical account of Adam and Eve as (unlike their Edenic neighbors) "two of far nobler shape erect and tall" a far more livable truth than Darwin's proposition that our original ancestor was "a hairy quadruped with a tail and pointed ears, probably arboreal in his habits"?

Liberal dogmatism has dominated American campuses for so many decades and with such dictatorialness that even a courageous truth-teller like Mary Lefkowitz at times shows herself eager to placate it. Many readers of *History Lesson* are likely to challenge her with Elijah's question: "How long halt ye between two opinions?"

Notes

1. Mary Lefkowitz, *History Lesson: A Race Odyssey* (New Haven, CT: Yale University Press, 2008), 4. Subsequent references to this work appear in parentheses in the text.
2. See Lionel Trilling, "The Princess Casamassima," in *The Liberal Imagination* (New York: Vintage Books, 1950), 84.

Tom Paulin:
Poetaster of Murder

Some have at first for wits, then poets passed,/Turned critics next, and proved plain fools at last.
—Alexander Pope, *An Essay on Criticism*

Preamble

On March 11, 2011, five members of the Fogel family, two adults and three of their children, were massacred in Itamar, a small Israeli settlement in the Samaria mountains. A few days later (March 15) Bret Stephens, in an editorial entitled "Are Israeli Settlers Human?" reminded *Wall Street Journal* readers that Oxford poet Tom Paulin had, "several years earlier," insisted that West Bank Jewish settlers "should be shot dead." Back in 2003, in the wake of Mr. Paulin's declaration, I had published, in the Israeli journal *Nativ*, an essay urging that, instead of being appointed (as he had been) to lectureships and visiting professorships at Harvard and Columbia, he should be prosecuted as "an accessory to murder." Now that we have had yet another instance of the existential realization of the "ideas" of Palestinophiles and Judeophobes in crimes of which animals would be ashamed, I take the liberty of reprinting that essay. It argues that "progressives" like Paulin should not be reciting poems at Harvard or tutoring English majors at Columbia University or Hertford College (Oxford), but contemplating the fitness of things inside a prison cell, perhaps Reading Gaol, in which better Oxford poets were once confined.

March 2011

If your interlocutor can't keep Hitler out of the conversation, ... feverishly turning Jews into Nazis and Arabs into Jews—why then, I think, you may well be talking to an anti-Jewist.
—Conor Cruise O'Brien, *Jerusalem Post* (July 6, 1982)

We are fed this inert/This lying phrase/Like comfort food/As another little Palestinian boy/In trainers jeans and a white teeshirt/Is gunned down by the Zionist SS/Whose initials we should/—but we don't—dumb goys/Clock in that weasel word/Crossfire.
—Tom Paulin, "Killed in the Crossfire,"
The London Observer (February 18, 2001)

George Orwell once posed the question of whether we have the right to expect common decency from minor poets. The prominence of Tom Paulin, whose verse fluctuates between political doggerel and free verse of the sort that reminded Robert Frost of "playing tennis with the net down," in the literary, cultural, and academic life of contemporary Britain, makes that question as compelling as ever it was. Paulin is a lecturer in nineteenth and twentieth-century English literature at Oxford University's Hertford College, an institution whose famous past members include William Tyndale, Thomas Hobbes, and Charles James Fox. He is a regular on the BBC2 arts program Newsnight Review and a nearly inescapable presence on that network's literary/cultural programming, including TV criticism and "The Late Show." (As a sign of respect for his cultural authority, one British rock band has named itself "Tompaulin.") His increasing influence in progressive circles in Britain—this despite (or perhaps because of) his involvement in IRA politics—helps to explain why England's "learned classes" are in the forefront of European efforts to paint Israel as the devil's own experiment station, the major obstacle to world peace.

As a literary critic, Paulin's chief distinction has been the aggressive politicizing of literature. He has viewed the work of D. H. Lawrence through the prism of "post-colonialism," a pseudoscholarly enterprise whose primary aim is the delegitimization of Israel; he thought Emily Dickinson an important poet because she criticized "mercantile values"; in an essay on T. S. Eliot he sternly warned that "Hate poems are offensive" and took it upon himself to accuse a host of critics (including Denis Donoghue) of "complicity" in Eliot's antisemitism because they had discussed his poetry without mentioning it.[1] In this failure to recognize that although politics may be "in" everything, not everything is politics, and that to see politics everywhere empties politics of meaning, Paulin was not much different from countless other academic insurrectionaries in the English departments. But when he found that the excitement of showing oneself politically superior to writers of the past was transitory, Paulin turned to "action."

Perpetually intoxicated—by the sound of his own extremism—Paulin persuaded himself that an Indian student for whom he served as "moral tutor" at Hertford College had been discriminated against by an Israeli professor of Islamic philosophy and Arabic at Oxford's Oriental Institute. In October 2000, the student, one Nadeem Ahmed, went to court to charge Fritz Zimmermann (of St. Cross College) with "discouraging" him, calling him "stupid," and being "biased." Since Paulin belongs to that sizable community of academics who would be rendered virtually speechless if deprived of the epithet "racist," he leapt into the fray, making 200 phone calls (none to Zimmermann) on behalf of his protege, to proctors, deans, and his numerous friends in the news media. He made a particular point of alleging that Zimmermann was "bunged off to Israel to get out of the way." When Judge Playford, QC, of Reading County Court, dismissed the case on April 23, 2002, he made a point of saying that "Dr. Zimmermann was not in any way motivated by race," that "neither Mr. Ahmed nor Mr. Paulin honestly thought there was any racial element in the complaint," and rebuked Paulin for "mischievously" making "cryptic" phone calls threatening to charge various university officials with "racism" and to initiate "legal action and unfavourable publicity." The judge also pointed out that Paulin's abstruse research into Zimmermann's ethnic and national identity was flawed: Zimmermann was neither Jewish nor Israeli, but a German Gentile.[2]

The court's judgment was, as it happened, handed down about ten days after Paulin made his most ambitious bid for world fame (and perhaps martyrdom at the hands of the implacable Jews). He told an interviewer for the Cairo weekly paper, *Al-Ahram*, that he abhorred Brooklyn-born Jewish "settlers" and believed "they should be shot dead. I think they are Nazis, racists, I feel nothing but hatred for them." He added, for good measure, that he had quit the Labor Party because Tony Blair presides over "a Zionist government" and that he had "never believed that Israel had the right to exist at all." Since the preferred form of Arab Jew-killing at the time of this April 2002 interview was suicide bombing rather than "shooting dead," Paulin indicated that, of course, he could "understand how suicide bombers feel"; his only objection to this particular form of murdering Jews was a strategic one: guerrilla warfare, he suggested to Palestinian Arabs needful of advice on the subject, would be more effective because direct attacks on civilians might create a sense of solidarity among Israelis.

Paulin's unambiguous incitement to raw murder was clearly in violation of British law. The Terrorism Act 2000, section 59, states: "A person commits an offence if he incites another person to commit an act of terrorism wholly or partly outside the United Kingdom . . . it is immaterial whether or not the person incited is in the United Kingdom at the time of the incitement." Once upon a time—and this long before there was such a thing as the Terrorism Act—incitement to murder was a serious offense in England. For example, in 1881, Johann Most was tried in Britain merely because his newspaper, *Freiheit*, exulted (after the fact) in the assassination of the Czar. Most was found guilty of libel and incitement to murder, and sentenced to sixteen months of hard labor—a sentence deemed "merciful" because Most was a foreigner and "might be suffering violent wrong." (The episode lurks in the background of Henry James' novel, *The Princess Casamassima* [1885–1886].) In fact, Most should have been kept in jail much longer; after finishing his term, he moved to America, where he was imprisoned for inciting the assassin of President McKinley.

But Paulin uttered his call for the murder of Jews living in Judea and Samaria with complete impunity. Oxford University said it was launching an investigation into his comments, and the Board of Deputies of British Jews threatened to prosecute Paulin in accord with the provisions of the Terrorism Act. Exactly why the British Home Secretary left the matter to be pursued (not very tenaciously, as it turned out) by private parties remains a mystery. Can one imagine a prominent British figure calling for the shooting "dead" of any other ethnic or national group—Pakistani Muslims, let us say, or Palestinian Arabs—and escaping prosecution, to say nothing of dismissal by his assorted employers, ranging from Oxford University to the "respected" (but not very respectable) BBC?

For decades, and especially since the June 1967 war, it has been a necessary if wearisome task to point out that a person need not directly advocate the murder of Jews in order to qualify as an antisemite. Yet here was somebody explicitly advocating that certain Jews be shot dead, and endless foolish debates ensued, on both sides of the Atlantic, about whether it was permissible to label the advocate an antisemite, or whether incitement to murder constituted "hate speech," or whether

Paulin should be invited (or disinvited or reinvited) to deliver a lecture or to recite his wretched poems.

Indeed, Paulin himself made it clear that he was not to be labeled an antisemite merely because he had advocated killing Jews and denying Israel the "right to exist," as if it were his privilege to decide whether the Jews or the Jewish state had a "right" to exist. Paulin not only declared himself a "philo-Semite," thereby confusing those who do not know that in Paulin's circles this is far more likely to mean love of everything Arab than of anything Jewish. He also took to the welcoming pages of the venomously anti-Israel *London Review of Books* in January 2003 with a 133-line poem called "On Being Dealt the Anti-Semitic Card." Here he spews forth, along with numerous incoherent and apoplectic utterances on the Crusades, on Joseph de Maistre, on the Enlightenment, on Christian fundamentalism, his extreme dissatisfaction with being called an antisemite: "the program though / of saying Israel's critics / are tout court anti-Semitic / is designed daily by some schmuck / to make you shut the fuck up." Without quite intending to do so, the terminally obtuse Paulin, in his most touching and beautiful language, thus confirms the assertion that "criticism of Israeli policy" is almost always a leftist euphemism for "advocating destruction of Israel and murder of its citizens."

Not a few readers now returned to Paulin's February 2001 scribblings on Israel, quoted above, and noticed that their key phrase of ironically flattering self-mockery about being deceived by the wily Zionists came from none other than Hitler himself. In a passage from *Mein Kampf* familiar to every student of this subject, Hitler wrote: "While the Zionists try to make the rest of the world believe that the national consciousness of the Jew finds its satisfaction in the creation of a Palestinian state, the Jews again slyly dupe the dumb Goyim." Did Paulin write "dumb goys" out of genuine illiteracy or out of a desire to conceal his source?

The publicity generated by the two British scandals in which Paulin became embroiled was, however, as nothing compared with what followed in America. In November 2002, Paulin, by this time a visiting professor in the English department of Columbia University, was invited to be the Morris Gray lecturer at Harvard by its English department. At about the same time, rumors circulated that Columbia was considering a permanent appointment for him there—perhaps because its English department's most famous member, the late

Edward Said, had lauded Paulin for being a "reader of almost fanatical scrupulosity."

Just how Paulin got himself invited to Harvard or Columbia in the first place remains a mystery. John Bradley, writing for the *Arab News* (November 18, 2002) suggested that "it was almost certainly [Seamus] Heaney himself who invited Paulin to give the lecture [at Harvard]." According to one student of Irish literary culture whom I consulted, "Heaney may have owed Paulin a large debt of gratitude: an old rumor had it that Heaney was in some sort of trouble with the IRA (for distancing himself from Irish politics) and needed a friend with bonafide Irish credentials." But then English departments are notoriously susceptible to the lure of extremist political views, especially if they have the leftist stamp of approval on them.

At Harvard the dispute over Paulin became one about free speech or hate speech or (perhaps) the constitutional right of a British subject to have an endowed lectureship bestowed on him. After a storm of criticism, the English faculty, with the blessing of Harvard President Lawrence Summers, rescinded its invitation to Paulin. But then Harvard's civil liberties absolutists weighed in on behalf of Paulin's "right" to lecture, and the English faculty reinvited him. Some urged that he should be encouraged to speak because they were confident that his egregious stupidity would expose him to deserved ridicule and keep him from wallowing in the (painless) martyrdom he sought.

The deeper significance of the Paulin affair was revealed, unintentionally to be sure, by Columbia's James Shapiro, a professor of English, the author of a book on Shakespeare and the Jews, and one of the most ardent defenders of Columbia's decision to embrace Paulin. Casting his mind's eye over Paulin's oral and written remarks about shooting Jews dead and destroying their country, Shapiro declared that these remarks "did not step over the line."[3] Apparently Shapiro's dividing line is like the receding horizon; he walks toward it, but can never reach it. And so the real question—which was not whether or not Paulin should be reciting poems at Harvard or tutoring students (morally or academically) at Columbia but whether or not he should be in prison—was almost entirely ignored. Public discourse about Jews and Israel has now crossed a threshold; the dividing line between the permissible and the possible has been erased. In the months following the Paulin affair, publications that had long been hostile to Israel did, in more "civilized" and literate form, what Paulin had already done in his unkempt Yahoo style: they moved from strident criticism of Israel to apologias for antisemitic violence and calls for the dissolution of the country. The liberal Berkeley historian Martin Jay in *Salmagundi* (Winter/Spring 2003) merely blamed Jews for "causing" the "new" antisemitism; the liberal journalist Paul Krugman in *The New York Times* (October 21, 2003) went a step further by "explaining" (away) the Malaysian Mahathir Mohamad's regurgitation of The Protocols of the Elders of Zion as "anti-Semitism with a Purpose"; and then the liberal historian Tony Judt outdid both of them in *The New York Review of Books* (October 23, 2003) by calling—no doubt to the general satisfaction of the readers of that High Authority of the American left—for the end of the State of Israel as the panacea for the world's ills. Tom Paulin may have failed to get himself a permanent academic appointment in America, but he helped American liberalism to redefine itself, in this age of suicide bombing, as an accessory to murder.[4]

Notes

1. See *Writing to the Moment: Selected Critical Essays: 1980–1996* (London: Faber and Faber, 1996).
2. "Tutor in Mischief," *Telegraph* (London), April 23, 2002. See also Neil Tweedie, "Oxford Poet 'Wants Jews Shot,'" April 13, 2002.
3. *Columbia Spectator*, November 20, 2002.
4. Black's Law Dictionary defines "accessory" as it is used in criminal law as follows:

   > Contributing to or aiding in the commission of a crime. One who, without being present at the commission of a felonious offense, becomes guilty of such offense, not as a chief actor, but as a participator, as by command, advice, instigation, or concealment; either before or after the fact of commission.

Jewish Israel-Haters Convert Their Dead Grandmothers: A New Mormonism?

Who is a Jew? A Jew is someone with Jewish grandchildren.
—Folk Saying

Jews have long objected to the Mormon practice of "vicariously" converting their deceased ancestors, especially those who perished in the Holocaust, to the Mormon faith, a practice (now less common than it once was) that has seemed to them more brazenly dogmatic than the worst excesses of the Inquisition. But now it seems that Jewish Israel-haters, people who define their "Jewishness" almost entirely by their repudiation of the Jewish state, have developed their own brand of Mormonism. It consists of converting deceased Zionist grandparents (especially of the female sort) to their own pseudoreligion, which starts from the premise that when a person can no longer be a Jew, he (or she) becomes an anti-Zionist.

In the December 21, 2010 issue of the *National Post* (Canada), the astute journalist Barbara Kay expressed the hope that "after I have shuffled off this mortal coil, none of my granddaughters will turn into useful idiots for a rotten political movement riddled with antisemitism." Kay was alluding to two unusually foul volleys of fire and vitriol shot in the direction of Israel and her Jewish supporters by Canadian Jewish women, Jennifer Peto and Judy Rebick.

Peto, a twenty-nine-year-old activist on behalf of lesbian and anti-Zionist causes (sometimes happily intermarried as "Queers against Israel") has gained notoriety for a master's thesis with the bombastic title (*The Victimhood of the Powerful: White Jews, Zionism and the*

Racism of Hegemonic Holocaust Education). It was submitted to and approved by the "sociology and equity" cranny of a minor branch of the University of Toronto called Ontario Institute of Studies in Education (OISE). In its regurgitation of hoary antisemitic tropes directed at "Jewish privilege," "Jewish racism," and the "apartheid" state of Israel, the thesis reminded many of the pseudoscholarly materials studied (and brilliantly dissected) in Max Weinreich's *Hitler's Professors* (1946), a book that showed how German academics were the first to make antisemitism both academically respectable and complicit in murder. Peto's malice toward and ignorance about Jews and Israel know no bounds. Jews who wish to remember the Holocaust are "racists" (the alpha and omega of her vocabulary) who want to monopolize all that beautiful suffering which other, especially darker skinned, peoples would very much like, belatedly, to share. Israel, not only a country in which Arabs and Jews share the same buses, beaches, clinics, cafes, soccer pitches, and universities, but the only country in history to have brought thousands of black people to its shores to become citizens and not slaves, is for her the quintessentially "apartheid" state. Chief among the multifarious abominations that Peto imputes to the wily Jews is "Hegemonic Holocaust Education." Professor Werner Cohn, the first to call attention to the scandal of Peto's thesis (and the still greater scandal that her academic advisor, one Sheryl Nestel, routinely encourages and approves such theses), noted that Peto uses the word "hegemonic" fifty-two times but defines it just once: "I am defining hegemonic Holocaust education as projects that are sponsored by the Israeli government, and/or mainstream Jewish organizations." Since Peto thinks (mistakenly) that "hegemonic" is a pejorative term, she defines it as whatever Israel and Jews do.

What distinguished Peto's rehashing of the ravings of the *Protocols of the Elders of Zion* as modernized by assorted Chomskys, Finkelsteins, and Walt-Mearsheimers, was her dedication of the thesis to her dead and defenseless grandmother, Jolan Peto: "If she were alive today, she would be right there with me protesting against Israeli apartheid." Like most dead people, Peto's grandmother is vulnerable to assaults on her memory by an unscrupulous and ruthless grandchild. (Jewish mothers, one notices, rarely receive these accolades from their Israel-hating daughters; often still alive, mothers constitute too great a risk.)

But, although unlucky in her granddaughter, Jolan Peto has been redeemed by her grandson, a Houston physician named David Peto. He published on December 16 an open letter to the press in which he urged his sister to respect the dead and cease to conscript their grandmother for her sordid vendetta against the Jews:

> It is not my desire to get involved with the details of my sister Jenny Peto's thesis, which has recently generated tremendous controversy. There are people far more qualified than I to debate the merits of the thesis, or lack thereof. There is, however, one point that I would like to contest. My sister dedicated her thesis to our late grandmother, Jolan Peto. She asserted that if our grandmother "were alive today, she would be right there with me protesting against Israeli apartheid." Our grandmother was the youngest teacher at the Jewish orphanage in Budapest during the Second World War. She, along with my grandfather, saved countless children from death at the hands of the Nazis. After the war, she saw firsthand the brutality and baseness of the communist regime that came into power. She, along with our grandfather and father, escaped to Canada, and celebrated the day of their arrival each and every year. Freedom was not an abstract idea to her; it was alive and tangible for her. Our grandmother was a soft-spoken woman, but she had an iron will. She taught us to abhor hatred, and to strive for excellence in everything we did. She was a woman of endless patience and generosity, and boundless love. She was uncompromising in her dedication to truth and honesty, and was also an ardent supporter of the state of Israel. My sister is simply wrong; our grandmother would have been entirely opposed to her anti-Israel protests. Our grandmother had a tremendous impact on my life, and her memory continues to be a source of strength and inspiration to my family. My daughter is named after her, and we pray that she will emulate her namesake. I cannot in good conscience allow my sister to misappropriate publicly our grandmother's memory to suit her political ideology.

For this act of decency, Dr. Peto was pilloried by his ever-predictable sister as "a right-wing fanatical, racist Zionist."

The other "useful idiot" (and cemetery desecrator) to whom Kay alluded is one Judy Rebick. She is a practitioner of no known discipline at all (not even the one prohibited by W. H. Auden's eleventh commandment: "Thou shalt not commit sociology"). Rather, she is a "chaired" professor (at Ryerson University in Toronto) of "Social Justice," that prolific generator of ferocious do-gooders, people who confuse doing good with feeling good about what they are doing. She is the author of a number of feminist tracts (including "Barack Obama is 'our sister's keeper'") and a book called *Politically Speaking* (coauthored with one Kike Roach). She too has a dead grandmother to sacrifice at the antisemites' new altar. A year before Peto vaulted to worldwide infamy,

Rebick came to the defense of yet another prodigiously busy Canadian-Jewish Israel-hater, Naomi Klein, by announcing in September 2009 that her own grandmother, who had survived a pogrom, indeed (she implied) *because* she had survived a pogrom, "would have been so proud of Naomi Klein" for exhorting the Toronto Film Festival to shun the city of Tel Aviv.

The line of succession among these anti-Zionist converters of their deceased grandmothers may, however, be traced a bit farther back than Kay's Canadians, to a public intellectual of far greater weight, moment, literacy, and prominence than either Rebick or Peto: England's Alain De Botton. Mr. De Botton is the author of several "self-help" books with titles like "How Proust Can Change Your Life," and to his actual publishing record has recently been added a fictional string of titles invented by Howard Jacobson, author of *The Finkler Question*. This satirical novel, to be discussed later in this book, portrays the spiritual anemia of England's anti-Zionist "ashamed" Jews, who are ashamed not of their own perfidy and cowardice but of Israel's existence. The character who gives the novel its name, Samuel Finkler, is a composite figure based in part on De Botton. Finkler has written such best-sellers as *The Socratic Flirt* and *The Existentialist in the Kitchen*. For declaring on the BBC (just as the pudgy little English character-actress Miriam Margolyes had done) that, "as a Jew," he is "ashamed" of Israel, Finkler is promptly rewarded with an invitation to join a group of "well-known theatrical and academic Jews" who offer to rename themselves, "in honour of his courage in speaking out—Ashamed Jews." Flattered by the attention of the third-rate actors, he accepts the honor. The narrator adds, for no readily apparent reason, that Finkler cares as little for the praise of his fellow academics as for "the prayers he had never said for his grandfather." The pointed acerbity of that remark about how Finkler cynically manipulates the memory of his grandfather is puzzling unless we are aware that, in this *roman à clef*, Finkler's exploitation of his grandfather is probably based upon De Botton's exploitation of *his* grandmother in the Anglo-Jewish and Israeli press.

We do not know whether De Botton—who is proud to call himself an atheist—has been more attentive to the soul of his grandmother than that of his grandfather, but, like his Canadian emulators, he has gone to the trouble of disinterring and resurrecting her, as if to invoke ancestral authority for his repudiation of his ancestors. In a September 22, 2009 interview with the London *Jewish Chronicle*, De Botton replied to a question about what Israel meant to him as follows: "Israel is for me a country I will always associate with my grandmother, Yolande Gabai, who played a central role in the founding of the state through her activities in Egypt with the Jewish Agency, a country whose current state she would deplore, for she knew that peace with the Arabs was at the core of the challenge facing the new country." We are all too familiar with the smug, self-satisfied assurance of these smelly little orthodoxies about "deplorable" Israel; they say, in effect, the following: "Despite superficial evidence to the contrary, such as the absence of peace since Israel's unilateral withdrawal from Lebanon in favor of Hizbullah or from Gaza in favor of Hamas, all of us thinking people who read *The Independent*, *The Guardian*, *The Observer*, and *The New Statesman* know that Israel is responsible for the absence of peace with her neighbors because she has not yet fully withdrawn from the disputed territories of Judea and Samaria (which, lest it be forgotten, were entirely in the hands of the Arabs, theirs to do with whatever they liked, from 1948-67, when they decided to go to war against Israel). But this is not quite blatant and gross enough for De Botton: he must also invoke the authority of his dead grandmother.

Yolande Gabai Harmor De Botton was indeed an important figure in the Zionist movement. Born in Alexandria, Egypt, she spied for the Jewish Agency during 1947–1948, risking both her own life and that of her son while posing as a *Palestine Post* journalist, and earning the nickname of "the Jewish Mata Hari." In July 1948, she was imprisoned in Egypt and later deported. In 1948–1949, she worked for the Middle East Department of the Israeli Foreign Ministry. She died in 1959, ten years before her grandson Alain was born, and left behind precious little evidence that she would have become a willing recruit to the view of Anglo-Jewish leftists that if Israel has a raison d'être at all, it is, as De Botton suggested in an egregious interview with *Ha'aretz* in October 2008, to "humiliate" Arabs and "kill" their olive trees. (Allegations of Israeli attacks on Arab olive trees flare up frequently in the propaganda war conducted by Arabs and Arabophiles in the west. Although never attaining the scale of such gigantic frauds as "Jeningrad" or "Mohammed al-Dura," they never go away either. In October 2002, for example, as a distraction from the news of the latest intifada savagery, *bien-pensant* Jewish leftists shrieked about "the cruel and vindictive destruction of . . . venerable olive groves under the pretext that they were hiding places for snipers." Alas, as Israel Radio reported, the terrorist who had just murdered two little Jewish girls and a woman in Hermesh exploited the olive trees to reconnoiter the area and then slip under the fence to do his murderous work.[1])

De Botton seems to take the fact that his grandmother got along nicely in Egyptian society (while concealing her work as a spy!) and believed the foundation of a Jewish state would benefit Arabs (toward whom she felt kindly) as well as Jews shows that she would now, if resurrected, be an avid conscript to his own trendy prejudices and the "Palestinian" irredentist cause.

Ben-Gurion, of course, believed the very same thing that Grandma Yolande did, but he has yet to be conscripted by the grave-robbers. Moreover, it does not occur to De Botton that the Palestinians have become one of the world's most ruined peoples not because Jews will not "make peace" with them but because, encouraged by the Petos, Rebicks, and De Bottons, they have devoted themselves not to the building up of their own society but to the destruction of the society of their neighbor.

In addition to being a writer (at times, as in *The Pleasures and Sorrows of Work*, a very good one), De Botton is the founder of an institution in central London called "The School of Life." Repudiating the Renaissance tradition of liberal (or "useless") education in favor of what John Henry Newman called the servile (or "useful") kind, the school offers courses in (to quote De Botton) "marriage, child-rearing, choosing a career, changing the world and death." The curriculum does not, however, appear to include a course in the fifth commandment, and De Botton's violation of the injunction to honor your father and mother (and, by extension, your grandfather and grandmother) suggests that he (and Peto and Rebick and all the other aspiring Jewish Mormons) would do well to make honest people of themselves before setting out to convert the dead and change the world.

Note

1. Palestinian Arab farmers frequently complain that "settlers" cut their trees and hurt them and their livelihoods. Most such complaints of olive tree damage are filed at or near the end of the harvest season. In November 2006, Palestinian youths were caught doing the cutting at the request of the owners of the grove, who had hoped for the usual generous government compensation.

The Antisemitism of Liberals: A Gentile's View

According to the famous eleventh edition of the *Encyclopedia Britannica* (1910), "Antisemitism is a passing phase in the history of culture." Since that sanguine declaration, antisemitism has had several very good rolls of the dice, culminating in the destruction of European Jewry. So horrendous was this event that a Jesuit priest once lamented, with touching simple-minded nostalgia, that the Holocaust had given antisemitism a bad name. Does the tenacity of antisemitism through the ages prove that, as their enemies claim, the Jews are indeed a very bad lot, or that, as England's Chief Rabbi Jonathan Sacks says: "Anti-Semitism exists whenever two contradictory factors appear in combination: the belief that Jews are so powerful that they are responsible for the evils of the world, and the knowledge that they are so powerless that they can be attacked with impunity."[1] This combination of an enormous image (Christ-killer, for example) with ridiculously small numbers has proved irresistible to predators. The "new" antisemitism is by now the subject of numerous books, published in America, England, France, Israel, and Italy. Their shared conclusion, set forth from a variety of perspectives, is that the physical violence of the new Jew-hatred is largely the work of young Muslims, but that the ideological violence is the work primarily of leftists, battlers against racism, professed humanitarians, and liberals (including Jewish ones).

Bernard Harrison's scintillating book—which deals almost entirely with the drift of liberals and leftists into fascist antisemitism—brings to the subject a distinct authorial identity, a unique academic background, an exhilarating voice. This is the best book on contemporary antisemitism by a gentile (of the British sort). According to Harrison, his gentile identity not only contradicts a major premise of the new antisemitism, i.e., that only Jews support Israel, but has also made him privy to the expression of antisemitic prejudice, political as well as social, by apparently respectable academic people, "when Jews are absent."[2] (I must, however, add that if Harrison hears more of this in England than Jews do, his ears must be badly singed by now. I heard more antisemitic remarks, privately uttered, during my three years of living in England than in my more than threescore and ten in America, including the deep South.)

Harrison is a philosopher trained in "habitual skepticism, bitterly close reading, and aggressive contentiousness contributed by forty years in the amiable sharkpool of analytic philosophy" (37). His merciless deconstruction of anti-Israel invective and smug cliché coming from the *New Statesman, Guardian, Independent,* BBC, and other bastions of anti-Jewish sentiment in England reminds one of the kind of literary scrutiny that in America was pioneered by the New Critics (Brooks, Warren, and Heilman) who arose in the thirties and dominated English studies until the seventies. He demolishes bad reasoning as they demolished bad poems.

Typically Harrison scrutinizes the statements of Israel-haters for internal contradictions, inconsistencies, specious reasoning, misstatements of fact, and outright lies. To wade through the fulminations of such people as John Pilger or Robert Fisk or Jacqueline Rose concerning Israel ordinarily requires the mental equivalent of hip boots; Harrison, however, approaches with a scalpel and dissects their ravings with surgical precision. He devotes all of Chapter Two, for example, to a single infamous issue of the *New Statesman* of January 14, 2002. The cover showed a tiny Union Jack, placed horizontally, being pierced by the sharp apex of a large Star of David, made of gold; below, in large black letters, was the question, posed with characteristic English understatement: "A Kosher Conspiracy?" It seemed right out of *Der Stürmer*, and the articles that followed it had at first suggested to Harrison that he entitle his analysis of them "In the Footsteps of Dr. Goebbels," but then he decided that would be "inadequate to the gravity of the case" (49).

Among the many left-liberal canards, slanders, slogans, and clichés that Harrison dismembers in the book are the following: "Israel is a colonialist state"; "Israel is a Nazi state, and the Jews who support it are as guilty as Nazi collaborators were"; "Anybody who criticizes Israel is called an antisemite"; "Jews do not express grief except for political or financial ends"; and so on and on ad nauseam. Some will say that, in response to these vicious or insane allegations, the best response would be: "Why did you kill your grandmother?" i.e., merely to go on the defensive is already to concede defeat. Harrison thinks otherwise, and those who do wish to engage the current enemies of the Jews and of Israel would do well to attend carefully to what he says. Take, for example, the way in which he draws out the implications of the omnipresent Israeli–Nazi equation, an old favorite of Israel-haters. The first is that to demonize Israel or Zionism is to demonize the Jews as well. The second is that "To attach the label 'Nazi' to Israel, or to couple the Star of David with the swastika is not just to express opposition to the policies of one or another Israeli government. It is to defame Israel by association with the most powerful symbol of evil, of that which must be utterly rejected and uprooted from the face of the earth" (68).

It is this Manichean tendency of contemporary left-liberal defamers of Israel that for Harrison is its defining trait. An old literary accusation against liberals is that they cannot comprehend tragedy, in which a hero is divided against himself, or two rights contend against each other, but prefer melodrama, the simplistic struggle of good people versus bad ones. Thus the central claim of the new antisemitism is that, from a humanitarian's perspective, the State of Israel is evil incarnate, to a degree that transcends the wickedness of any other state that exists or ever existed. But the overriding question of Harrison's remarkable book is why liberals, more than any other political group, have been drawn to this moral absolutism and mistaken their antisemitism for a moral virtue. The much-trumpeted (and largely self-induced) "plight of the Palestinians" can hardly make even the "Top Twenty" list of the world's current misfortunes. Contemporary liberals may be keen to address the endless list of grievances of Islam, but even here the Palestinian issue is not at the top. When Zacarias Mussaoui, the only person to be tried (in April 2002) for the 9/11 massacres, gave his fifty-minute oration in court, "he called for the return of parts of the world to Muslim rule, including Spain, Kashmir and Chechnya," and then also prayed "for the destruction of the Jewish people and state and the liberation of Palestine." Perhaps liberals sense that only prayers number four and five stand a good chance of being answered.

Harrison consistently criticizes contemporary liberals who have allowed their moral indignation on behalf of Palestinians to pass into something "very hard to distinguish from anti-Semitism of the most traditional kind" (11), yet he just as consistently refrains from calling them antisemites. (He does, however, wonder whether, in their dreams, they call themselves antisemites.) Thus the editor of the *New Statesman* who approves a cover worthy of Julius Streicher, one Peter Wilby, is "an entirely honest, decent man," and both Dennis Sewell, whose essay on the Anglo-Jewish "Kosher Conspiracy" is worse than Goebbels, and others like him belong to the rank of "sincere humanitarians" (74). Two factors seem to lead Harrison into implying that one can have antisemitism without antisemites. One is his assumption, oft-repeated, that liberals and leftists in the past were almost always opposed to antisemitism. But surely this is open to question. In France, for example, the only articulate friends of the Jews prior to the Dreyfus affair were conservative writers who regularly denounced anti-Jewish attitudes as "one of the favorite theses of the eighteenth century." Nineteenth-century French leftist movements had been outspoken in their antipathy to Jews until the Dreyfus affair forced them to decide whether they hated the Jews or the Catholic Church more, and so they become Dreyfusards. In England, as we have seen, the famously liberal Dr. Arnold called English Jews "lodgers" and wanted them barred from universities and citizenship. Gladstone would refer to Disraeli as "that alien" who "was going to annex England to his native East & make it the appanage of an Asian empire"; Ernest Bevin, Labor foreign minister from 1945 to 1951, was notoriously venomous toward Jews. James G. McDonald, first American ambassador to Israel, wrote in his diary for August 3, 1948, that Bevin, then Labour's foreign secretary, exhibited "blazing hatred" for "the Jews, the Israelis, the Israeli government" (as well as for President Truman).[3]

But perhaps there is a more positive motive at work in Harrison's delicate epithets for his adversaries. He seems to believe in the humanist ideal of self-correction, according to which a man vacillates between his ordinary self and his best self, and can be wooed by reason into embracing the latter. Let us hope that he is right. My own, darker view is that ultimately philosophy is no more than character. If Harrison believes that he can reason into decency people like his fellow philosopher Ted Honderich, the devout believer in "Violence for Equality" who extols Palestinian suicide bombers, I wish him joy of his efforts. Deductions have little power of persuasion.

These quibbles apart, Harrison's book is one of the crucial utterances on the subject of the new, liberal antisemites (as I would call them), the people who are busily making themselves into accessories before the fact of Ahmadinejad's plan "to wipe Israel off the map." The fact that this eloquent and elegantly argued book (by someone with a formidable reputation as a literary critic as well as philosopher) was largely ignored by book review editors is itself testimony to the liberal dogmatism and dictatorialness that Harrison has so vividly portrayed.

Notes

1. Sacks, "Lecture of 28 February 2002 to Inter-Parliamentary Committee Against Antisemitism," in *A New Antisemitism?* ed. Paul Iganski and Barry Kosmin (London: Profile Books, 2003), 40.
2. Bernard Harrison, *The Resurgence of Antisemitism: Jews, Israel, and Liberal Opinion* (Lanham, MD: Rowman & Littlefield, 2006), 80. Subsequent references will be given in parentheses in the text.
3. Robert S. Wistrich, "A Deadly Mutation: Antisemitism and Anti-Zionism in Great Britain," in *Antisemitism on the Campus: Past and Present*, ed. Eunice G. Pollack (Boston, MA: Academic Studies Press, 2011), 55.

IV
Literature

Lionel Trilling: The (Jewish) Road Not Taken

In 1950, Lionel Trilling published *The Liberal Imagination*,[1] a collection of essays that established him as the most subtle and influential mind in contemporary American culture. Sixteen discussions of the interplay between literature and society taught a generation of Americans to believe in the power of literature (for mischief as much as elevation). Trilling's subjects ranged from Tacitus to Wordsworth, Mark Twain, F. Scott Fitzgerald, Theodore Dreiser, and Henry James. The essays were not political, but they assumed an intimate connection between literature and politics. They also staked out, on "the dark and bloody crossroads where literature and politics meet," (8) an adversarial position with respect to the liberalism that had hardened into Stalinism in the early years of the Cold War.

Trilling's first mature critical undertaking had been his book entitled *Matthew Arnold* (1939), which he called a biography of Arnold's mind. He had been drawn to Arnold, he said, for two reasons: a desire to understand Arnold's melancholy (exemplified in "Dover Beach") and a sense that, like Arnold, he was a liberal whose major effort in criticism was to call into question the substance of contemporary liberal thought. He felt himself to be, in Arnold's words from the Introduction to *Culture and Anarchy* (1869), "a Liberal, [but] a Liberal tempered by experience, reflection, and renouncement, and . . . above all, a believer in culture." Arnold's critique of Victorian liberalism deplored certain habits of mind, especially the herd instinct. Trilling, similarly, declared, in his Preface to *The Liberal Imagination*, that "a criticism which has at heart the interests of liberalism might find its most useful work not in confirming liberalism in its sense of general righteousness but rather in putting under some degree of pressure the liberal ideas and assumptions of the present time" (viii). Trilling also had a target: those American liberals who had been living contentedly as supporters of Stalinist totalitarianism.

There was a third, unacknowledged reason for Trilling's attraction to Arnold. If you sat in Trilling's undergraduate course in nineteenth-century English literature, as I did in 1956–1957, you could notice his keen interest in Arnold's justification, in the 1865 essay "The Function of Criticism at the Present Time," of his career move from poetry to criticism, from creative to critical activity. Readily admitting that the critical faculty is lower than the inventive, Arnold asked: "Is it true that Johnson had better have gone on producing more *Irenes* instead of writing his *Lives of the Poets*; is it certain that Wordsworth himself was better employed in making his Ecclesiastical Sonnets than when he made his celebrated Preface so full of criticism, and criticism of the works of others?" Some of us in the class were aware that Trilling had published several short stories as well as a novel, and we assumed he was invoking the precedent of Arnold to justify his own shift from creation to criticism. (By creation, Arnold of course meant poetry, not fiction. Indeed, he once haughtily remarked that "No Arnold could write a novel.") We have known for a long time that Trilling was far from content with his role as a critic. In notes for a talk he gave at Purdue University in 1971, Trilling wrote: "I am always surprised when I hear myself referred to as a critic. My early conception of a life in literature did not include criticism. What it envisaged was the career of a novelist."[2]

Posthumously published excerpts from Trilling's notebooks show that he contrasted himself unfavorably with Hemingway and used the word "writer" as if it were synonymous with "novelist." On July 3, 1961, he wrote: "Death of Ernest Hemingway. Except Lawrence's 32 years ago, no writer's death has moved me as much—who would suppose how much he haunted me? How much he existed in my mind—as a reproach? He was the only writer of our time I envied. I respected him in his most foolish postures and in his worst work (except *The Old Man and the Sea*)."[3] In her memoir of 1993, Diana Trilling recalled that her husband believed he had sacrificed his hope of being a novelist to conscience: "Conscience had not made a coward of him, it had made him a critic. Was I the only person in the world who knew this about Lionel? Did his friends and colleagues have no hint of how deeply he scorned the very qualities of character—his quiet, his moderation, his gentle reasonableness—for which he was most admired in his lifetime and which have been most celebrated since his death?"[4]

Until a few years ago, it was assumed that Trilling had written only one long fiction, *The Middle of the Journey* (1947). Now, thanks to

Geraldine Murphy, a learned and imaginative editor, we know that Trilling was a third of the way through another novel, begun years earlier, when *The Middle of the Journey* appeared in 1947. The manuscript of the unfinished work, which Murphy has entitled *The Journey Abandoned*,[5] had lain for decades in Trilling's papers at Columbia University. Was it ignored because the critic Trilling's grave eloquence and beautiful reflective calm had made him seem a mere belle-lettrist to literary theorists in the Age of Stupefying Opacity? Or did researchers examine it and conclude that its publication would not help his reputation? In any case, its appearance affords us the opportunity to reflect not only on Trilling's inner division but on the way in which the virtues of critical work may turn into the defects of creative work.

The title of Trilling's first novel, *The Middle of the Journey*, derived from the opening of Dante's *Inferno*: "Midway along the journey of our life I had wandered off from the straight Path." The book dealt mainly with, in Trilling's words, "the moral and intellectual implications of the powerful attraction to Communism felt by a considerable part of the American intellectual class during the Thirties and Forties." The protagonist, John Laskell, a fellow-traveler of the Communist cause who had given up a literary career to become a city planner, has survived a nearly fatal illness. His rehabilitation is conjoined with a spiritual recovery from the characteristic weaknesses of liberalism, though not from liberalism itself. His friends Arthur and Nancy Croom do all they can to help him recover, but they do not want to hear talk of death, a "politically reactionary" subject. They do want to hear about their mutual friend Gifford Maxim, who has defected from the Communist party. The Crooms embody the follies, hypocrisies, and failures of imagination that Trilling imputes to liberalism in his discursive essays. They cannot believe that Maxim's life is in danger; they will not believe that the Communist party is controlled by the Soviet Union; and they are full of the liberal condescension (a favorite Trilling target) that imputes all bad behavior by the poor and members of minority groups to inescapable environment and circumstances. Nancy, a repository of jejune clichés, speaks of the Stalin regime as "a great social experiment" that cannot be judged by old-fashioned moral standards.

The most richly conceived character in *Middle of the Journey* is Maxim, modeled on Trilling's old college acquaintance Whittaker Chambers (as Trilling knew him before the Alger Hiss spy case, which commenced in 1948). Maxim challenges all that the Crooms believe in, by his polemical sharpness as much as by his defection. He enters the novel to unmask the inflated rhetoric of the Communist party. No, he tells them, the party has nothing to do with equal rights or trade unionism, only with cruelty, oppression and mass murder. Like Camus, Maxim has come to believe that the deepest desire of every progressive intellectual is to rule by force, to follow in the footsteps of the Grand Inquisitor.

Laskell too had been a liberal fellow-traveler, refusing to acknowledge the ruthlessness of the Communists and the danger to Maxim's life. But he is swayed not so much by Maxim's arguments as by the obtuseness of Nancy Croom's resistance to them. True, he is repelled by Maxim's newly adopted religious and authoritarian views, but more appalled by the Crooms' imbecilic reaction to them. They bristle at the suggestion of religion (derided as "mysticism") as the alternative to Communism. The moral shallowness and intellectual dimness of the Crooms shock Laskell more than Maxim's conversion. At the novel's end, Laskell finds himself with a great vacancy in his thought. In Stalinist liberalism, he now sees "an absolute freedom from responsibility" that he no longer wants, but Maxim's insistence on the doctrine that "we are all part of one another" is also unpalatable: "An absolute responsibility—that much of a divine or metaphysical essence none of us is." When Trilling reprinted the novel in 1975, he stated that its "polemical end" had been to show how Stalinist Communism had negated political life among intellectuals. Looking back upon it now, one may usefully view the book's themes as a foreshadowing of what today is called neoconservatism, especially in its embrace of Trilling's definition, given in 1943 in his book on E. M. Forster, of liberalism's fatal flaw:

> Surely if liberalism has a single desperate weakness, it is an inadequacy of imagination: liberalism is always being surprised. There is always the liberal work to do over again because disillusionment and fatigue follow hard upon surprise, and reaction is always ready for that moment of liberal disillusionment and fatigue—reaction never hopes, despairs or suffers amazement. . . . The liberal mind is sure that the order of human affairs owes it a simple logic: good is good and bad is bad. . . . Before the idea of good-and-evil its imagination fails; it cannot accept this improbable paradox.[6]

In *The Middle of the Journey*, the philosophical difficulty that a great many liberals have in recognizing and confronting evil, and their vulnerability to the ideological bullying of authoritarian leaders are given existential realization in the Stalinism of the protagonist's progressive ex-friends.

Trilling's letters of 1947–1948 expressed the hope of establishing himself as a novelist rather than a critic. As *The Middle of the Journey* was going to press, he told a colleague, Richard Chase, that he was at work on another novel, which he expected to be "better, richer, less shaped, less intellectualized, more open."[7] The new book (of which we have 24 chapters, or about 150 pages) left the realm of politics for that of the literary life in the late 1930s, and placed Vincent Hammell, an ambitious young teacher and would-be biographer, at its center. In a document that Murphy calls Trilling's preface, he defines the hero's literary pedigree. "His ambitions are intellectual and, at 24, he has won some intellectual distinction in his own city. Think of him as practical, energetic, not a dreamer or a moon-calf. He has real talent and he does not have the mechanical 'shyness' of a sensitive young hero.... He has what in a young man passes for maturity. He is decent, generous; but he is achingly ambitious ... he wishes to be genuine, a man of integrity; yet he also wishes to be successful. His problem is to advance his fortunes and still be an honest man. He is conscious of all the dangers; he is literate and knows the fates of Julien Sorel, of Rastignac, of Frederic Moreau—all the defeated and disintegrated young men of the great 19th century cycle of failure. He ... is determined not to make their mistakes."[8]

This Young Man from the Provinces is very much a "programmed" character in a *Bildungsroman*, which may explain why he never quite comes alive. Trilling came to feel, after he had completed "a very decent third of the book," that he was "experiencing discouragement because this kind of unconscious movement of the mind isn't now going on."[9] In the course of the story, Vincent, having given up his projected history of late nineteenth-century American literature, is rescued from unrewarding part-time teaching jobs by Harold Outram. Outram has, after successes as a critic and novelist, given up literature to head the Peck Foundation. A Stalinist in opinions, though not practice, he is the only major character in the book who seems to have wandered in from the pages of *The Middle of the Journey*: "Literature is dead.... Russia is our future and our hope. And Russia has not produced one single notable work of art."[10] It is he who selects Vincent to become the biographer of the octogenarian Jorris Buxton, "the last manifestation of heroism in the human race."[11]

Buxton's life too was shaped by a daring shift away from the arts—poetry, painting, and novels—into (of all things!) mathematical physics. Trilling says that Buxton was modeled on the English Romantic poet Walter Savage Landor (previously fictionalized in Dickens' *Bleak House* as Boythorn), whose numerous eccentricities included a reckless fondness (very like John Ruskin's) for women much younger than himself. But Murphy, in her ingenious reading of the book as a *roman à clef*, suggests that it is not Landor but Henry James (with a large admixture of brother William) who is Buxton's model, and that this "anti-Stalinist version of James"[12] was Trilling's way of carrying on the Cold War struggle against fellow-traveling liberals who derided the novelist James as reactionary, "impotent in matters sociological," and inferior to Dreiser.[13] She suggests that Trilling's 1948 essay on *The Princess Casamassima* provides a key to his own novel's intentions. That essay argued that James' political vision anticipated the collapse of European civilization in World War II and the Holocaust. "Henry James in the Eighties understood what we have painfully learned from our grim glossary of wars and concentration camps, after having seen the state and human nature laid open to our horrified inspection."

But since one can't publish a novel with marginalia signaling biographical and historical parallels, the book must stand on its own, and this it does not do well. Parading Buxton's mistresses does not exactly establish his intellectual potency. Moreover, Trilling's critical virtues here often dwindle into irritating verbal idiosyncrasy and what must (astonishingly) be called bad writing. "Nor was she pretty. But she was remarkably good-looking." "He would formerly have said that Marion Cathcart was a quick graceful person and tall. But now she seemed rather short than tall." "Like any foreigner, observation and understanding were his means of defense against his alien position."[14]

There are some vividly realized scenes: Vincent's childhood, his creative-writing class for women, his discovery that having the papers of the man whose biography you are writing gives you only what people have written to him, not what he has written to them. But too often we are told that an experience is "intense" for a character without being shown why it is so. Frequently the supremely intelligent narrator analyzes and explains a character before that character has had a chance to open his or her mouth. If James had reviewed this novel, he might have said what he did of George Eliot's *Middlemarch*: "Certainly the greatest minds have the defects of their qualities and as George Eliot's mind is preeminently contemplative and analytic, nothing is more natural than that her manner should be discursive and expansive."[15]

And there is something more. Murphy reports the astonishing fact that, in 1948, Trilling, reflecting on the burgeoning career of Irving Howe (born, let us recall, Horenstein), thought: "How right for my Vincent!" and by 1952 considered reviving his moribund novel by making Vincent "specifically Jewish."[16] How he could have done this without rewriting the entire book is hard to say. Whatever obstacles impede Vincent's career, being Jewish is not one of them; yet, as everyone knows, Trilling's career at Columbia nearly fell victim to the then deeply entrenched opposition to hiring Jews in English departments.

Trilling had always bristled at the suggestion he might be a Jewish writer. In 1944, he wrote: "I know of writers who have used their Jewish experience as the subject of excellent work; I know of no writer in English who has added a micromillimetre to his stature by 'realizing his Jewishness,' although I know of some who have curtailed their promise by trying to heighten their Jewish consciousness."[17] He was stung by Robert Warshow's criticism of *The Middle of the Journey* in *Commentary* for concealing the Jewish background of the world of fellow-travelers. He responded to Elliot Cohen's invitation to join the board of *Commentary* with the sad, foolish remark that this was an attempt by Cohen to "degrade me by involving me in [a] Jewish venture."[18] When Howe began working on his *Treasury of Yiddish Stories* in the early 1950s, Trilling told him that he was altogether "suspicious" of Yiddish literature, a remark that (so Howe wrote to me in 1983) "hurt and angered me deeply, and I never forgave him for it." Did Trilling now, in a startling reversal, come to think that, as Cynthia Ozick has famously said, literature springs from the tribe, not from the urge to Esperanto? Did he think he had taken a wrong path as a novelist in keeping distant from his deepest personal experience? We shall never know.

Notes

1. *The Liberal Imagination: Essays on Literature and Society* (New York: Doubleday, 1950). Subsequent references to this work appear in parentheses in the text.

2. "Some Notes for an Autobiographical Lecture," Appendix to Lionel Trilling, in *The Last Decade: Essays and Reviews, 1965–75*, ed. Diana Trilling (New York and London: Harcourt Brace Jovanovich, 1979), 227.
3. Diana Trilling, *The Beginning of the Journey: The Marriage of Diana and Lionel Trilling* (New York: Harcourt Brace, 1993), 371.
4. Ibid., 372–73.
5. Lionel Trilling, *The Journey Abandoned: The Unfinished Novel*, ed. Geraldine Murphy (New York: Columbia University Press, 2008).
6. Lionel Trilling, *E. M. Forster* (New York and London: Harcourt Brace Jovanovich, 1943), 8.
7. Trilling to Chase, June 1, 1947, Richard Chase Papers, Columbia University Library.
8. "Preface," *Journey Abandoned*, l–li.
9. "Trilling's Commentary," *Journey Abandoned*, 160–61.
10. *Journey Abandoned*, 56.
11. Ibid., 59.
12. Ibid., xxi.
13. See Trilling's essay on *The Princess Casamassima* in *Liberal Imagination*.
14. *Journey Abandoned*, 111, 135, 136.
15. *Galaxy* 15 (March 1873), 424.
16. *Journey Abandoned*, xxxiii.
17. *Contemporary Jewish Record* 7 (February 1944): 16–17.
18. *Journey Abandoned*, xv.

Metaphor and Memory in Cynthia Ozick: Pro and Con

Throughout her career as an essayist—in which capacity she has been called "the most accomplished and graceful literary stylist of our time"[1]—Cynthia Ozick has both celebrated metaphor and warned of its excesses, praised it for converting memory into conscience and pity, imagination into morality, and deplored its licentious use by "scribblers" who have neither memory nor pity. In her Phi Beta Kappa oration of 1985 at Harvard called "Metaphor and Memory," she elaborated on Matthew Arnold's distinction between Hebraism and Hellenism (the fourth chapter of *Culture and Anarchy*) by crediting the Greeks with "inspiration" and the Hebrews (i.e., the Jews) with memory—and metaphor. "Inspiration," she asserted, "has no memory . . . its opposite is memory, which is history as judgment." The Greeks' much-praised "civilization" did not preclude slavery and intense xenophobia because "they did not, as a society, cultivate memory, or search out any historical metaphor to contain memory."[2]

By contrast, the Jews, despite being a mixed multitude, a "slave rabble," brought something new into the world by turning their memory of enslavement in Egypt "into a universalizing metaphor of reciprocity . . . a way to convert imagination into a serious moral instrument." Her chief example of this was Leviticus 19, verse 34: "The stranger that sojourneth with you shall be unto you as the home-born among you, and you shall love him as yourself; because you were strangers in the land of Egypt." The metaphor of memory and history enabled the Hebrew to imagine the life of the stranger, of "the Other." Thus does metaphor, in its highest capacity, act as a universalizing force that enables one to see into the heart of the stranger.[3]

But there is for Ozick a darker side to the history of metaphor, and one in which the Jews also figure prominently, albeit disastrously. In an essay of 1975 (a decade before the Harvard lecture) called

"A Liberal's Auschwitz," cited earlier in this book, she sharply condemns the liberal (including, or perhaps especially, the Jewish liberal) habit of "universalizing" Jewish experience. "If the Jew is ground into the metaphorical dust of 'humanity,' or of 'victim,' if he is viewed only as the emblematic 'other,'" then ideological and polemical mischief is afoot.[4] This is especially evident in the polemical distortion (beloved of universalists the world over) of what happened at Auschwitz, the one which says that the victims of the Nazis were "human beings" or "humanity" at large, or else applies the term "Auschwitz" to every instance, real or imagined, of "man's inhumanity to man." On this issue, Ozick is the enemy of universalizing, the enemy of metaphor. "Jews," she insists, "are no metaphors—not for poets, not for novelists, not for theologians, not for murderers, and never for anti-Semites" (128). Auschwitz is not a metaphor, and there are no metaphors for Auschwitz.

Ozick is hardly the first compulsively metaphorical writer to warn of the dangers of metaphor. Shakespeare does so in *Julius Caesar* when Brutus, in a classic example of specious reasoning, convinces himself that Caesar must be murdered, and does so through a series of ludicrously inappropriate similes and metaphors, culminating in this: "think him as a serpent's egg/Which, hatch'd, would, as his kind, grow mischievous,/And kill him in the shell" (II, 1, 32–34). Caesar had, of course, long before emerged from his shell and is now a fully grown and very familiar "serpent" in Rome. George Eliot's *Middlemarch* (1871–1872), in its texture perhaps the most pervasively metaphorical novel ever written, also warns (in Chapter 10) that "we all of us, grave or light, get our thoughts entangled in metaphors, and act fatally on the strength of them." Eliot is here generalizing from the specific instance of Edward Casaubon, the devotee of futile mythological research into the Key to All Mythologies, who, as we shall see, is (metaphorically) omnipresent in Ozick's novel, *Heir to the Glimmering World*.[5]

"Metaphor and Memory" at first uses the word "metaphor" expansively, rather than in the narrower (I. A. Richards tenor/vehicle) sense. For example, Ozick alludes to medical doctors as people generally "appalled by metaphor . . ., by fable, image . . . obliqueness, double meaning, the call to interpret . . ." (268). But later, after crediting the Jews with giving birth to metaphor in its largest sense, she turns to strict definition: "it is now time to ask what metaphor is" (280). Again she links it to history—because it transforms the strange into what we already know and have long known—but also to language, specifically the language of interpretation: "Metaphor is . . . a priest of interpretation; but what it interprets is memory."[6]

Interpretation and metaphor are at the center of *Heir to the Glimmering World*. Indeed, Ozick explicitly tells us as much in her epigraph from Frank Kermode—"Yet the world is full of interpreters. . . . So the question arises, why would we rather interpret than not?"—and in her comments (outside of the book) about the scholarly interests of a central character in the novel, Professor Rudolph (Rudi) Mitwisser. Mitwisser and his wife Elsa and their children fled Nazi Germany in 1933; when the novel opens in 1935, we find him in America pursuing his research into the subject of the heretical Jewish sect called the Karaites. "I was drawn to the Karaites," Ozick has said in an interview, "not so much as a subject (the obsession is Mitwisser's, not mine), but far more usefully . . . as a metaphor."[7] Ironically, however, the metaphorical meaning of the Karaites is precisely their opposition to metaphor and interpretation. As the novel's narrator observes: "They scorn metaphor and the poetry of inference" (74). A sect founded at the beginning of the eighth century, they were what nowadays might be called fundamentalists or literalists, adhering only to the text of the Bible and rejecting all Biblical commentary and interpretation, that is, the Talmud and the whole complex structure of rabbinical Judaism built upon it.

We know that Ozick was not "drawn" to the Karaites in this novel by any sympathy for them. In an essay called "Literature as Idol," for example, she argues that normative Judaism's adoption of "interpretation" represented a middle way between the Karaites' devotion to the doctrine of standing still, and the opposite extreme of displacement, deviation, substitution, and revisionism. "'Torah' includes the meanings of tradition and transmittal together. . . . Transmittal signifies the carrying-over of the original strength, the primal monotheistic insight . . . In Jewish thought there are no latecomers."[8] For Ozick, the striking modern instance of Karaitism is not anything Jewish at all, but rather what she calls "the Christian Karaites," better known in the history of literary criticism as the New Critics, who would allow neither tradition nor history to be attached to a literary text.[9]

Although an Ozick novel exists more than most fictions in the realm of imagination, its characters are not free from the shaping pressures of history; they have their historical actuality and rootedness. But history, in the best novels, makes itself felt not as a mere reproduction of the familiar world or "a slice of life," but as moral, perhaps also political, criticism. This helps to explain why we see Mitwisser and his somewhat zany family (including wife, two girls, and three boys) not only through the eyes of the first-person narrator Rosie Meadows, but also through the eyes of the omniscient narrator. Although the novel has reminded some critics of *Jane Eyre*, it differs sharply from Brontë's novel because it spurns formal unity; rather than consistently filtering everything through the limited perspective of the eighteen-year-old governess–amanuensis–nanny–copyist–typist who is the book's central figure, it shifts when necessary to the omniscient narrator—dare we call her Ozick?—for historical perspective, longer memory.

It is from the omniscient narrator that we learn the circumstances of the Mitwissers' persecution by and ejection from Nazi Germany and also of its lingering effects. Rosie, intelligent and observant, can tell us of how Professor Mitwisser, though he appears to her eyes "densely, irrevocably German" (4), nevertheless resolutely opposes the use of German in his household in the northeastern outposts of the Bronx, and attempts "the obliteration of German in every room of the house except his own" (85), in which he reads Schiller. Rosie goes to the New York Public Library to find out about the Mitwissers' past in a travel book that shows a splendid Berlin hotel Mrs. Mitwisser has mentioned to her. But in order really to know their past we rely on the all-seeing and historically knowledgeable narrator. It is she who explains, for example, why the oldest Mitwisser child, Anneliese, refuses to attend school in America. Anneliese's recollection, given far from the purview of Rosie, of how Jews were expelled from the life of their native land is one of the book's memorable passages:

> Frau Koch's desk was on a raised platform. A short metal bar lay in the drawer of this desk. The lesson was on Bismarck: name two achievements that can be attributed to Chancellor von Bismarck. Frau Koch broke the bones of the left hand. Not with a ruler. The ruler was for the others. The ruler would not have been so savage. With the short metal bar Frau Koch smashed two narrow bones. Because I gave the answer. Because I forgot that I was forbidden to speak. Because by then it was forbidden to be in that school at all. Because I would soon be thrown out of that school. Because it was imperative to be silent. Because it was imperative to be invisible. Because I spoke aloud. Because I gave the answer. (267–68)

Anneliese's recollections of Nazi Germany make her both wiser and more ignorant than native-born Americans. Her boyfriend James

A'Bair, a character inspired by Christopher Robin (Milne) whose ironic relationship (as an American and metaphorical "Karaite") to her father is central to the novel, laughs at her childish ignorance because she thinks one needs passport and papers to cross from New York into Pennsylvania. But she thinks him typical of how "the Americans were like children" (265) because "he did not comprehend what it was to be without papers, to have no passport, to cower before a uniform, to pay for forged papers . . . never to have good papers, valid papers, a genuine passport!" (265) What do Americans know of "the bonfires in the streets at night, and the broad black leaves of charred books, like spread-out bats' wings, and the smoke" (270). Anneliese's childhood memory confirms what Edelshtein, the protagonist of Ozick's 1969 story "Envy" thinks about European civilization: "that pod of muck." The willed American distancing from modern Europe may also be hinted at in the novel's insistence on the ancient provenance of the names of upstate New York towns: "Syracuse," Rosie recalls, "was to the north of us, Troy to the east, Carthage to the west" (11). The geographer Erich Isaac has suggested that "the classical place-naming enthusiasm reflected an urge to create a classical republican past, since they had no use for their real European antecedents."[10]

The Jewishness of the Mitwisser family was not much to live by in Germany, and it barely exists in America, except in the Hebrew texts in Mitwisser's library. Although a student of the history of religion, his own life is without any sign of belief, even in fossilized form. "In that family there was no rite or observance, no Sabbathday or Passover or sacral new year" (67). His oldest child Anneliese senses that "her papa's people [i.e., the Karaites] . . . believed in God" (239) but that her parents probably did not (and her physicist mother said the universe was made of atoms, and God had nothing to do with the matter). The same holds for the American Jews in the novel, the "secularized" Jews who get little sympathy in Ozick's essays. Rosie observes that "It had been the same—the same absence—for my father and me, and for Bertram [her distant cousin and halfhearted wooer]. . . ." But Europe was different because if the Mitwissers had not escaped early in the Nazi era the Jewishness which was not much to live by would have been more than sufficient to die for.

The Mitwisser parents had felt the lash of the Nazi regime early because both Rudolph and Elsa were academics expelled from their profession by the April 1933 decree dismissing Jewish academics from their posts. Ozick forcefully conveys the swiftness with which their status was reduced to nothing in the land of their birth:

> At home in Berlin, at the University, he had been surrounded by a haze of attentive acolytes; his students bowed to him, waiters in restaurants recognized him from newspaper photographs and bowed to him, he was Herr Doktor Professor, esteemed lecturer before the Religionswissenschaftliche Vereinigung, honored by his colleagues all over Germany. And then—overnight—they threw him out. His poor wife, a respected senior fellow of the Kaiser Wilhelm Institute, her too they threw out . . . (55)

Here Ozick's fiction is firmly rooted in history. In Freiburg, for example, the local Nazi paper *Der Allemanne* published lists of Jewish doctors and dentists who were to be boycotted, and a few days later a list of Jewish members of the university's medical faculty. On April 10, the rector of the university, none other than Martin Heidegger, instructed his deans to dismiss all faculty members of Jewish religion or origin. Whether by accident or intention, Ozick's novel about (among many other things) Jewish refugees from Germany appeared at the very time (2004) when university academics and researchers across Europe (but especially in England) were calling for a moratorium on all cultural and research links with Israel, the world's only Jewish state. In this sense, *Heir to the Glimmering World* has (at least) as much immediacy as Philip Roth's blatantly political novel, *The Plot Against America*, also starting in the 1930s, which appeared at the same time as Ozick's.

Rudolf Mitwisser is the book's most richly conceived character. Gradually, Rosie comes to see that the man she serves is both more and less than a dryasdust scholar sorting through moldy futilities. "Boiling rebellion," she observes, "was Mitwisser's subject. He was drawn to schismatics, fiery heretics, apostates—the lunatics of history. Below the scholar's skin a wild bellows panted . . ." (64). His is an imperial intellect, laying claim to hitherto unconquered realms of interpretation, in opposition to "the arrogance of received interpretation" (5). But when Rosie one day decides to follow him to his regular niche at the New York Public Library where he is assumed to be pursuing his research (into a medieval scholar named Jacob al-Kirkisani and the possibility that he may have been a Hindu heretic—from Karaite heresy) she finds him staring into space, his briefcase "propped, limp and unopened," looking very much "like a mummy exposed" (99).

"He's no better than a mummy," says James Chettam in *Middlemarch* about Edward Casaubon, George Eliot's great character who serves both as model for and antithesis to Mitwisser. We get a strong hint of their connection early in *Heir* when cousin Bertram—years before Rosie has become Mitwisser's research assistant—picks up her copy of *Middlemarch* and opens to an illustration of Casaubon and his youthful research assistant and wife Dorothea (27). The two scholars are antithetical in that Casaubon is a clergyman, and his research is motivated in part by a desire to demonstrate Christianity's hegemony over all other religions; Mitwisser, by contrast, is likened by Rosie to a biologist studying the very disease to which he is immune—that is to say, religion. The great gap in Casaubon's scholarship is his avoidance of "the Germans" and their "Higher Criticism"; Mitwisser, by contrast, is (apart from the little inconvenience of being Jewish) German of the Germans, the "towering Teuton" (200).

On the other hand, there is a striking resemblance in the paradoxical contrast between what Casaubon and Mitwisser study and what they are. The impotent Casaubon, for example, "in an agitated dimness about the Cabeiri [Samothracian fertility gods], or in an exposure of other mythologists' ill-considered parallels, easily lost sight of any purpose which had prompted him to these labours. With his taper stuck before him he forgot the absence of windows, and in bitter manuscript remarks on other men's notions about the solar deities, he had become indifferent to the sunlight" (*Middlemarch*, Chapter 19). But, lest her readers press too hard on the novel's link to this aspect of *Middlemarch*, Ozick, in her last chapter, has Rosie declare that "It was not my destiny to be planted in a single spot of the earth, like that other discarded amanuensis of another century, Dorothea Casaubon..." (308).

Measuring the heroine and Mitwisser against literary forebears indicates the extent to which most major characters in the novel have a significant relationship to literature, and to literature's power not only to elevate and ennoble, but also to damage.[11] Rosie, when we first meet her, is a student who has already absorbed *Jane Eyre*—whose "sad orphanhood" (10) she had admired—and is now "reading night after night, Dickens and Trollope and George Eliot, one after another" (27). (Although ironic echoes of Brontë's novel may be glimpsed in the omnipresent word "heir" and in the fact that Mitwisser keeps a mad wife in the attic, the echoes prove a false clue. Mitwisser is hardly a Bluebeard figure like Rochester, and Rosie's narration lacks the mixture of self-criticism with self-respect that characterizes Jane Eyre's. Whereas fathers are virtually absent from *Jane Eyre*, Ozick's novel has at its center a trio of bad fathers: Rosie's father deceived her by saying that her mother (like Cathy in *Wuthering Heights*) died giving birth to her; James' father exploited him for a book; and Anneliese Mitwisser's father virtually sells her to James. In any case, one should remember Ozick's own warning against submitting to the influence of past writers: "To be any sort of competent writer one must keep one's psychological distance from the supreme artists."[12]

Rosie's romantic rival for the attention of her cousin Bertram is Ninel, a stupid and fanatical revolutionary (her adopted name—chosen to replace the "Jewish" Miriam—is Lenin spelled backward) with strong literary opinions. She reads Jane Austen as Edward Said (in *Culture and Imperialism*) taught hordes of his academic acolytes to do: "'Jane Austen, wouldn't you know. Now that's what I call a provocation. Do you realize,' she demanded, 'how the servants in those big houses lived? The hours they had to put in, the paltry wages they got? Chicken-feed! And where the money to keep up those mansions came from? From plantations in the Caribbean run on the broken backs of Negro slaves!'" (24) Rosie, by contrast, hits upon *Sense and Sensibility* as therapy for the (apparently) mad Elsa Mitwisser precisely because—and one detects the quintessential Ozick voice here—"what was wanted for Mrs. Mitwisser—was simply Story; a story about men and women free of history, except their own" (83). And for a time the Austen bibliotherapy works: "Mrs. Mitwisser understood all this very well; it glimmered with unfamiliar familiarity; none of it was beyond her comprehension. She understood it pleasurably . . . she warmed to the affinities she instantly felt: the loss of money, the necessity of money, the hope of money; standing, expectation, repute" (84). Eventually, however, she tears the novel to shreds.

The character most firmly tied to a book and indeed to its author is James A'Bair, who arrives from another world, spiritually even more than geographically, to become thematically kin to Dr. Mitwisser, a "metaphorical" Karaite like those who dominate the professor's inner life. Ozick's attention had been caught by an obituary of Christopher Robin Milne, the grown-up son of A. A. Milne, the author of the *Winnie the Pooh* stories, and the "model" for Christopher Robin. Christopher Milne died on April 20, 1996. The (London) *Times* obituary of him mentioned that he "had always had a close relationship with his father, but after being away for some time when he was discharged from the army the boy seemed to have been broken and he grew to resent his father's exploitation of him, and he hated the books that had made him famous." Despite the "damage that Christopher had suffered because of books," he and his wife moved to Dartmouth in the north of England in 1951 to start a bookshop, precisely the place where people were most likely to remind him of his fictional existence. (One wonders whether he displayed in his shop the two books by Frederick Crews—*The Pooh Perplex* [1965] and *Postmodern Pooh* [2001]—which fiercely satirize much of contemporary literary theory by lampooning its imagined excesses in interpretation of the Pooh stories. The cover of Crews' earlier book carries this subtitle, much to the point of Ozick's story: "In Which It is Discovered that the True Meaning of the Pooh Stories is Not as Simple as is Usually Believed, But for Proper Elucidation Requires the Combined Efforts of Several Academicians of Varying Critical Persuasions.")

From reading obituaries of Milne Ozick concluded that the author's son had spent much of his life trying to escape identification with his father's fictional inventions and the drawings of them, in particular trying to escape the fate of being a lifelong five-year-old, forever wearing a laced collar and sporting rouged knees (so they would be red for sketching). At first little Jimmy—Ozick's fictional recreation of Christopher R. Milne—loved the pictures his father drew of him and the stories that seemed to grow out of his father's doting on him. Perhaps the double buckles on his shoes and the rouge on his knees troubled him, but the excitement of fame was adequate compensation for the uneasiness:

> "Well!" his father said. "There you are!" It wasn't an ordinary book, it was like no other book in the house or in the world, his mother explained, because it had Arrived From The Publisher and his father had Written and Illustrated it. (117)

But when he passed the age of five, he sensed that he was no longer "himself," no longer Jimmy but "the A'Bair Boy," later simplified to "the Bear Boy," as he was called by other children at school (and is in the novel). Soon he came to hate his father's books and felt that "he would never be Jimmy again, he would have to be the Bear Boy in buckled shoes and long bangs and flounced collars all the rest of his life, like a Raggedy Andy doll that never changed its clothes" (118). His father had, in effect, "interpreted" him out of existence; fiction exists in a parasitical relationship to its "real-life" subjects. (Parasite is a word used frequently in the novel, in its German as well as English form. For Elsa Mitwisser, James is himself a parasite, and for Ninel everybody from Albany, the seat of New York State government, is a parasite.)

For a long time, Rosie, who herself labors to escape "the wilderness of my father's imagination," knows neither the actual relationship of the Bear Boy to her own father nor his relationship—as their financial provider—to the Mitwissers. Eventually she discovers that "the Bear Boy had gambled with my father, and my father had won, or had slyly been permitted to win, the Bear Boy's own relic [the first copy of his father's The Boy Who Lived in a Hat], spotted with the Bear Boy's own jam. The relic could be turned into gold, and I was its heir" (111). She also learns that it is the fabulously wealthy (from royalties on his father's books) James who supports the Mitwisser family (and so indirectly pays Rosie's salary, and in that limited sense makes her once again an "heir").

What Rosie never discovers, however, and what (again) the narrator must reveal to us, is the metaphorical connection between Mitwisser, the researcher into anti-interpretation Karaitism, and James A'Bair, the victim of an excess of interpretation and also, like Mitwisser, imprisoned by the past. "This James," observes his enemy Elsa, "dieser Säufer [this drunkard] . . . believes he is Karaite. Consequently, he loves my husband" (115). In his reaction, or over-reaction, to his parents' attempt to keep him the eternal child, and under the tutelage of hashish, "he did not want to be or to become" (159). Although Professor Mitwisser scoffs at his wife's allegation as an absurdity, "It was not absurd. How was he, the counterfeit tutor, different from the Karaites, who rejected graftings on the pristinely God-given? He too rejected graftings. He was born unencumbered, nakedly himself, without a lace collar. The author of the Bear Boy had grafted on the lace collar. The moment he was free he tore it off. From then on he was all impulse" (212). This impulse leads him to travel the world, forever in flight; his insuperable problem is that, as Oedipus and many other literary fugitives since Oedipus have discovered, the man who leaves town still has an insuperable problem: he takes himself with him.

The identity of James with Dr. Mitwisser is the novel's chief example of metaphor, that is, the discovery of similitude in dissimilitude. Although just fourteen and a half, Anneliese recognizes that James, though he too does not believe in God, is as much in the grip of the Karaites as is her father. One wears his shirt with a great deal of starch, the other is a pot-smoking, disheveled, vagabond, playboy millionaire bum. Nevertheless, she discerns that "Her papa and James! They were exactly alike . . ." (240). By reaction against what his father's commentary and interpretation have done to his body and brain, James becomes a devotee of Karaite anticommmentary, anti-interpretation, a formless, unpredictable, and purposeless being.

One might expect that in between the extremes of Karaite anti-interpretation—"no metaphors"!—and literary excess of interpretation the novel would present, in the person of heroine (and sometimes narrator) Rosie, the mean, but no, we must (as so often in literature, from Don Quixote onward) infer the mean from the extremes. Rosie, although emotionally intelligent and a keen observer, does not represent or even recognize the thematic, metaphorical link between the scholar she serves and the unpredictable scoundrel who supports them, and is not conscious of the need to find a via media between too little and too much interpretation.

In fact, Rosie tends to be surprised even by what seems to be within her purview, like her cousin Bertram. In the early chapters of the book, he is a weak-willed airhead. His most significant action at the outset of the tale is to allow Ninel to evict Rosie, an orphaned teenager, from his apartment. As a result, she is forced to look for work, which she finds with the Mitwissers in the rural wastes of the Bronx (probably the one setting of the novel that is based on Ozick's own experience).[13] Thereafter, and indeed until Chapter 50, he is a distant presence, sending vapid letters to Rosie, whom he relentlessly addresses as "kid" (193).

But when Bertram returns to the novel after losing his job as a hospital chemist because he is a leftist and getting kicked out of his apartment (by Communists) because he is not leftist enough, he quickly emerges—to the amazement of Rosie, of the reader, and perhaps of the writer herself—as responsible, omnicompetent, directorial, and indeed the master of the novel's remaining action. His transformative powers exceed those of Nature herself: "Bertram could convert downstream to upstream, Anneliese the fallen to Anneliese the wife, mad Mrs. Mitwisser to mundanely triumphant Elsa" (307). He imposes order on the chaotic Mitwisser household, becomes guardian of the bastard child Anneliese has had with James (now dead by suicide), and even changes from whining socialist to adroit capitalist.

The novel seems to end precariously poised between life and death. On the one hand, there is a new baby and a marriage, on the other the third death, and this one self-inflicted, of a prominent character. James "lay now in the troublesome grave Mr. Brooks [executor of the family fortune] had painfully contracted for . . . Not far off, under the sanctified earth of Troy, my father lay in disgrace. Somewhere in Spain lay Ninel . . ." (309). Bertram, with characteristically shallow cheerfulness, sends Rosie "Off to the big world," but a normally attentive reader will recall that the year is 1937, well into the Hitler era and the "big world" of mass murder and universal war. Rosie's observation that "Things have been put right" (304) is an instance of dramatic irony.

In one of the most acute essays written about this novel, Hillel Halkin has used the suicide of James, the Bear Boy, to raise the question of the conflict between Ozick the essayist and Ozick the novelist. He alleges that there is no organic reason for James' suicide, and that he is killed off not by Ozick the novelist, who serves Hellenism and imagination, but by Ozick the essayist, servant of Hebraism and of conduct and its consequences.[14] Although Halkin has not chosen a good example of this conflict in Ozick—James is hardly the magnetically "appealing" rogue Halkin takes him to be (both Rosie and Mrs. Mitwisser see through him)—the conflict is a real one, often acknowledged by Ozick herself, as in this "Forewarning" to *Metaphor and Memory*: "a fiction writer who also writes essays is looking for trouble . . . If a writer of stories is also a writer of essays, the essays ought not to be seized as a rod to beat the writer's stories with; or as a frame into which to squeeze the writer's stories. . . ."[15]

Another way of stating this conflict is to observe that few essayist–moralists as passionately committed to a political or religious outlook as Ozick is have been able to achieve the willing suspension of disbelief required of a novelist. In the Victorian period, for example, such writers as Carlyle, Macaulay, and Newman possessed, to a very high degree, many of the gifts of the novelist, but were too powerfully committed to their philosophies of life or (supposedly) prophetic revelations to be able to imagine the inner world of people indifferent to their views or unvisited by their revelations.[16] George Eliot, on the other hand, though highly contentious and polemical and uncharitable in her discursive essays in the *Westminster Review*, could be sympathetic in her fiction to the very people (evangelicals, for example) she scourged in her essays. In this respect, though she disclaims Victorian "influence" almost as frequently as she reveals it, Ozick has in *Heir to the*

Glimmering World, a novel largely about marginal or deracinated Jews, shown herself to be "our" George Eliot, a novelist whose work embodies her predecessor's view that "If Art does not enlarge men's sympathies, it does nothing morally. . . . Opinions are a poor cement between human souls; and the only effect I ardently long to produce by my writings, is that those who read them should be better able to imagine and to feel the pains and the joys of those who differ from themselves in everything but the broad fact of being struggling erring human creatures."[17]

Notes

1. John Sutherland, "The Girl Who Would Be James," *NYTBR*, October 8, 2000.
2. "Metaphor and Memory," in *Metaphor and Memory* (New York: Knopf, 1989), 276–77. Subsequent references to this essay appear in parentheses in the text.
3. Ibid., 278, 277.
4. "A Liberal's Auschwitz," *Confrontation* X (Spring 1975): 126.
5. *Heir to the Glimmering World* (Boston, MA: Houghton Mifflin, 2004). Subsequent references to the novel will be given in parentheses in the text.
6. "Metaphor and Memory," 268, 280. In an interview about this novel, and in explanation of why her heart is more in her fiction than in her essays, Ozick observed that a novel exists essentially not in sociology but in "the most fearful intimations of language, when setting down a phrase feels tantamount to ingesting the blood of demons . . ." In "Metaphor and Memory" she had described herself as "a word-besotted scribbler"(MM, 265). This word-besottedness often expresses itself in *Heir to the Glimmering World* with metaphorical brilliance and the force of revelation. In Chapter 50, for example, she wants to convey Dr. Mitwisser's fear that Rosie will leave him, as his eldest daughter and (in a different way) his wife already have: "he feared the ambush of the vacuum that waits beyond commotion" (249). Elsewhere, she alludes to the Nazis' "insect-leg flags" (295), a perfect convergence of image and meaning. But some of her critics, though acknowledging her verbal brilliance, allege that some of its examples merit the censure that Dr. Johnson leveled at the metaphysical poets: "Their thoughts are often new, but seldom natural; they are not obvious, but neither are they just; and the reader, far from wondering that he missed them, wonders more frequently by what perverseness of industry they were ever found." Johnson's strictures (in his essay on Abraham Cowley in *Lives of the Poets*), might be called an eighteenth-century version of "Metaphor and Memory," although the history against which Johnson measures metaphysical wit is really the collective mind of the human race.
7. "A Conversation with Cynthia Ozick," on the Houghton Mifflin website. The professor's name may recall that of Ruth Puttermesser [butter-knife in Yiddish] of Ozick's earlier novel, and could mean "accessory" or (taken more literally) "co-knower."

8. *Art and Ardor* (New York: Knopf, 1983), 194.
9. "Toward a New Yiddish," in *Art and Ardor*, 163.
10. Letter from Isaac to EA, November 1, 2004. See also Wilbur Zelinsky, "Classical Town Names in the United States," *Geographical Review* 57 (1967): 463–95.
11. This fact has led foolish reviewers of the book to conclude that Ozick writes not "from life" but from literature. Needless to say that the novelistic genre, starting with *Don Quixote*, is (even more than other literary forms) about other books and how "life" imitates art.
12. "The Lesson of the Master," in *Art and Ardor*, 297.
13. "I lived in a neighborhood in the northeastern Bronx where there was no public library at that time, but there was a travel library, a green truck that would come and stop in front of the house that had a pig in its backyard . . . and the librarians would throw into a muddy grass . . . two boxes . . ." No wonder that in the novel Ozick plays on the ironic contrast between the classy classical names of (very shabby) upstate New York towns—Troy, Thrace, Carthage, Ithaca, and Rome—and the wilderness to which Rosie moves.
14. Hillel Halkin," What Is Cynthia Ozick About?" *Commentary* 119 (January 2005): 55.
15. *Metaphor and Memory*, ix–xi.
16. See on this topic George Levine, *The Boundaries of Fiction: Carlyle, Macaulay, Newman* (Princeton, NJ: Princeton University Press, 1968).
17. *The Letters of George Eliot*, ed. G. S. Haight, 7 vols. (New Haven, CT: Yale University Press, 1954–1955), III, 111. It is worth noting that, as we shall see later in this book, Ozick published her own version of George Eliot's famous essay of 1887 "The Modern Hep! Hep! Hep!" in the *New York Observer* (May 10, 2004) in the same year that *Heir to the Glimmering World* appeared. Both essays deal with the plague of antisemitism.

Foreign Bodies: Americans Abroad in Post-Holocaust Europe

> "But there is some kind of advantage in the roughness of a place like Chicago, of not having any illusions either. Whereas in all the great capitals of the world there's some reason to think humanity is very different. All that ancient culture and those beautiful works of art right out in public, by Michelangelo and Christopher Wren, and those ceremonies, like trooping the color at the Horse Guards' parade or burying a great man in the Pantheon over in Paris. You see those marvelous things and you think that everything savage belongs to the past. So you think. And then you have another think, and you see that after they rescued women from the coal mines, or pulled down the Bastille and got rid of Star Chambers and lettres de cachet, ran out the Jesuits, increased education, and built hospitals and spread courtesy and politeness, they have five or six years of war and revolutions and kill off twenty million people. And do they think there's less danger to life than here? That's a riot."
> —Saul Bellow, *The Adventures of Augie March* (1953)

Cynthia Ozick's *Foreign Bodies* opens with an epigraph from *The Ambassadors* (1903), the most ambitious of Henry James' fictions about the "international" theme (in which provincial Americans experience Europe or actually mate with Europeanized Americans and, in later books, real Europeans):

> But there are two quite distinct things—given the wonderful place he's in—that may have happened to him. One is that he may have got brutalized. The other is that he may have got refined.[1]

In James' novel, a Mrs. Newsome of Woollett (roughly Worcester), Massachusetts dispatches ambassadors or emissaries to restore to his home town and the family business a son (Chad) who has been detained in Paris by what she assumes to be a sordid passion. Thus a private problem becomes an exercise in diplomacy, with reports and cables going back and forth between the home office and the ambassador, who might desert and go over to the enemy. The first of her ambassadors and the hero of James' novel is Lambert Strether, her intimate friend and a man of letters who edits a highbrow Review with a small but loyal readership. For him Paris proves a school of reality. Chad Newsome turns out to be the center of an attractive circle of artists and aristocrats, and so Strether—leaping to the opposite naivete—assumes (mistakenly) that the older woman responsible for Chad's improvement must be far better than he had supposed. Mrs. Newsome loses confidence in her first ambassador and gives his portfolio to her married daughter Sarah, who is now charged with saving Strether as well as Chad from Europe; Chad indicates he might return home if Strether would advise him to.

In *Foreign Bodies*, the protagonists are mainly Jews and their relatives, including their non-Jewish children. Marvin Nachtigall replaces Mrs. Newsome as the wealthy American trying to get his son Julian, an unemployed waiter, *luftmensh*, would-be theologian of atheism, and pedestrian writer (in *Botteghe Oscure* but not *Paris Review*), out of the clutches of an older woman (Lili) and back from Paris to take over the family business (plastic parts for airplanes). Marvin is imperious and boorish and aggressively assimilated into "America, his newfound land" (155), but has the laudable instinct to want his son "out of Europe, out of the bloody dirt of that place, and back home in America where he belongs" (10). Marvin's first ambassador is his divorced, graying schoolteacher (of English) sister Bea Nightingale (a name-changer). She fails as an ambassador in large part because she despises both her nephew and niece, "their alien bodies and whatever effluvium might pass for their souls" (41); she is replaced by Julian's gullible sister Iris. Most of the characters contribute letters to telling a story that is otherwise Ozick's third-person narrative. Whereas the *fin de siècle* Paris of Strether and James was populated exclusively by artists and members of the nobility in search of pleasure, enlightenment, and art, Ozick's is populated mainly by two kinds of foreigners or "foreign bodies." The first comprises self-intoxicated young Americans trying to summon up the past and calling themselves "expatriates"; the second is made up of polyglot "ghosts," Europe's "wailing wall" (71), the displaced persons of many nations whom Europe had defined as foreign bodies, had spat out and hunted down, and who will forever wear "Europe's tattoo" (2–3). The former, in a way, aped the latter: "The ground was scorched, the streets teemed with refugees, and these Americans," so Lili (a genuine DP) thinks, "were playing at fleeing!" (102)

Foreign Bodies, unlike James' Parisian novel, is a tale of *three* cities—Paris, New York, and Los Angeles—and takes place (two world wars after James' story) in 1952, seven years after Germany's Third Reich had murdered many millions of people, including most of European Jewry. Ozick's book is many things, but it is above all a condemnation, very much in the manner of the aforementioned speech in *Augie March*, of post-Holocaust Europe. That this fact received very little attention in reviews of the novel shows just how far we have traveled towards becoming what Bea Nightingale calls "Amnesiac America" (78). A great deal has been written about the ways in which *Foreign Bodies* reworks, extends, and also reverses *The Ambassadors*. But very little mention has been made of the fact that Julian Nachtigall, Ozick's young American who is to be "rescued" from his extended "year abroad" in Paris and brought back to California, is married to a Romanian Jewish Holocaust survivor named Lili, whose parents and husband Eugen and three-year-old son Mihail were murdered and she herself shot (by the Iron Guard, Romanian Nazis) in Transnistria, a mélange of camps (governed by one Professor Alexianu) that contained Romania's greatest and most barbaric killing centers.

Unlike Julian and his sister Iris, another ambassadorial deserter seduced by Europe's "beckoning cities . . . great public statues pitted by age, spires, ancient bridges over ancient rivers" (139), Lili is constantly haunted by memories of the singular savagery of the Romanian destruction process, which shocked even the Germans. One of them described it thus: "In the Bucharest morgue, one can see hundreds of corpses, but they are mostly Jews . . . The victims had not merely been killed, they had been butchered. In the morgue bodies were so cut up that they no longer resembled anything human, and in the municipal slaughterhouse bodies were observed hanging like carcasses of cattle. A witness saw a girl of five hanging by her feet like a calf, her entire body smeared with blood."[2] When Lili weeps at the sight of "that old *boucherie* [in her workplace] with the hooks for carcasses still on one wall" (128), she sees the bodies of wartime Bucharest, which we too may glimpse in the novel's relentlessly grotesque and revolting images of "foreign bodies." (The protagonist of Saul Bellow's *Ravelstein* also

197

called up "the massacre in Bucharest when they hung people alive on meat hooks in the slaughterhouse and . . . skinned them alive. Just give a thought now and then to those people on the meat hooks.")

As if all this were not enough to impress upon the reader that *Foreign Bodies* is centrally (though not exclusively) about post-Holocaust Europe, Ozick arranges a marriage for Marvin Nachtigall (Yiddish for Nightingale) with one Margaret Breckinridge, who has "relatives in the State Department" (14). Here Ozick alludes—one would have thought to say "of course" if the reviewers of *Foreign Bodies* had not proved otherwise—to Breckinridge Long, a ferocious antisemite who, when European Jewry was being systematically destroyed, used his position as assistant secretary of state in charge of refugee affairs to oppose European Jewish immigration to America and to block rescue proposals.[3] (In the novel, his cousin Margaret is run over by a bus on the LA Freeway as she flees from a psychiatric nursing home, mischievously named by Ozick The Suite Eyre Spa to call up the memory of Edward Rochester's mad wife in Brontë's *Jane Eyre*.)

Although Lili and Julian eventually leave Paris for New York, the real foil to Europe, and probably their ultimate destination, is not America but Israel, where Lili has an uncle in Jaffa, the city adjacent to Tel Aviv. She has come to think of Europe as Nineveh, described in the biblical book of *Jonah* as a city fully meriting destruction by fire from above if it does not repent of its sins. Jaffa (Joppa) is the biblical city in which Jonah, the appointed instrument of Nineveh's rescue, boards a ship destined for Tarshish.

As an astute observer of the political scene, Ozick knows that the international theme of *Foreign Bodies* gained a special immediacy when America acquired, perhaps for the first time in its history, a president who not only exhibited strong signs of Europhilia but bristled at the mere mention of "American exceptionalism."[4] Perhaps, in reinterpreting James' international theme in such a way as to excoriate post-Holocaust Europe and even sympathize with vulgar Marvin's effort to save his son from it, Cynthia Ozick remembered another classic utterance about "refinement," from a literature whose very existence James could never imagine. The Yiddish writer Shmuel Niger, in 1945, criticizing American-Jewish literati who throughout World War II had repudiated any responsibility for their fellow Jews being done to death in Europe, said: "We suffer not only from Jews who are too coarse, but also from Jews who are too refined."[5]

Notes

1. *Foreign Bodies* (Boston, MA and New York: Houghton Mifflin Harcourt, 2010). Subsequent references to the novel appear in parentheses in the text of the essay.
2. Raul Hilberg, *The Destruction of the European Jews* (Chicago, IL: Quadrangle Books, 1961), 489.
3. See on this subject David S. Wyman and Rafael Medoff, *A Race Against Death: Peter Bergson, America, and the Holocaust* (New York: The New Press, 2002).
4. See, earlier in this book, the essay on Obama's demotion of the Jews.
5. Niger was commenting, in *Der Tog*, on an article in the *Saturday Review*. See *Contemporary Jewish Record* (June 1945).

Saul Bellow's Jewish Letters

"We shall receive no letters in the grave," said Dr. Johnson during his final illness in 1784. To read Saul Bellow's letters in Benjamin Taylor's collection[1] is to understand that Johnson's remark was not a sigh of expected relief from nuisance and obligation but an anticipatory lament over loss of a supreme pleasure. It is said that nobody ever threw out a letter from Voltaire (whose published correspondence of 20,000 letters fills 102 volumes), and one would like to believe that nobody except Isaac Rosenfeld, Bellow's old friend from Chicago days at Tuley High School, ever discarded one from Bellow. The letters are replete with wit, wisdom, and Bellow's trademark mixture of erudition, sidewalk eloquence, Yiddish intonation, rhythm, and diction. "If you can bear to get to know them you learn about these *Nation*-type gnomes that they drink, drug, lie, cheat, chase, seduce, gossip, libel, borrow money, never pay child support.... Yet to vast numbers of people they are very attractive... That's because those vast numbers are the rank and file of nihilism, and... want to hear from Hitchens and Said, and consume falsehoods as they do fast-food. And it's so easy to make trouble for the Jews. Nothing easier. The networks love it, the big papers let it be made, there's a receptive university population for which Arafat is Good and Israel is Bad, even genocidal" (456). The letters confirm what Bellow once said about the letters of a great writer: "It is extraordinarily moving to find the inmost track of a man's life and to decipher the signs he has left us." That Bellow is a master of the epistolary art was already evident by 1964, when he published *Herzog*, a novel made up partly of letters written (not mailed) by the book's protagonist.

Taylor's collection contains 708 letters, forty percent of Bellow's known output, but none by his correspondents, unless we count the poignant one from his father (Abram Belo) quoted in the introduction: "Wright me. A ledder. Still I am the Head of all of U. Signed, Pa." (xii)

Omission of Bellow's interlocutors is a pity, the more so when Bellow alludes (as in writing to Cynthia Ozick in 1988) to "your beautiful letter" (450).[2] The reason why Taylor entirely omits correspondents' letters is likely the reason why they are omitted by most editors of writers' letters: you save yourself much time and labor. This is not because of the difficulty of finding them—if you have access to a writer's papers, you will likely find there hundreds of letters from his correspondents—but the enormous difficulty of securing permission to publish them. A letter is legally the property of the person who writes it or heirs and executors, not its recipient.

Taylor's introduction to the *Letters* is fine, his chronology and index excellent, his annotation adequate but quirky. In so ambitious book, there are bound to be errors, as in Taylor's very last sentence, where he thanks Bellow "for the privilege of spending each afternoon of the last three years with him" (558). Bellow died in 2005, five years before the book's publication.

Bellow, like most first-rank American-Jewish writers, resented being labeled an American-Jewish writer. I. B. Singer (whom Bellow made instantly famous by translating "Gimpel the Fool" into English) appears at first to be an exception to the rule; Singer *was* willing to be called a Jewish writer, so long as he was not called a Yiddish one, even though he wrote almost exclusively in Yiddish. (Bellow's translation had, ironically, indeed changed him from a Yiddish writer into a modernist American one.) In 1969, Bellow expressed his irritation with the American-Jewish label in a now famous quip: "This tendency to turn Malamud, Roth, and me into the Hart, Schaffner & Marx of American literature is ridiculous."[2] Disavowal of the "Jewish writer" label was to some extent the literary version of that distinctly Jewish form of parochialism known as "universalism." But it also expressed Bellow's resistance to being conscripted for Jewish ethnic vanity or accused (by such resentfully jealous anti-Jewish types as Truman Capote or Leslie Fiedler) of Jewish conspiracy. In an angry letter of June 1960, Bellow scolded Fiedler: "What is this 'marketable' Jewishness you talk about? And who are these strange companions on the bandwagon that plays *Hatikvah*? . . . What you think you see so clearly is not to be seen. It isn't there. No big situations, no connivances, no Jewish scheme produced by Jewish Minds. Nothing. What an incredible *tsimis* you make of nothing! You have your own realities, no one checks you and you go on and on. You had better think matters over again, Leslie. I'm dead serious" (197).

Still, even if Bellow was not an American-Jewish writer, everyone has to start somewhere. And how had Bellow begun? Perhaps as a *Chicago*-American writer. He first gained acclaim (and revolutionized American prose) with *The Adventures of Augie March* (1953), which opens thus: "I am an American, Chicago born—Chicago, that somber city—and go at things as I have taught myself, free-style . . ." Over forty years later, in a 1996 letter, he placed himself in relation to such Chicago icons as Carl Sandburg and Studs Terkel. "I've always liked Studs. We grew up in the same Chicago neighborhood . . . Humboldt Park. . . . [But] Studs's Chicago certainly was not mine. His Chicago was mythical. . . . A convenient way to describe it is to refer you to Carl Sandburg. Sandburg had his gifts as a poet, but he was also a gifted advertising man. . . . The image of Chicago they held up to the world was stylized. It was The People. Yes! Populism was the source of their mythology. It was not necessary for them to wonder how to describe any phenomenon because they had ideological ready-mades, cutouts, stereotypes, etc. Poets and street-corner orators can make use of slogans, but slogans will not do for writers" (526).[3] Seeing Chicago as it really was proved crucial to Bellow's worldview, but in an unexpected way: "There is some kind of advantage in the roughness of a place like Chicago, of not having any illusions either." Among those advantages was a clear-eyed view of the far greater shortcomings of European civilization: "Europe is not the Great Good Place for me," he wrote in a letter of late 1949 from Paris. French intellectuals, for example, "understood less about . . . left-wing politics than I had understood as a high-school boy," as for New Yorkers: "old-time Chicagoans . . . had fuller or, if you prefer, richer emotions" (92, xxv).[4]

Disavowal of the Hart–Schaffner–Marx label did not keep Bellow away from distinctly Jewish subjects, or indeed from returning often to the question of what constitutes a Jewish literary language. In his introduction to the anthology *Great Jewish Short Stories* (1963), he recounted his 1960 meeting in Jerusalem with the great Hebrew writer S. Y. Agnon. "While we were drinking tea, he asked me if any of my books had been translated into Hebrew. If they had not been, I had better see to it immediately, because, he said, they would survive only in the Holy Tongue. His advice I assume was only half serious. This was his witty way of calling my attention to a curious situation. I cited Heinrich Heine as an example of a poet who had done rather well in German. 'Ah,' said Mr. Agnon, 'we have him beautifully translated into Hebrew. He is safe.'"[3] Bellow was amused, but not convinced—even though, at some level, he too recognized that Hebrew was not only the Holy, but also the Eternal, language.

Mr. Sammler's Planet (1970), winner (like both the aforementioned novels) of the National Book Award, confronted the Holocaust, and *To Jerusalem and Back* (1976) dealt with Israel, especially its literary and political culture. Bellow took a keen interest in the work of other members of the firm—Bernard Malamud and Philip Roth—as well as the younger, female partner: Cynthia Ozick. In all three he found what he called "the real thing" in fiction, though he was not bashful about criticizing shortcomings, such as Roth's softness on Stalinism in *I Married a Communist*: "When I landed in Paris in 1948 I found that the intellectual leaders (Sartre, Merleau-Ponty, etc.) remained loyal [to Communism] despite the Stalin sea of blood. Well, every country, every government has *its* sea, or lake, or pond. Still Stalin remained *the* hope—despite the clear parallel with Hitler.... The reason lay in the hatred of one's own country. Among the French it was the old confrontation of 'free spirits,' or artists, with the ruling bourgeoisie. In America it was the fight against the McCarthys... that justified the Left, the followers of Henry Wallace, etc.... If you opposed the CP you were a McCarthyite, no two ways about it" (540).

The only one of the firm to whom Bellow wrote about Jewish as well as distinctly literary matters was Ozick. The earliest letter to her published by Taylor, dated July 19, 1987, expresses Bellow's sense of literary affinity with Ozick:

> I know you through your books, which I always read because they are written by the real thing. There aren't too many real things around. (A fact so well-known that it would be tedious to elaborate on it.) You might have been one of the dazzling virtuosi.... I might have done well in that line myself if I hadn't for one reason or another set my heart on being one of the real things. Life might have been easier in the literary concert-hall circuit. But Paganini wasn't Jewish.[4] (438)

Uttering that word leads Bellow to observe that "although we have never discussed the Jewish question... and would be bound to disagree (as Jewish discussants invariably do), it is certain that we would, at any rate, find each other Jewish enough." The particular aspect of that question which Bellow and Ozick were now discussing in their letters was why Jewish intellectuals, and especially Jewish writers, had failed to respond (or even attend) to the Holocaust, the systematic destruction of European Jewry.

Here is Bellow responding to what we can safely assume was Ozick's accusation:

> It's perfectly true that 'Jewish Writers in America' (a repulsive category!) missed what should have been for them the central event of their time, the destruction of European Jewry. I can't say how our responsibility can be assessed. We (I speak of Jews now and not merely of writers) should have reckoned more fully, more deeply with it. Nobody in America seriously took this on and only a few Jews elsewhere (like Primo Levi) were able to comprehend it all. The Jews as a people reacted justly to it. So we have Israel, but in the matter of higher comprehension ... there were no minds *fit* to comprehend. And intellectuals ... are trained to expect and demand from art what intellect is unable to do. All parties then are passing the buck and every honest conscience feels the disgrace of it. I was too busy becoming a novelist to take note of what was happening in the Forties. I was involved with 'literature' and given over to preoccupation with art, with language, with my struggle on the American scene, with claims for recognition of my talent or, like my pals of the *Partisan Review*, with modernism, Marxism, New Criticism, ... with anything except the terrible events in Poland. Growing slowly aware of this unspeakable evasion I didn't even know how to begin to admit it into my inner life. Not a particle of this can be denied. (438–39)

At first this strikes the reader as a rare confession of guilt from a member of a fraternity famous for passing the buck; we are likely to think that Bellow deserves credit for making it, and Ozick for provoking it. But Ozick herself, in a *New Republic* review essay on the letters in March 2011, argued that, in fact, there was no "unspeakable evasion" and Bellow's "I was too busy becoming a novelist" apologia struck a false note. She recalled the biographical facts: in 1948, Bellow and Anita Goshkin, a social worker who became his first wife, went to live in Paris. There she worked with the American Jewish Joint Distribution Committee, which helped Holocaust survivors to repair their shattered lives. How could Bellow *not* have learned from her, perhaps every day, about "the terrible events in Poland"? Bellow was, Ozick infers from the data available, at once too severe upon himself—he did see and he did know—and too lenient: his (relatively) early awareness of the death camps "here fades into the metaphorical abstraction of 'a crime so vast that it brings all Being into Judgment.'"[5]

Notes

1. *Saul Bellow: Letters*, ed. Benjamin Taylor (New York: Viking Penguin, 2010). Subsequent references to this work will be given in parentheses within the text.
2. James Atlas, *Bellow: A Biography* (New York: Random House, 2000), 290.
3. *Great Jewish Short Stories*, ed. Saul Bellow (New York: Dell, 1963), 14–15.
4. Bellow's fear of being turned into a traveling virtuoso surfaced early in his career, as in the following letter of April 9, 1953 (not in Taylor's collection) to Robert B. Heilman: "*Augie*'s coming out in September. By December I'll be looking for asylum, if Ralph Ellison's experience is a common one. You write a book and you become a sort of radio and book-panel trained seal."—*Robert B. Heilman: His Life in Letters*, ed. Edward Alexander, Richard J. Dunn, and Paul Jaussen (Seattle: University of Washington Press, 2009), 277.
5. Cynthia Ozick, "Lasting Man," *New Republic*, March 3, 2011, 13–25.

Lublin Before It Became Majdanek: Jacob Glatstein's Autobiography

> We received the Torah on Sinai/and in Lublin we gave it back./Dead men don't praise God,/the Torah was given to the living./And just as we all stood together/at the giving of the Torah,/so did we all die together at Lublin.
> —"Dead Men Don't Praise God," by Jacob Glatstein[1]

Jacob Glatstein may be the only major writer of the twentieth century better known (at least until now) by another writer's fictional representation of himself than in his own person and words. Widely respected, especially among Yiddish readers, for a powerful body of Holocaust poetry like the passage quoted above, he appears in Cynthia Ozick's satirical but affectionate story "Envy; or, Yiddish in America" (first published in *Commentary* in November 1969) as a Yiddish poet named Edelshtein. Unlike his rival Ostrover, modeled on Isaac Bashevis Singer, who only *writes* in Yiddish (and, in Glatstein's view, writes mainly unpleasant stories of horror and eroticism), Edelshtein *believes* in it. In the wake of the Holocaust, Yiddish, the *mameloshen* or everyday language of a majority of Hitler's victims, had, in Glatstein's view, replaced Hebrew as the Jews' *loshen koydesh* (holy tongue). By 1948, Hebrew was an everyday language in Israel, used by peddlers of unkosher meat in Tel Aviv, while Yiddish had become the holy tongue of martyrdom, demanding perpetuation: "In Talmud," says Edelshtein, "if you save a single life it's as if you saved the world. And if you save a language? Worlds maybe. Galaxies. The whole universe."[2]

Glatstein was no less eloquent on the crucial place of Yiddish in the aftermath of the Holocaust. In an interview of 1955, he told Abraham Tabachnik that "the obligation of a Yiddish poet today is to seek a place in that circle of . . . Jewishly responsible human beings, who, through art, want to express, to become a voice, a tongue for our generation. The Yiddish poet must become the aesthetic chronicler of what happened, and he must fix it for all time. In comparison with what we have hitherto regarded as poetry, the responsibility of a Yiddish poet today . . . is a fearsome responsibility."[3] This made Glatstein all the more bitter about the fact that he, one of the last defenders of the Yiddish word and the major post-Holocaust Yiddish literary figure in America, was obliged to know the poetry of W. H. Auden but Auden was under no obligation to read his, or even to know of his existence.

The Glatstein Chronicles[4] (edited with a superb introduction by Ruth Wisse), a hybrid of autobiography and fiction first published in Yiddish, comprises two novellas describing Glatstein's return in 1934, after twenty years' absence, from America to Lublin, Poland to visit his dying mother. The first volume, entitled *Ven Yash iz geforn*, appeared in Yiddish in 1937, the second, *Ven Yash iz gekumen*, in 1940. Book One, now entitled *Homeward Bound*, has been finely translated by Maier Deshell, former editor of the Jewish Publication Society (and winner of the Leviant Prize in Yiddish Studies for his translations); Book Two, now called *Homecoming at Twilight*, was translated by the late Norbert Guterman in 1962. A projected third volume, which would have described a postwar return to Lublin, never appeared because postwar Lublin had for Jews become what it is in "Dead Men Don't Praise God": the nearby killing center called Majdanek.

In 1934, one year into Hitler's rule and what Lucy Dawidowicz named "The War Against the Jews," Glatstein (fictionalized as "Yash") and his fellow-travelers were sailing to Europe on a British ship. Katherine Anne Porter's famous novel *Ship of Fools* (1962) was set in 1931 aboard a ship headed to Germany, and there are some striking similarities between the two books.

Although filial duty is the motive for Glatstein's trip, he does not hold back from conversations with his fellow-passengers. From them we learn that the narrator writes for a Yiddish newspaper, that his poetry shows tendencies both erotic and nationalistic, that he sides with religious Jews in their skirmishes with Bundists, Bolsheviks, and other socialists who threaten Jewish unity more than Christian proselytizers do (and are as prone to violence as Gentile soldiers). Unlike those who now think that "loving Yiddish" requires hating Israel, Glatstein admired Zionism.[5] Yash's own heroes are literary figures such as Sholom Aleichem and Haim Nachman Bialik, "the greatest Jewish poet since Yehuda Halevi" (141).

The ship is well-supplied with fools, especially the Jewish sort. Prominent among them is "a Dutch Jew, pure and simple, a descendant of generations of Dutch Jews." He is little concerned with the rise of Hitler, which he blames on the *ostjuden*, who "always attract attention to themselves"; he imputes Jewish problems in Holland to "the affliction of Zionism, which [is] spreading among the youth like an epidemic" (30). Several passengers sing the praises of "the brave new world of the USSR" (137), where Jew-hatred has (so they believe) vanished, a great experiment is in process, and humanity is being reborn in collectivist test tubes. Others worry not so much about the rise of Hitler or other political menaces but about Glatstein himself, "a writer over there who's eavesdropping on every word you say [in order to] write about you" (93). That writer is obsessed by an eerie foreboding about things to come: "In twenty-five years such travelers returning to pay respects to the graves of forefathers will have disappeared. . . . The familiar Poland will have died, and with it the longing or the hatred for that Poland. There will be tourists, but no one going home to see a dying mother or father, or to mourn dead parents" (137).

Volume Two leaps over the details of Glatstein's mother's funeral to his last days in Europe prior to returning to New York. In the manner of Thomas Mann's *The Magic Mountain* (1924), which had recently been published in a Yiddish translation by Singer, Glatstein gathers his Jews into a resort-sanatorium, located near Lublin. (Aharon Appelfeld would later, in 1980, use the same device in *Badenheim 1939*.) As one character says: "Nearly all the guests in this resort are sick. I'd say nine out of ten . . ." Many seek a cure for "arteriosclerosis," which is elusive because "in this resort . . . the word is used in a different sense, to signify a hardening of the brain" (195). Several are consumed by resentment of their brethren who have abandoned their families for the promised land of America. They entrust Yash (Glatstein) with such charming messages as: "If you see my brother, who is ashamed of his own flesh and blood, tell him that I hope he falls from the highest cliff" (270).

Yet many of these sick Jews, unlike Mann's doomed Europeans, have rich blood, powerful personalities, and prophetic potentiality for intellectual heroism. Prominent among them is a sixteen-year-old Chassid who gives vivid reports of his discussions with the ghosts of heretics Sabbatai Zevi and Jacob Frank. Brazenly immodest, he lays claim to a majestic intellect that has mastered "all of Jewish literature" and aspires to a science of the sciences that integrates all branches of knowledge: "We must do away with Gentile forms. A Jewish creation must be everything—poetry, prose, philosophy, drama, psychology, astronomy, epigrams—everything. We have no use for neat little compartments. We must be a creative encyclopedia" (286).

Even more striking among the sanatorium's residents is Steinman, an elderly German-trained historian who survived a pogrom, and whose personal impressions of the diverse vitality of Jewish intellectual life at the turn of the century would be the high point of this book, were they not overshadowed by his premonitions of the looming "extermination." Anyone who doubts that at least some Jews were fully aware of the genocidal intentions of Germans and their sympathizers when World War II began should attend closely to this passage published in 1940. "Yes," says Steinman, "they want to destroy us, nothing less. Yes, to destroy us. For instance, take me—I am a patriotic Pole. And yet they'd destroy me too. They want to exterminate us, purely and simply." But why, asks his interlocutor, one Finkel: surely there must be a reason. "Why?" replies an exasperated Steinman, and (in a classic utterance) answers as follows:

> For the Sabbath. . . . They hate us for observing the Sabbath, and they hate us for violating the Sabbath. They hate pious Jews, and they hate freethinkers who eat lobster. They hate our capitalists and they hate our beggars, they hate our reactionaries and they hate our radicals, those who earn their bread and those who die three times a day from starvation. . . . Sometimes the ringleader is called Pharaoh, sometimes Torquemada, and sometimes Hitler. . . . (226)

Steinman tells the guests of the (quixotic) efforts by Israel Hildesheimer and Heinrich Graetz to "reform" the spiritual life of Polish Jewry on the German model. He gives a withering critique of the assimilationist ideas of Jacob Gordin, whose "bloodless new Judaism," encapsulated in the slogan "Be a Jew at home, and a man in the street," flourished—until Jewish blood flowed in pogroms. He calls Jewish life in the 1880s "a sorry spectacle" until "suddenly a new light dawned in our exile" (238): Theodor Herzl. Steinman's impassioned account of the first Zionist congress in 1897 and being inspired by Herzl and Nordau to preach Zionism in crowded tailors' and shoemakers' synagogues moves one of the guests to say that "It's to Paradise you have just taken us." His story reminds us that Israel was created not *because* of the Holocaust, which destroyed the most Zionist-inclined Jews in the world, but in spite of it.

The book's crucial autobiographical segment is Glatstein's account of his education, which pursued the ideals of Haskalah, the Hebrew Enlightenment. Whereas I. B. Singer recalled that his father accused all secular writers, *especially* Yiddish and Hebrew ones, of leading Jews to heresy via "sweetened poison,"[6] Glatstein's secular teacher Goldblat "never tried to diminish what I learned at cheder, [but] added to it." Moreover, Glatstein loved Goldblat's lessons because they "had no relation whatever to plans for a career, they had no purpose at all" (305). Thus did Glatstein absorb, in a profoundly Jewish setting, the meaning of Aristotle's distinction between liberal and servile knowledge, that of the free man seeking escape from ignorance, and that of the slave, pursuing utility.

But these Enlightenment ideals, like Polish Jewry itself, would be turned to dust and ashes in the Holocaust. Glatstein repudiated them all in a bitter poem of 1938: "Good night, wide world,/big stinking world,/Not you but I slam shut the gate./With a long gabardine,/ with a fiery yellow patch,/ . . . I'm going back to the ghetto . . . to my crooked streets, humped lanterns,/my sacred pages, my Bible, /my Gemorra."[7]

Notes

1. *The Selected Poems of Jacob Glatstein*, trans. Ruth Whitman [from Yiddish] (New York: October House, 1972).
2. Ozick has often denied that the character Edelshtein was based on Glatstein, insisting that she really had the internecine squabbles of the American Hebrew poets in mind, but nobody, least of all Glatstein, has believed her.
3. A. Tabachnik, "A Conversation with Jacob Glatstein," *Yiddish* (Summer 1973): 41. (This interview was taped in 1955.)
4. Jacob Glatstein, *The Glatstein Chronicles* (New Haven, CT and London: Yale University Press, 2010). Subsequent references to the book will be given in parentheses in the text.
5. See, for example, his statement of 1955: "We stand before a divine revelation, a revelation with so much divine destruction and so much divine redemption, and we see it happening before our eyes, the miracle of our times. And we see a Jewish people that has more right on its side than any other people in the world today. Nor was there ever a people at any time in the history of the world that was more sinned against. Every living Jew had a father burned or a mother killed. Such a people has great responsibilities. It has an unforeseen new mission."—"A Conversation with Jacob Glatstein,"

40. Volume Two of *The Glatstein Chronicles* was not the writer's only book of 1940 about the predicament of European Jewry facing the Holocaust. He also published in that year *Emil un Karl*, a novel set in Vienna during the early days of the destruction process. It has been translated into English by Jeffrey Shandler as *Emil and Karl* (New Milford, CT: Roaring Book Press, 2006).

6. Joel Blocker and Richard Elman, "An Interview with Isaac Bashevis Singer," *Commentary* 36 (November 1963): 368.

7. See note 1 above.

Abba Kovner: Partisan, Poet, Curator, Avenger

My place of work is a wooden hut between the graveyard and the children's house. There I am writing something that has no beginning and no end. But if there is a central thread that goes through the empty pages, it is the leitmotif of those who survived, those who were destroyed, and those who come after them.
—Abba Kovner, March 7, 1975[1]

Abba Kovner, ghetto resistance commander (at age twenty-five) of Jewish partisans in Vilna and the forests during World War II, leading figure in the postwar *Brichah* movement that brought the remnant of European Jewry to Palestine, Givati Brigade information officer in Israel's War of Independence, major Hebrew poet, founder-designer of several Jewish museums, was at the storm-center of Jewish history from 1939 to 1949, a decade that determined (his critics alleged over-determined) his subsequent nearly four decades in Israel. Yet most Americans, including American Jews, first became aware of him in the early 1960s as a prominent figure in Hannah Arendt's *Eichmann in Jerusalem*. In reporting on the 1961 trial in Jerusalem, this haughtiest of German Jews reluctantly conceded that a segment of Kovner's testimony provided the greatest "dramatic moment" of the whole trial. He told the story of a German officer named Anton Schmidt who had helped the Jewish partisans, including Commander Kovner, with forged papers and military trucks; moreover, Kovner emphasized, Schmidt "did not do it for money." Those two minutes of Kovner's testimony, the first and last about a *German* in the entire trial, were "like a sudden burst of light in the midst of impenetrable, unfathomable darkness" and prompted Arendt to think "how utterly different everything would be today in . . . all countries of the world, if only more such stories could have been told."[2]

This glimpse of Kovner may have given Arendt's readers the impression that he was an early promoter of the (mischievously misleading) myth that World War II Europe was teeming with Righteous Gentiles. In fact nothing could be farther from the truth—either about that myth or Kovner's promotion of it. At the end of World War II, Kovner alienated many Jews by devoting himself not only to rescue but to revenge. From August 1945 to December 1947, he thought of little else but his plan "to kill six million Germans" because "the idea that Jewish blood can be shed without reprisal must be erased from the memory of mankind."[3] This plan, which involved poisoning Germany's water supply, was usually called *nakam* (vengeance) by Kovner. Like every other aspect of his life, it is fully described in Dina Porat's fine book. She is at once biographer and historian, with a vision at times microscopic, probing Kovner's inner world, at times telescopic, surveying the larger world that he inhabited and also shaped. Originally published in Hebrew in 2000, and now available in Elizabeth Yuval's translation, her book is for English-speaking readers the most important point of entry into Kovner's world since Shirley Kaufman's book of poetic translations, *A Canopy in the Desert* (University of Pittsburgh Press, 1973).

Kovner was the Jewish embodiment of Walt Whitman's creed: "Do I contradict myself?/Very well then, I contradict myself, /I am large, I contain multitudes." In his famous speech of December 31, 1941, by which time thousands of Lithuanian Jews had already been murdered—either in random killings or systematic depopulation by mass shootings in Ponary, a desolate village ten kilometers away—Kovner exhorted members of Vilna's Zionist youth groups to join what would become the first Jewish resistance group in Europe. "Let us not go like lambs to the slaughter. . . . Better to fall in the fight for human dignity than to live at the mercy of the murderers!" But when the image of European Jews passively going like cattle to slaughter became a cliché of small Jewish minds in Israel and America, Kovner felt obliged to declare, repeatedly: "I never thought a woman who had her child taken out of her arms had gone like a sheep to the slaughter."[4] Indeed, the separation of a mother from her child was the unresolved contradiction in Kovner's own life. When he ordered the headquarters of the Vilna resistance sealed off, his mother fell against the gate and asked her son in terror whether she should remain in Vilna or flee with him into the forests: "And I, the commander of the ghetto fighters, could not look into her eyes as I answered, 'Mother, I don't know!' And so to this very day I don't know whether I am worthy of the honor of a ghetto resistance fighter, or the curse of a son who abandoned his mother and did not go with her on her last road."[5]

When World War II ended, Kovner was fiercely critical of Jews who wanted to rebuild Jewish life in the continent that had just spat them out: Jews, he insisted, should not settle in a graveyard.[6] When he returned to the liberated—and destroyed—Vilna, he found amidst the ruins only the eastern wall of the old synagogue, and on it an ancient inscription with a modern message: "Lift up the miracle-banner for the ingathering of our exiles."[7] Yet when he came to Israel he redirected his anger at Israelis who were at once ignorant and contemptuous of the Jewish Diaspora, who believed in what he derided as the "infantile" myth of "It starts with me," and failed to understand that there is no Jewish future without rootedness in the past. He believed, passionately, in the Zionist principle of "negation of the Diaspora," but founded and organized a now famous Tel Aviv museum called Beit Hatefutsot (House of the Diaspora), dedicated to the proposition that Diaspora Jews were a dispersed, but not a dismembered, people. He had the richest, most integrative imagination of any Israeli writer; he joined Israel with Diaspora, present with past, the huge brown leather volumes of the Talmud which he took from the great Jewish library of Vilna with the life-preserving sandbags he had made out of them. This synthesizing imagination was never more evident than in his two major books of 1967: *The Seventh Day*, his conversations with soldiers about the recently concluded Six Days' War, and the ambitious poem *My Little Sister*, in which he confronted the central fact of his life: the half-dead, half-crazed girl from Ponary's mass grave.

Kovner was a man of paradoxes. He was a lifelong member of the dogmatically left-wing and atheist Zionist movement Hashomer Hatzair and the Mapam Party, but he rejected the movement's commitment to international class solidarity in favor of his overriding concern, the survival of the Jewish people. In trying to be a bridge between secular and religious Jews, he suffered the fate that bridges always do: he was stepped on. Gershom Scholem's wife Fania (sent by her husband from Rehavia in Jerusalem to evaluate Beit Hatefutsot) reported disparagingly that Kovner's museum, which stresses the centrality of Jewish religion, was "a synagogue built by atheists."[8] His ostensibly secular conception of literature had a distinctly religious element. He was fond of pointing out that in classical Hebrew there was no single word for literature: rather, it was called *chayyim she-bi-khtav*, life in writing. (He once scolded me roundly for foolishly using the word "kotev" instead of "sofer" for "writer." "A journalist," he bristled, "is not a writer.") Ever "a faction of one, a born *misnagid*,"[9] Kovner also repudiated Mapam's idolatrous worship of the Soviet Union. In Vilna, from June 1940, he had faced the choice between "life imprisonment among the Soviets and the death sentence handed out by the Germans."[10] He had seen and experienced enough of Soviet brutality, Jew-hatred, and cynicism in World War II to know better.

Kovner was a man of great, almost prophetic vision and prescience. As a young man in Vilna, his imagination had been captured by a little girl who had nearly died, and yet lived. She was one of the 47,000 Jews taken from Vilna to the shooting pits of Ponary. Incredibly, she managed to crawl out from among the thousands of dead and dying bodies to tell her story. Like countless other survivor-witnesses whom we now know from the history and literature of the Holocaust, she was believed by nobody—except for Abba Kovner. He did not suffer from the gullibility that *disbelieves* everything, and so he became probably the first person to declare as fact the planned destruction of all European Jewry. He organized armed resistance not because he expected victory, but because he instinctively knew that the apparently futile struggle against the Nazis (and their collaborators) in Vilna and Warsaw would have its effect not in Europe but in *Eretz Yisrael* because nothing that is done for the sake of justice is, in the long run, practically useless: "Israel was born in the last bunker of the ghetto."[11] He also began, planned, and provided the impetus for the exodus of European Jewry to the Land of Israel.

Yet *realpolitik* was never his strong card. Once, when he and I were arguing about "the Palestinian problem," he said: "How can I, as a member of the Jewish people, deny a homeland to another people?" But then—to my astonishment—he added: "Of course, if even a single gun or dagger is smuggled into the Palestinian state, we should immediately reoccupy." Nevertheless, what for many years seemed the most radical of all his ventures, the pursuit of vengeance against Germany, was based on a foreboding that now seems far less absurd than it did sixty years ago. He believed that vengeance was not only repayment for the past but also a warning for the future. Without it there would be a second Holocaust. When he learned of the existence of atomic weapons, he wanted them for Israel, in order to put the world on notice that "those who survived Auschwitz could destroy the world. Let them know that! That if it ever happens again, the world will be destroyed."[12] As the international noose today tightens around Israel's throat, those words may seem less extreme than they once did.

Perhaps the ultimate paradox of Kovner's life was that he was an imperious, commanding personality—critics said he "acted like Napoleon" and admirers typically recalled how "needless to say, we took our orders from Abba Kovner"[13]—but also a man content to paint walls, unclog drains, and wait on tables in his kibbutz. Indeed, the renowned partisan, poet, and golden-tongued orator was cleaning tables when my wife and I first met him at Ein Hachoresh many years ago. One is therefore tempted to address Kovner's ghost as Wordsworth addressed another great poet (John Milton): "Thou hadst a voice whose sound was like the sea . . . and yet thy heart/The lowliest duties on herself did lay."

Notes

1. Speech at an international conference on "The Holocaust—A Generation After." Quoted in *New York Post*, March 7, 1975.
2. *Eichmann in Jerusalem: A Report on the Banality of Evil* (New York: Viking, 1963), 210–11.
3. Dina Porat, *The Fall of a Sparrow: The Life and Times of Abba Kovner*, trans. Elizabeth Yuval (Stanford, CA: Stanford University Press, 2010), 212.
4. Interview in *New York Times*, March 6, 1975.
5. Quoted in *New York Times* article of March 4, 1975 on aforementioned NYC Holocaust conference.
6. Porat, *Fall of a Sparrow*, 196.
7. "A First Attempt to Tell," 32, of the typescript of an unpublished English translation of a speech Kovner made in 1944, in a synagogue in Vilna, on the liberation of Vilna by the Russians. The speech was published in Yiddish in *Yiddishe Kultur* in 1946.
8. Porat, *Fall of a Sparrow*, 293.
9. Ibid., 264.
10. Ibid., 19.
11. Ibid., 281.
12. Ibid., 236.
13. Ibid., 153, 181.

Ashamed Jews:
The Finkler Question

When a man can no longer be a Jew, he becomes a Zionist.
—a character named Yudka in "The Sermon,"
by Haim Hazaz (1942)

I am a Jew by virtue of the fact that I am not a Zionist.
—a character named Kugle in *The Finkler Question*,
by Howard Jacobson (2010)

The Finkler Question is a profoundly serious comic novel. Seriousness, let us remember, is not the same as solemnity; it does not require pince-nez spectacles and grave demeanor. Howard Jacobson's primary subject is the English version of Jewish hatred of Israel, otherwise known as the antisemitism of Jews in its most recent incarnation. It is a serious subject because Jewish Israel-haters and Jewish "anorexics" (who wish the Jews to live without a body) play an enormously disproportionate role in the blackening of Israel's image and the relentless campaign to expel her from the family of nations. If they have not set it in motion, they have certainly accelerated a process that may turn out to be the antecedent of a second Holocaust within a single century. Such Jews have already made a large contribution to antisemitic agitprop and the raw violence consequent upon it in England. Jacobson presents both with a specificity, courage, and candor rare among Jewish novelists, although they had already been the subject of several books, most notably *The Resurgence of Antisemitism* (2006), by the philosopher and literary critic Bernard Harrison, and *Trials of the Diaspora* (2010) by literary critic and historian Anthony Julius.

At the novel's center stands a womanizing Gentile named Julian Treslove, formerly a programmer for the BBC (the butt of relentless and well-deserved derision throughout the novel) and then a double for various celebrities. When at school, he had befriended a Jew (the first he had ever known) named Samuel Finkler; both were students of the transplanted Czech Jew Libor Sevcik, who later became a celebrity journalist. Treslove came to think of Finkler as representing (although in ways he finds difficult to define) Jews in general, and it is this misapprehension that explains the novel's title: a "Finkler" is for Treslove a Jew, and *The Finkler Question* really means *The Jewish Question*. Partly because his own life has been a series of romantic misadventures, partly because he convinces himself that he has been mugged by a woman who thinks he is a Jew, and partly because he aspires to substitute the Jewish tragedy for his private farce, Julian aspires to (yet never does) become a Jew. The novel is full of his (often jejune) questions about what it means "to think Jewishly," to speak Jewishly, to eat Jewishly. But he also is puzzled—and one really should sympathize with him and with all the Gentiles he represents for their understandable befuddlement—by the fact that so many of the Jew-haters he has known are Jews: "I remember what anti-Semites they all were there [at the BBC], especially the Jews."[1]

Finkler, who studied moral philosophy at Oxford and has named two of his children after Kant (Immanuel) and Pascal (Blaise), has become rich and famous by publishing a series of self-help books of moral philosophy. Among the more delicious titles are: *The Existentialist in the Kitchen*, *The Little Book of Household Stoicism*, and *The Socratic Flirt: How to Reason Your Way into a Better Sex Life*. (The titles call to mind some of the writings of Alain De Botton, discussed elsewhere in this book. De Botton is another "proud" Jewish atheist and author of such "practical" manuals as "How Proust Can Change Your Life.") We enter the story shortly after Finkler has vaulted to still greater fame by concluding his appearance on the popular BBC program *Desert Island Discs* with the declaration that, "as a Jew," he was "ashamed," that is to say, ashamed of Israel (a word that he did not, however, allow to soil his lips, sticking to "Palestine," or even "Canaan"). For this gesture he is promptly rewarded with an invitation to join a group of "well-known theatrical and academic Jews" who offer to rename themselves "in honour of his courage in speaking out—Ashamed Jews." Flattered by the attention of (mostly third-rate) actors—for the professors' praise he cares as little as for "the prayers he had never said for his grandfather" (113–15)—he accepts, on the condition (quickly agreed to) that they slightly change their name to

ASHamed Jews to show off their contempt for Holocaust memory: "Holocaust fucking Holocaust" (291). (Jacobson's unfortunate addiction to this epithet is on the Gargantuan scale of Hollywood directors and other linguistically deprived and morally anemic types who believe people actually talk like this.)

"ASHamed Jews" is a wonderful comic invention, on a par with Philip Roth's Antisemites Anonymous in *Operation Shylock*. It produces (and is produced by) Jacobson's best writing:

> The logic that made it impossible for those who had never been Zionists to call themselves ASHamed Zionists did not extend to Jews who had never been Jews. To be an ASHamed Jew did not require that you had been knowingly Jewish all your life. Indeed, one among them only found out he was Jewish at all in the course of making a television programme in which he was confronted on camera with *who he really was*. In the final frame of the film he was disclosed weeping before a memorial in Auschwitz to dead ancestors who until that moment he had never known he'd had. 'It could explain where I get my comic genius from,' he told an interviewer for a newspaper, though by then he had renegotiated his new allegiance. Born a Jew on Monday, he had signed up to be an ASHamed Jew by Wednesday and was seen chanting 'We are all Hezbollah' outside the Israeli Embassy on the following Saturday. (138–39)

Readers unfamiliar with the current English scene may assume that Jacobson's comic triumph derives from his exaggeration of "reality." Is there actually a liberal rabbi in St. John's Wood who always wears a PLO scarf when riding his motorbike to shul every morning? Can there be a real-life model for Alvin Poliakov, who presides over an anticircumcision website called "ifnotnowwhen.com" which recounts his valiant struggle to reverse his circumcision and—for no extra charge—tells his readers how "sexual mutilation . . . is just one more of the countless offences against humanity [along with Zionism] to be laid at the gates of the Jews" (201). In fact, Jacobson exaggerates nothing; quite the contrary. To some extent, *The Finkler Question* is what the French call a *roman à clef*, a novel with a key in which the knowing reader is expected to identify, within the work, actual people or events. Thus most of Jacobson's English readers immediately recognized that Finkler's despicable confession of shame on *Desert Island Discs* exactly duplicated that of Miriam Margolyes, the pudgy little character actress, a few years earlier, and that the tearful comedian who discovered his "Jewishness" while making a TV program was

Stephen Fry, a stalwart of Jews for Justice for Palestinians. Among British precursors in the *roman a clef* genre are Thomas Love Peacock's *Nightmare Abbey* (1818) and Aldous Huxley's *Point Counter Point* (1928). But the more important literary point here is that the ancient task of literature is to begin with the actual world, which is far more fantastic than even the most imaginative writer can contrive, and try to make it more plausible, which is to say more in conformity with what Hannah Arendt, in the *Antisemitism* volume of *The Origins of Totalitarianism*, called "the wheedling voice of common sense." Thus, the novel's Holocaust-denying Israeli *yored* drummer is in fact based upon one Gilad Atzmon, who is better known in England for endorsing the ideology of the *Protocols of the Elders of Zion* and describing the burning of British synagogues as a "rational act" in retaliation for Israeli actions. Another of Jacobson's fictional inventions, the play called *Sons of Abraham*, which gets a standing ovation for its equation of "Gaza" with Auschwitz, is not quite as blatant in its deranged espousal of the blood libel as the actual (ten-minutes long) play upon which it is based: Caryl Churchill's highly popular 2009 monstrosity called *Seven Jewish Children—A Play for Gaza*, in which the aforementioned Margolyes appeared. (When, because of this, a Jewish nursing home in Australia withdrew its invitation to her to perform there, she was shocked, simply shocked, that anybody could consider a play showing Jews deliberately killing Arab babies and thirsting for their blood to be antisemitic.)

What is true of these secondary examples of apparent "exaggeration" in the book is still more striking in its primary conceit, the Jews of shame who blush for the existence of a Jewish state. Such displays have been a device of self-aggrandizement by Jewish Israel-haters (and not only in England) for many years. In 2003, the late Tony Judt, one of England's booby-trapped gifts to America, in an almost laughable display of insecurity and self-pity, petulantly complained that "non-Israeli Jews feel themselves once again exposed to criticism and vulnerable to attack for things they didn't do . . . The behavior of a self-described Jewish state affects the way everyone else looks at Jews."[2] In 2005, Jacqueline Rose, who appears in *The Finkler Question* as Tamara Krausz (for whom Zionism is a Coleridgean "demon lover" [230] and she its psychoanalyst), "appalled at what the Israeli nation perpetrated in my name," expressed the wish to live "in a world in which we did not have to be ashamed of shame" and looked forward to curing her shame-sickness by destroying its cause: Israel.[3] When, in the novel, she reaches the point of endorsing the old Christian belief that male Jews menstruate, Finkler's revulsion actually carries him to the other side of a public debate between the ashamed and unashamed Jews. Krausz-Rose is the book's most lurid example of Libor's generalization that "We [Jews] have become a sick people" (193).

These ashamed Jews are in many respects like the assimilated Jews of old, insisting that Jewish particularism, Jewish peoplehood, and a Jewish state constitute the sole obstacles to universal brotherhood and peace. But there is a difference. Whereas the motto of the assimilationists, as far back as the 1880s, was "Be a Jew at home and a man in the street," the motto of Jews ashamed of Israel is the opposite: "Be a man at home and a Jew in public." At every opportunity, the Jewish anti-Zionist who can no longer be a Jew at home now introduces his self-righteous and self-loving public display of outrage against Israel with "As a Jew . . ." But here too Jacobson, except for a hint or two, substitutes believable fiction for incredible reality: the introduction now, more often than not, is: "As the Jewish child [or grandchild] of Holocaust victims, I am ashamed of Israel and hope to see it boycotted, punished by sanctions, and removed from the family of nations."

The novel's most incisive and severe critic of Finkler and the Jews of shame in general is Finkler's wife Tyler—or rather her ghost, because she is already dead when the story begins. Finkler's bereavement binds him to Libor, who is also a widower, despite their (apparent) disagreement over Israel and blushing Jews. A convert (against her husband's wishes, of course) to Judaism, Tyler insists that she is the real Jew in their marriage because she knows the difference between culture and biology, religion and stupid ethnic vanity. She sees Finkler and his anti-Zionist comrades as "profoundly self-important" more than "profoundly ashamed"; she knows why Jews pray every morning that "we may never be put to shame"; for her Finkler and his comrades are "*shande* Jews," which is to say *shame* as in "disgrace . . . they brought shame" (270). It is she who must explain to the puzzled Treslove the grotesque and brazen fakery of anti-Zionists who insist that if Jews do not exist as "a light unto the nations" they do not deserve to exist at all (271).

Although nearly every part of this novel has its comic dimension, the single exception that tests the rule (and also Libor Sevcik) comes more than halfway into the story, and shocks all the more precisely *because* it is an exception. Libor agrees to meet with an old (in both senses of the term) girl friend of his named Emmy Oppenstein after a hiatus of half a century. As usual with Jacobson, whose sex obsession is on a par with Philip Roth's (and equally wearisome to readers who have long been freed from this mad and cruel master—sex, not Roth), we get a resume of their long-ago affair, with the usual speculation about who undressed whom, etc. But then, in the book's greatest dramatic moment, comes this:

> ... She told him, without tears, without false sentiment, that her twenty-two-year-old grandson had been stabbed in the face and blinded by an Algerian man who had shouted 'God is great' in Arabic, and 'Death to all Jews.'
>
> 'I'm very sorry,' Libor said. 'Did this happen in Algeria?'
>
> 'It happened here, Libor.'
>
> 'In London?'
>
> 'Yes, in London.'
>
> ... Libor had been lucky in love but in politics he was from a part of the world that expected nothing good of anybody. Jew-hating was back—of course Jew-hating was back. Soon it would be full-blown fascism, Nazism, Stalinism. These things didn't go away. There was nowhere for them to go to. They were indestructible, non-biodegradable. They waited in the great rubbish tip that was the human heart.
>
> It wasn't even the Algerian's fault in the end. He just did what history had told him to do. God is great ... kill all Jews. It was hard to take offence—unless, of course, the blinded boy was your child or grandson. (153–54)

The grandmother has arranged to meet Libor solely in order to ask him, as a one-time writer about show business luminaries, to speak out against the famous film director who declared that he "understood" why the Algerian blinded her grandson: "Because of Gaza, he says he understands why people hate Jews and want to kill them."

The moviemaker goes unnamed but he is almost certainly based upon Ken Loach. A Trotskyist, Loach collaborated with author Jim Allen to produce the "poisonously" (thus Arnold Wesker) antisemitic play *Perdition*, which depicted the Holocaust as the product of a Zionist–Nazi conspiracy. We do not learn until nearly the end of the book that Libor fails Emmy because he too had succumbed to the anti-Jewish tsunami, now so powerful in England that both the Jew

Finkler and the non-Jew Treslove discover that they have produced antisemitic sons. Libor's apparent Zionism had been no more than "lifeboat" Zionism, a place of refuge when Europe returned to its default ideology. By the time Emmy asks for his help against the moral desperadoes of England's artistic/learned classes, he has decided that the Jews must disappear: "I will have no more Jews." And he practices what he preaches, committing suicide in Eastbourne.

The Finkler Question is not quite the literary masterpiece that numerous reviewers have declared it to be. It is full of verbal tics, small jokes that are amusing when first told but become cloying by the fourth or fifth repetition, and resort to words (like "methodology") that usually betray a virgin mind seduced by the temptation of a few extra syllables into saying what the writer does not mean. Nevertheless, the work has what John Ruskin called "noble imperfection" and a great truth-telling power.

The last few pages of this *comic* novel include the following: the suicide of Libor; a somber gathering at his grave in London; the near lynching of a Sephardic Jewish boy in Regent's Park; the opening of a Museum of Anglo-Jewish Culture in St. John's Wood attended by twelve people, a greater number of anti-Israel demonstrators led by "the Jew in the PLO scarf," and watchful police; and a recitation of the *Kaddish*. The very English Jacobson appears to have adopted the wise slogan of his cross-channel neighbors: *Il faut rire pour ne pas pleurer*.

Notes

1. Howard Jacobson, *The Finkler Question* (New York: Bloomsbury, 2010), 162, 195. Subsequent references to this work will be given in parentheses in the text.
2. On Judt, see *The Jewish Divide over Israel: Accusers and Defenders*, ed. Edward Alexander and Paul Bogdanor (New Brunswick, NJ: Transaction Publishers, 2006), xv, 65–71.
3. On Rose, see Benjamin Balint's essay, "What Zionism Is Not," *Weekly Standard*, November 14, 2005, 37–39.

Daniel Deronda: "The Zionist Fate in English Hands" and "The Liberal Betrayal of the Jews"

In Chapter Seven of *The Modern Jewish Canon*, "The Zionist Fate in English Hands," Ruth Wisse veers slightly from her attempt to define the literary canon to a consideration of how well English literature has been able to admit the autonomy of modern Jewish people. Wisse limits her canon to Jewish writers who, whether they write in Yiddish, Hebrew, or some Gentile tongue, evince respect for the autonomy of Jewishness and the centrality of Jewish national experience. Their work must "attest to the indissolubility of the Jews," although not necessarily in a positive way. Another requirement for admission to Wisse's canon is that "in Jewish literature the authors or characters know and let the reader know that they are Jews." But here she announces that before considering how Jewish literature has dealt with the Zionist enterprise she will discuss two works by non-Jewish authors, George Eliot's *Daniel Deronda* (1876), "the classic of Zionism," and James Joyce's *Ulysses* (1922), "the classic of modernism," to discover "how Jews can, and cannot, survive the dilemma of English generosity."[1]

In the event, Wisse gives a low grade to Joyce and a very high one to George Eliot, whose novel (begun in 1874) she deems "the imaginative equivalent of the Balfour Declaration" (238), which in 1917 gave the British government's formal recognition of a historical Jewish claim to Palestine and so provided the basis for the Palestine Mandate given to Britain in 1920. One might also add that the novel anticipated the rationale for a Jewish state given in the same year by the most important Englishman of modern times, Winston Churchill: "If, as may well happen, there should be created in our own lifetime by the banks of the Jordan a Jewish State under the protection of the British Crown which might comprise three or four millions of Jews, an event will have occurred in the history of the world which would from every point of view be beneficial, and would be especially in harmony with the truest interests of the British Empire."[2]

Wisse did not raise the question of whether *Deronda* itself, by virtue of the fact that some of its characters do know and let the reader know they are Jews, belongs in the Jewish canon, even though written by a non-Jew who—with one notable exception—knew little from experience about Jews except for the deracinated ones who, then as now, frequented intellectual coteries. "Is it not," George Henry Lewes observed, "psychologically a fact of singular interest that she was never in her life in a Jewish family, at least never in one where Judaism was still a living faith and Jewish customs kept up? Yet the Jews all fancy she must have been brought up among them . . ."[3]

George Eliot as the celebrator of Jewish autonomy and indissolubility, and nearly an honorary Jew! Who that looked over her shoulder as she wrote her letters or diary entries in 1848 could have predicted this? At age twenty-nine, Mary Ann Evans (Eliot's real name), infuriated by the idea of "race fellowship" among Jews, which she thought she detected in Benjamin Disraeli's novel *Coningsby* (1844), told a friend that she was "almost ready to echo Voltaire's vituperation. I bow to the supremacy of Hebrew poetry, but much of their early mythology and almost all their history, is utterly revolting. Their stock has produced a Moses and a Jesus but Moses was impregnated with Egyptian philosophy, and Jesus is venerated and adored by us only for that wherein he transcended or resisted Judaism . . . Everything specifically Jewish is of a low grade." This being so, she could even ruminate about how "Extermination . . . seems to be the law for inferior races," including "even the Hebrew caucasian."[4]

Nevertheless, a mere twenty-eight years later the young Lithuanian Jew Eliezer ben-Yehuda was telling his friends that what they had derided as his "new heresy" of the rebirth of the people Israel, speaking its own language (Hebrew) in its own land was, in his view, being massively endorsed by the English novelist George Eliot, who had written of "a man who had a vision similar to my own." "After I had read the story a few times [!]," Ben-Yehuda wrote in his autobiography, "I went to Paris . . . to learn and equip myself there with the information needed for my work in the Land of Israel."[5]

And exactly one hundred years after Mary Ann Evans' Voltairean fulminations of 1848, the three main cities of the newly founded state of Israel—Jerusalem, Tel Aviv, and Haifa—all boasted a George Eliot Street. (None of this should be taken as confirmation of the absurdities of Edward Said, who in *The Question of Palestine* [1979] based his entire discussion of the origins of Zionism on Eliot's novel, to which he devoted six pages while ignoring Pinsker, Herzl, Smolenskin, Ahad Ha'am, Gordon, Syrkin, Jabotinsky, and Ben-Gurion.) The development of Eliot's Jewish sympathies was made possible by her turn, not taken until 1857, when she was almost thirty-eight, from discursive writing to fiction, at whose heart, she believed, was the capacity for imaginative sympathy. "If Art does not enlarge men's sympathies, it does nothing morally. I have had heart-cutting experience that opinions are a poor cement between human souls, and the only effect I ardently long to produce by my writings, is that those who read them should be better able to *imagine* and to *feel* the pains and the joys of those who differ from themselves in everything but the broad fact of being struggling erring human creatures."[6]

In 1858, she and Lewes, with whom she was by now living happily in sin, traveled to Prague, where she found that "the most interesting things" in the city were the Jewish burial ground (Alter Friedhof) and the old (Altneu) synagogue. The multitude of quaint tombs in the cemetery struck her as the existential realization of Jewish history, "the fragments of a great building ... shaken by an earthquake." But could these fragments still, as Ezekiel had foretold, live? Perhaps. "We saw a lovely dark-eyed Jewish child here, which we were glad to kiss in all its dirt. Then came the somber old synagogue, with its smoked groins, and lamp forever burning. An intelligent Jew was our cicerone and read us some Hebrew out of the precious old book of the law."[7]

But the real turning point in George Eliot's attitude toward "everything specifically Jewish" came in 1866, when she met Emanuel Deutsch, the Talmudic scholar born in Prussian Silesia and educated both by the University of Berlin in theology and by his rabbinic uncle in Talmud. He gave her weekly Hebrew lessons and also conveyed to her the excitement he felt upon visiting the Holy Land in 1869. When he saw Jews leaning against the Western Wall in prayer he thought less of the past than of the future, and expressed his conviction that the destiny of "the once proscribed and detested Jews ... is not yet fulfilled."[8] (*"Od lo avdah tikvateinu."*)

So intimate did the relationship between Deutsch and the novelist become that Eliot, during the years when her friend began to suffer terribly from the cancer that would eventually, in 1873, kill him, felt personally obligated to keep him from suicide. This she did, in part, by casting herself as "a fellow Houyhnhnm who is bearing the yoke with you" and who had herself (perhaps) once considered self-destruction. "I have been ailing and in the Slough of Despond too . . . [but] remember, it has happened to many to be glad they did not commit suicide, though they once ran for the final leap. . . ."[9]

Although it is generally supposed that Deutsch's vision of national revival first made itself felt in the character of Mordecai in *Daniel Deronda* (1876), there is evidence that, for whatever reasons, Eliot was being drawn toward the affirmation of a national idea some years earlier. One hint of the forces stirring within her appears in the famous Prelude to *Middlemarch* (1871–1872), the novel Eliot began to work on in 1867, the year after she met Deutsch. The Prelude's opening sentences allude to the way in which Spain's national identity was forged in an ostensibly religious struggle against Muslim Arabs, but they do so by briefly telling the story of Saint Theresa as a little girl, "walking forth one morning hand-in-hand with her still smaller brother, to go and seek martyrdom in the country of the Moors." Their children's hearts were "already beating to a national idea."[10]

Given the prominence of the "national idea" on the first page of the novel, one looks, but in vain, for its development in the nearly 900 pages of *Middlemarch*. The novel's heroine Dorothea Brooke yearns intensely for "something . . . by which her life might be filled with action at once rational and ardent; and since the time was gone by for guiding visions and spiritual directors, since prayer heightened yearning but not instruction, what lamp was there but knowledge?" (Chapter 10, 112–13) But since, unlike Theresa, she lives in the nineteenth rather than the sixteenth century, her yearning can only be satisfied (and, as it happens, not very well at all) in marriage. Fulfillment of a protagonist's larger spiritual ambitions was not to come until *Deronda*.

When she began *Middlemarch*, Eliot would also have been aware of a recently published novel dealing with Jewish–Christian relations called *Nina Balatka* (1867), by Anthony Trollope. Trollope concealed his authorship of the book, but gave a curious hint of it by naming its Jewish protagonist Anton Trendellsohn. Set in both the Christian and Jewish sections of Prague, including the very Altneu synagogue ("the oldest place of worship belonging to the Jews in Europe"[11] and the location for its most powerful scene) that had engaged Eliot's interest and sympathy, *Nina Balatka* can be linked, though by contrast as much as by likeness, to *Daniel Deronda*.[12]

Although Trollope displays at least as much knowledge and sympathy for an existing Jewish community as will be found in *Deronda*, he follows the convention of marrying his Jewish protagonist to the Christian heroine: Catholic Nina wins out (in part because she does not have black hair and dark eyes) over her Jewish rival Rebecca. The novel acknowledges that "the Jews of Prague were still subject to the isolated ignominy of Judaism" and that "In Prague a Jew was still a Pariah" (69) but also assumes that raw, violent Jew-hatred is a thing of the past—"In her time but little power was left to Madame Zamenoy to persecute the Trendellsohns other than that which nature had given to her in the bitterness of her tongue" (3–4). *Nina Balatka's* awareness of Jewish national aspirations in Palestine does not go beyond such comments as "most of us [Jews] are dark here in Prague. Anton says that away in Palestine our girls are as fair as the girls in Saxony" (10). So much for this Jewish hero's Zionism.

A good deal of what has come to be called the "Zionist part" of *Daniel Deronda* is actually no more than what the writer Avi Erlich calls "ancient Zionism," that is, traditional orthodox beliefs about the importance of the Holy Land in Jewish ethics and self-definition that may underlie political Zionism but could have been held (then) by many orthodox Jews who opposed political Zionism as itself a thinly veiled form of assimilation.[13] The book of Ezekiel, for example, promises that "I will take you from among the nations, and gather you out of all the countries, and will bring you into your own land" (Ezekiel 36:24). Nevertheless, there is a specifically political Zionist element in the novel, both in the few scenes where Mordecai holds forth and in Deronda's own aspirations and ideals. Here, for example, is Mordecai's proposal for a Jewish national revival, an expression of the idea that the Jews are dispersed but not disintegrated.

> Revive the organic centre: let the unity of Israel which has made the growth and form of its religion be an outward reality. Looking towards a land and a polity, our dispersed people in all the ends of the earth may share the dignity of a national life which has a voice among the peoples of the East and the West—which will plant the wisdom and skill of our race so that it may be, as of old, a medium of transmission and understanding.[14]

This is quite different from both the Christian Zionism of Victorian English Evangelicals who proposed the Jews' return to the Holy Land, the better to convert them to Christianity, and from that of Moses Montefiore, who wanted "the return of thousands of our brethren to the land of Israel" to better observe their own religion.[15]

Mordecai, who also resembles Emanuel Deutsch in being fatally ill, sets forth his ideas in the discussions at the "Hand and Banner" workingmen's club, discussions which are remarkable in their prescient foreshadowing of the modern war of ideas over the Jewish state. Two of Mordecai's antagonists, for example, sound very like Arnold Toynbee condemning Jews as a culturally degenerate historical "fossil" or like Tony Judt disparaging the state of Israel as an "anachronism" and the only impediment to a postnationalist world or like modern "progressive" Jews who believe that liberalism and Judaism are the same thing:

> "Whatever the Jews contributed at one time, they are a standstill people," said Lilly. "They are the type of obstinate adherence to the superannuated. They may show good abilities when they take up liberal ideas, but as a race they have no development in them." (Chapter 42, 590)

When Mordecai envisions a time when the Jews, no longer a dispersed people, "shall have a defence in the court of nations, as the outraged Englishman or American" (595), one thinks immediately of the rationale for the trial in Jerusalem of Adolf Eichmann—for "crimes against the Jewish people." Already the Zionist idea that the Jews should be *not* a chosen people but a normal one *k'chol ha-goyim*, like the Gentiles, in the sense of belonging to the family of nations, was being derided by those who believed that the era of nationality was (almost) at an end, a belief as chimerical in 1876 as it is today.

A good deal less prescient or sophisticated is the process whereby Daniel discovers his Jewish identity. Although reared as an English aristocrat, and believing himself to be of Spanish "blood," he finds himself drawn, by apparent accidents that prove to be inevitabilities, to other Jews. This movement of the novel, as Lionel Trilling acerbically complained in 1939,[16] shows Eliot's susceptibility to Victorian race-thinking (of the sort exhibited, for example, in Matthew Arnold's Oxford lectures *On the Study of Celtic Literature*). Indeed, Daniel is often asked by London Jews, within five minutes of meeting him, whether he belongs to their "race." He eventually discovers his Jewish identity, and not by looking down.[17]

Rather, in the novel's great ironic moment, Daniel hears his mother (whose melding of [Jewish] Jew-hatred with feminism is yet another prescient touch of George Eliot's) boast of how she (now turned Christian) saved him from his Jewish fate, or, as Daniel sees the matter, deprived him of his birthright. "And the bondage I hated for myself I wanted to keep you from. What better could the most loving mother have done? I relieved you from the bondage of having been born a Jew" (Chapter 51, 689). Wisse correctly observes that "though the book's thematic sympathies are not with the princess [Daniel's mother], Eliot invests her with the dramatic and intellectual powers to express this position better than it has ever been done in fiction."[18]

Daniel, once sure of his Jewish identity, offers a more specifically English rationale than Mordecai's for a Jewish national home: "restoring a political existence to my people, making them a nation again, giving them a national centre, such as the English have, though they too are scattered over the face of the globe" (Chapter 69, 875). Here Daniel raises the question of the relation between the potentiality of Jewish nationhood and the actuality (which is shown to be in a very dismal state in the novel) of English nationhood.

Eliot seems to have looked to the Jewish tradition, more specifically to the Zionist version of national renaissance, for revival of an idea brought to ruin—at least according to *Daniel Deronda*—in Victorian England by its system of dehumanized relations, epitomized in the treatment of Gwendolen by Grandcourt. In the famous fifteenth chapter of *Middlemarch*, Eliot had expressed her dissatisfaction with the English novel's endless obsession with "romance" and her intention to direct it toward a nobler subject, that of "vocation." She was, of course, not entirely successful in doing so; four romances are still at the heart of that novel, despite its profound exploration of one protagonist's calling to medicine, the "noblest of professions." But one senses Eliot's earnestness about changing the genre's direction in the way she baffled Victorian readers by keeping the novel's true heroine, Dorothea, and the novel's true hero, Dr. Lydgate, on quite separate romantic–marital tracks. Similarly, in *Deronda*, the romantic attraction between Daniel and Gwendolyn is overcome (on his part) by "vocation," except that Daniel is called not to medicine or to law but to the Jewish national idea.

Daniel's linkage of a yet unrealized Jewish national idea to a tarnished and desiccated English one also implicitly raises the by now endlessly discussed question of the relation between the "English" and the "Jewish" halves of the novel in which he appears. Eliot herself complained that readers "cut the book into scraps and talk of nothing in it but Gwendolen."[19]

Some of the hostility to what Henry James derided as the "Jewish" part of the novel, and later critics, especially English ones writing after 1948 (when the yishuv drove the British from Palestine), as the "Zionist" part derives from genuinely aesthetic motives or principles. H. M. Daleski, the Israeli critic (and soldier in the War of Independence), while arguing for the essential thematic unity of the novel, also observed that "the Gwendolen Harleth part must surely rank as among the best things George Eliot ever did, while the Jewish part has no mean claim to being among the worst."[20] Barbara Hardy also wrote in good faith when she criticized Eliot for suspending her characteristic critical irony and humor (exercised even at the expense of Dorothea Brooke) in presenting the relentlessly solemn Daniel.[21] Irving Howe, to whom Ruth Wisse attributed perfect pitch as a literary critic, and who could hardly be accused of hostility to Jewishness, objected that Daniel is "abundantly virtuous but only intermittently alive.... No wonder he comes to seem a mere figment of will or idea, a speechmaker without blood, a mere accessory to the prophetic Mordecai, the dying spokesman of Jewish rebirth."[22]

But there has always been another, less "aesthetic," far nastier, a priori hostility to the "Jewish/Zionist" element of the novel, and one that appears to foreshadow the fierce hostility of England's current liberal and learned classes to the state of Israel. In a now famous letter, Eliot wrote to her American friend Harriet Beecher Stowe in 1876:

> As to the Jewish element in *Deronda*, I expected from first to last in writing it that it would create much stronger resistance and even repulsion than it has actually met with. But precisely because I felt that the usual attitude of Christians toward Jews is—I hardly know whether to say more impious or more stupid when viewed in the light of their professed principles, I therefore felt urged to treat Jews with such sympathy and understanding as my nature and knowledge could attain to.... Can anything be more disgusting than to hear people called "educated" making small jokes about eating ham, and showing themselves empty of any real knowledge as to the relation of their own social and religious life to the history of the people they

think themselves witty in insulting? . . . I find men educated at Rugby supposing that Christ spoke Greek.[23]

To George Eliot's inner circle, that "Rugby" allusion might have called to mind her young admirer (and later to be husband) J. W. Cross, who had been educated at Rugby (and whose lack of Hebrew—he "knew little of *hiphil* and *huphal*"—she sometimes lamented). But to the general reader that letter, when it appeared, is more likely to have suggested the most famous of all Rugby figures, Dr. Thomas Arnold, whose fierce hostility to Jews has been discussed earlier in this book. Dr. Arnold, had he lingered in the world long enough to read *Daniel Deronda*, might have said of Daniel and his bride Mirah as they sail off to the Holy Land, "good riddance to them." No need to guess what Henry James said of the novel's Jewish protagonist, through one of his invented characters (one Pulcheria) in "Daniel Deronda: A Conversation": "I am sure Daniel had a nose, and I hold that the author has shown great pusillanimity in her treatment of it." But James' unpleasantness has no political dimension, as does that of the formidable liberal Leslie Stephen, father of Virginia Woolf, whose discussion of Daniel's Jewish quest, according to Eliot's biographer Frederick Karl, "borders on a barely-controlled anti-Semitism."[24]

Eliot's own critique of what Ruth Wisse would later call "the liberal betrayal of the Jews," (the subtitle of *If I Am Not for Myself* . . .) comes in her essay of 1878: "The Modern Hep! Hep! Hep!" In it Eliot observes that English liberals often seem keen to promote every nationalism except the Jewish one. The new crop of what she calls "anti-Judaic advocates" are "liberal gentlemen," who "belong to a party which has felt itself glorified in winning for Jews, as well as Dissenters and Catholics, the full privileges of citizenship, laying open to them every path to distinction." In this sense, they are far different from Dr. Arnold. But now, she says, they have been brought up short by the prospect of Jewish autonomy and the desire of (some) Jews to retain a culture and an inner world of their own. "Too late enlightened by disagreeable events," these liberal gentlemen now regret that they were mistaken and the foes of emancipation correct. They are eager to celebrate the dignity of populations of which they have never seen a single specimen—she cites as an instance the liberal glorification of "grim marriage customs of the native Australians"—but "sneer at the notion of a renovated national dignity for the Jews," and impatiently demand (as the youthful Mary Anne Evans had) the "complete fusion" of the Jews with the various peoples among whom they are dispersed.[25]

Lest there be any doubt that she is alluding not just to typically English social prejudices and snobbishness but to sanctified liberal doctrine, Eliot proposes to "nationalize" the sacred text of English individuality, John Stuart Mill's *On Liberty* (1859). "A modern book on Liberty has maintained that from the freedom of individual men to persist in idiosyncrasies the world may be enriched. Why should we not apply this argument to the idiosyncrasy of a nation, and pause in our haste to hoot it down?" (423) Showing no patience with the utopian liberal fantasy—the antithetical twin of the aforementioned liberal respect for newly formed nationalities—that the nation-state is about to disappear, Eliot argues that the "organized memory" and distinctive national consciousness of the Jews require, if they are to be preserved and expressed in the modern world, a sovereign state:

> Are there, in the political relations of the world, the conditions present or approaching for the restoration of a Jewish State planted on the old ground as a centre of national feeling, a source of dignifying protection, a special channel for special energies, which may contribute some added form of national genius, and an added voice in the councils of the world? (422)

However painful to Eliot the "resistance" and "repulsion" with which the Zionist element of *Deronda* was met in 1878, they were a mere pinprick compared with the fusillades that the Zionist idea and the state of Israel provoke in England (and still more in Scotland) today. Indeed, the very title of Wisse's chapter, "The Zionist Fate in English Hands," which seemed innocent enough when *The Modern Jewish Canon* appeared in 2000, today seems ghoulishly ironic, especially when viewed in the light of Wisse's allusion to "the world's most hospitable culture." If we take "English hands" to refer to England itself, then the Zionist fate is in mortal danger. Contemporary England, most especially its literary culture, and within that culture most particularly its liberals and battlers against "racism," has declared war upon Zionism and the Jewish state and its inhabitants (unless they happen to be Israeli Arabs). Not many years ago London had a mayor (Ken Livingstone) who during his eight-year tenure considered vituperative abuse of Israel (and of British Jews) one of his primary municipal duties; England as a whole has become the most anti-Zionist and perhaps most antisemitic country in Europe, although it falls well behind France, with its much larger Muslim population, in acts of physical violence.²⁶

Such animosity is not entirely new in England. As far back as 1982, the *Observer* reporter who attended the London performance of George Steiner's *The Portage to San Cristobal of A.H.* said that it was received with raucous applause, and he wondered how much of that applause was intended for Hitler's monologue justifying himself and declaring that he, not Herzl, founded the Jewish state. Years later, when Norman Finkelstein's squalid tract *The Holocaust Industry* (2001), which depicted the Holocaust as in essence a Jewish–Zionist invention, appeared in England, every major British paper devoted at least a full page to this updated version of *The Protocols of the Learned Elders of Zion*, and the book was actually serialized in the *Guardian*. By 2003, a columnist in that paper's sister publication *The Observer* was demanding that Jewish journalists declare their "racial" origins when writing about the Middle East: "I have developed a habit," announced Richard Ingrams, "when confronted by letters to the editor to look at the signature to see if the writer has a Jewish name. If so, I tend not to read it." In 2002, it was English intellectuals who organized the boycott of Israeli academics and researchers. The English (also Jewish) playwright Harold Pinter spoke for a great number of English writers when he called Israel "the central factor in world unrest" and accused it of using nuclear weapons against the Palestinians.

Back in the summer of 1947, at the height of Jewish resistance to British rule in Palestine, the anti-Jewish riots in London, Glasgow, and Manchester were largely the work of working-class thugs; today the battle against Israel and British Jewry more generally is conducted by the devotees of George Eliot's own Religion of Humanity, humanists adept in the reversal of memory, passionate defenders of Islamic suicide bombers, whom they call "the victims of victims." The equation of Zionism with Nazism, a commonplace slander among British colonial officials as early as 1941, is now a central dogma of British liberals and leftists. Indeed, England's Chief Rabbi Jonathan Sacks labeled it "one of the most blasphemous inversions in the history of the world's oldest hate."²⁷

Amidst this ocean of English hostility to the Zionist idea and its realization in Israel, the pointed omission of "The Modern 'Hep! Hep! Hep!'" from A. S. Byatt's 1990 edition of Eliot's *Selected Essays, Poems and Other Writings* constitutes no more than a ripple, but one worth noticing in this context. Eliot's essay first appeared in what was to be her last book, *Impressions of Theophrastus Such*, a collection of eighteen pieces, ostensibly edited by Eliot. Although most Eliot scholars consider the "Jewish" essay by far the strongest in the collection, Byatt, a member in good standing of England's literary establishment (and not one of its ardent Israel-haters[28]) finds space for selections of nine of those essays but none at all for so much as a word from "The Modern 'Hep! Hep! Hep!'" On this particular subject, the voice of George Eliot is not welcome in the contemporary British world of letters.

And yet the voice continues to resonate. If, for example, we wonder what the author of *Daniel Deronda* would have made of this resurgence of Jew-hatred precisely in the midst of "the world's most hospitable culture," we need not do so for long. In May of 2004, the literary section of a New York newspaper carried a lengthy essay entitled—"The Modern 'Hep! Hep! Hep!'" which linked past and present:

> As an antisemitic yelp, *Hep*! is long out of fashion. In the eleventh century it was already a substitution and a metaphor: Jerusalem meant Jews, and 'Jerusalem is destroyed' was, when knighthood was in flower, an incitement to pogrom. Today, the modern *Hep*! appears in the form of Zionism, Israel, Sharon. And the connection between vilification and the will to undermine and endanger Jewish lives is as vigorous as when the howl of *Hep*! was new. The French ambassador to Britain, his tongue unbuttoned in a London salon, hardly thinks to cry *Hep*!; instead, he speaks of 'that shitty little country.' European and British scholars and academicians, their Latin gone dry, will never cry *Hep*!; instead they call for the boycott of Israeli scholars and academicians.... Lies shoot up from the rioters in Gaza and Ramallah. Insinuations ripple out of the high tables of Oxbridge. And steadily, whether from the street or the salon, one hears the enduring old cry: *Hep! Hep! Hep!*[29]

The words are those of Cynthia Ozick, the vision still that of the noble, long-nosed, omnipresent sibyl, "the first great godless writer of fiction" in England: George Eliot.

Notes

1. *The Modern Jewish Canon: A Journey through Language and Culture* (New York: The Free Press, 2000), 239. Subsequent references to this work appear in parentheses in the text. Perhaps Wisse should have qualified her allusions to the apparently welcoming arms of "English generosity" with mention

of the fact that the most vividly realized Jewish character in nineteenth-century English fiction, Fagin, an ancestor of Nazi antisemitic caricature, was the creation of the ardently liberal Charles Dickens.

2. *Illustrated Sunday Herald*, February 8, 1920. Quoted in Martin Gilbert, *Exile and Return* (Philadelphia, PA: J. P. Lippincott, 1978), 128–29. Many years later, Churchill said that the creation of the State of Israel might in time be considered the major historical event of the twentieth century. He respected the fact that virtually no nation-state anywhere in the world was more solemnly founded in international consent than Israel; yet his words strongly suggested that the significance of the State is rooted in deeper and more ancient foundations than those modern covenants or the modern Zionist movement: "The coming into being of a Jewish state . . . is an event in world history to be viewed in the perspective not of a generation or a century, but in the perspective of a thousand, two thousand or even three thousand years."
3. Richard Owen, *The Life of Richard Owen*, 2 vols. (London: John Murray, 1894), I, 231–32.
4. J. W. Cross, *Life of George Eliot* (New York: Thomas Y. Crowell, 1884), 84, 87, 88.
5. Eliezer Ben-Yehuda, *The Dream Come True*, trans. T. Muraoka, ed. George Mandel (Boulder, CO: Westview Press, 1993), 27.
6. *Letters of George Eliot*, ed. G. S. Haight (New Haven, CT: Yale UP, 1954–1955), III, 111.
7. Cross, *Life of George Eliot*, 274–75.
8. *Literary Remains of the Late Emanuel Deutsch*, ed. Emily Strangford (London: John Murray, 1874), 169.
9. *Letters of George Eliot*, V, 160–61.
10. *Middlemarch*, ed. W. J. Harvey (New York: Penguin Books, 1965), 25. Subsequent references to this work appear in parentheses in the text. Was Eliot aware, one wonders, of Theresa's Jewish ancestry?
11. *Nina Balatka*, ed. Robert Tracy (New York: Oxford University Press, 1991), 9. Subsequent references to this work appear in parentheses in the text.
12. See Murray Baumgarten's excellent discussion of the two novels in "Seeing Double: Jews in the Fiction of F. Scott Fitzgerald, Charles Dickens, Anthony Trollope, and George Eliot," in *Between Race and Culture*, ed. B. Cheyette (Stanford, CA: Stanford University Press, 1996), 44–61.
13. Avi Erlich, *Ancient Zionism: The Biblical Origins of the National Idea* (New York: Free Press, 1995). Professor David Mesher's unpublished work on this topic has also been of great use to me.
14. *Daniel Deronda*, ed. Barbara Hardy (Baltimore, MD: Penguin Books, 1967), Chapter 42, 592. Subsequent references to this work appear in parentheses in the text.
15. See Naomi Shepherd, *The Zealous Intruders* (San Francisco, CA: Harper & Row, 1987), 229, 239.
16. Lionel Trilling, *Matthew Arnold* (New York: Columbia University Press, 1939), 233.

17. On the intriguing subject of whether Daniel was circumcised as an infant, see John Sutherland, "Is Daniel Deronda circumcised?" in *Can Jane Eyre Be Happy?* (New York: Oxford University Press, 1997), 169–76.
18. *Modern Jewish Canon*, 242.
19. *Letters of George Eliot*, VI, 290.
20. "Owning and Disowning: The Unity of *Daniel Deronda*," in *Daniel Deronda: A Centenary Symposium*, ed. Alice Shalvi (Jerusalem: Jerusalem Academic Press, 1976), 67.
21. Introduction to *Daniel Deronda*, 20.
22. *Irving Howe: Selected Writings, 1950-1990* (New York: Harcourt Brace Javanovich, 1990), 361.
23. *Letters of George Eliot*, VI, 301–2.
24. Frederick R. Karl, *George Eliot: Voice of a Century* (New York: W. W. Norton, 1995), 556n.
25. "The Modern Hep! Hep! Hep!" in *Impressions of Theophrastus Such* [1879] (New York: Doubleday Page, 1901), 413, 421. Subsequent references to this work appear in parentheses in the text.
26. See Robert Wistrich, "Cruel Britannia: Anti-Semitism among the Ruling Elites," *Azure* no. 21 (Summer 2005): 100–24.
27. Jonathan Sacks, "A New Anti-Semitism?" in *A New Anti-Semitism?* ed. Paul Iganski and Barry Kosmin (London: Profile, 2003), 46.
28. By English standards, she is something of a trimmer. She has said (in the *Guardian*, April 27, 2002) that she "[understands] the anxieties of American Jews who, while not supporting all of Israel's actions, are disappointed by the way disapproval in Europe seems to shade very easily into anti-semitism."
29. Cynthia Ozick, *The New York Observer*, May 10, 2004.

Index

Abbas, Mahmoud, 84, 85n
Abonyi, Zsuzsi, 76–80
Acre (Akko), 60
Addison, Joseph, 55
Agnon, S. Y., 203
Ahad Ha'am, 229
Ahmadinejad, Mahmoud, 67, 123, 136, 168
Ahmed, Nadeem, 153
Ajami, Fouad, 120
Al-Arabiya, 116
Al-Azhar University, 119
Al-Dura, Mohammed, 97
Allen, Jim, 224
Alter, Robert, 90, 92
American exceptionalism, 88, 113–15, 198
American Jewish Committee, 3, 89, 121
American Jewish Congress, 3
Améry, Jean, 96, 99-100
antisemitism, xiii–xiv, 1–2, 53, 56, 81, 88, 96, 99, 109, 114–17, 121, 123, 125–26, 135–36, 147, 152, 157, 159–60, 194
    in American universities, 65–69
    anti-Zionism as modern version of, 47–50, 99, 109
    in England, 43–51, 53, 219–25
    euphemism invented by Jew-haters, xiii, 53–54
    Europe's most effective political ideology, 109, 115–16
    George W. Bush vs., 114, 121n
    in Germany, 81, 88, 136
    "Islamophobia" and, 117
    of Jews, 47–50, 135, 159–64, 219–25
    of liberals, 15–21, 165–69, 235–36
    Noam Chomsky and, 123
    "secret weapon" of WWII, 88

antisemitism (*continued*)
    in Spain's "Golden Age," 62–63
    T. S. Eliot and, 152
    Wilhelm Marr and, 109
Appelfeld, Aharon, 98, 209
Arafat, Yasser, 74, 120, 129–30, 134, 136, 139, 201
Arendt, Hannah, 1, 3, 8, 55, 75, 89, 96, 109, 213–14, 222
Aristotle, 145, 211
Armstrong, Karen, 96, 133–35
Arnold, Matthew, xiii–xiv, 21–27, 68, 78–79, 124, 148, 173, 181, 232
Arnold, Thomas, xiii, 15–21
Arrow Cross (Hungarian), 77
Auden, W. H., 161, 208
Austen, Jane, 188

Babel, Isaac, 127
Bacon, Francis, 119
Baker, James, 121
Baker, Mona, 140
Balfour, Arthur, 48, 57, 71, 120, 227
Balint, Benjamin, 87–93
Barnard College, 67
Bauer, Yehuda, 76, 96
BBC, 81, 125–26, 154, 162, 166, 219–20
Begin, Menachem, 57
Beit Hatefutsot, 215
Bellow, Saul, 1, 2, 5–7, 9, 68, 195, 201–206
Belo, Abram, 201
Ben-Gurion, David, 4, 110, 164, 229
Bentham, Jeremy, 33, 111, 132
Ben-Yehuda, Eliezer, 228
Bergen-Belsen, 98
Berman, Paul, 130
Bernal, Martin, 147

Bevin, Ernest, 168
Bialik, Haim Nachman, 209
Bitburg, 96
Blair, Tony, 123, 153
Blake, William, 54
Botteghe Oscure, 196
Bradley, John, 156
Braham, Randolph, 76
Brichah, 213
Buber, Martin, 89
Buchanan, Patrick, 121
Bucharest, 69, 197–98
Bund, 3
Burke, Robert, 66
Bush, George W., 105, 114, 121n
Butler, Judith, 5
Butler, Nicholas M., 66
Byatt, A. S., 237

Cairo University, 119
Cambridge University, 20
Camus, Albert, 176
Canning, George, 48
Capote, Truman, 202
Carlyle, Thomas, xiii, 15–16, 31, 44, 56, 192
Chamberlain, Neville, 71
Chambers, Whitaker, 175
Chamfort, Nicolas, 124
Chase, Richard, 177
Chaucer, Geoffrey, 43–44
Chomsky, Noam, 5, 67, 92, 105, 123, 140
Churchill, Caryl, 44–46, 222
Churchill, Winston, 7, 23, 57, 82, 227, 239n
Clermont-Tonnerre, Count Stanislaw de, 108
Cockburn, Alexander, 125, 132
Cohen, Elliott, 10n
Cohen, Stephen, 119
Cohn, Werner, 160
Coleridge, S. T., 27–28, 33, 53, 222
Columbia University, 65–67, 124, 126, 132, 151, 155–56, 157n, 175
Conant, James, 66
Considerations on Representative Government (Mill), 33
Constantine, Emperor, 22, 106
Cooper, Anthony Ashley (Lord Shaftesbury), 56–57

Cordoba, 63
Coser, Lewis, 91
Crews, Frederick, 189
Cromwell, Oliver, 54
Cross, John Walter, 235
Culture and Anarchy (Arnold), 21

D'Eichthal, Gustave, 32
Dafni, Reuven, 96
Daleski, Hillel M., 234
Daniel Deronda (Eliot), 227-28, 230–38
Dante, 175
Dawidowicz, Lucy S., 89, 96, 100n, 208
De Botton, Alain, 162–64, 220
De Maistre, Joseph, 155
Deir Yassin, 83
Derfner, Larry, xiv
Deshell, Maier, 59, 208
Deutsch, Emanuel, 24, 229–32
Dewey, Thomas, 68
Dickens, Charles, 43–44, 46, 51n, 58, 78, 124, 131, 178, 187, 239n
Disraeli, Benjamin, 47, 55–57, 168, 228
Disraeli, Isaac, 55
Disraeli, Jacobus (James), 55
Disraeli, Raphael (Ralph), 55
Dissent Magazine, 91
Donne, John, 44
Dostoevsky, Fyodor, 132
Dreiser, Theodore, 173, 178
Dreyfus, Alfred, 1, 36, 48, 109, 168

Eichmann, Adolf, 3, 73, 76, 213, 232
Ein Hachoresh, 217
El-Husseini, Haj Amin, 8, 71–74, 62
Eliade, Mircea, 68–69
Eliot, T. S., 44, 152
Ellis, Marc, 96
Encyclopedia Britannica, 165
Endelman, Todd, 20
Epstein, Joseph, 91
Erdogan, Recep, 118
Evans, Mary Ann (George Eliot), 228–29, 235
Ezrahi, Sidra, 62

feminism, 133, 233
Fiedler, Leslie, 202
Finkelstein, Norman, 96, 125, 160, 237
Fisch, Harold, 51n
Fisk, Robert, 166

Index

Fitzgerald, F. Scott, 173
Foreign Bodies (Ozick), 9–10n, 69n, 195–99
Forster, E. M., 176
Forster, John, 43
Fox, Charles James, 152
Foxman, Abraham, 121
Frank, Anne, 89, 98–99
Frank, Jacob, 210
Freedman, Samuel, 126
Freeman, Charles, 117
Froude, James A., 15

Gabai, Yolande, 163–64
Galloway, George, 118
Gay, Peter, 68
Geniza (Cairo), 62
George, Lloyd, 57
Germany, 25, 56, 66–68, 72, 74–75, 77, 81, 99, 110, 114, 116, 125–26, 143, 183–86, 197, 208, 214
Ghanem, As'ad, 142
Gildersleeve, Virginia, 67
Gladstone, William, 168
Glatstein, Jacob, 9, 207–11
Glazer, Nathan, 91
Goebbels, Josef, 66, 166, 168
Goering, Herman, 144
Goethe, J. W. von, 78, 99
Goodman, Paul, 90
Gordin, Jacob, 210
Gordon, Aaron D., 229
Goshkin, Anita, 205
Graetz, Heinrich, 210
Gray, Hannah, 68
Greenberg, Clement, 89
Greenberg, Hayim, 2–3
Greenblatt, Stephen, 140
Greenfield, Susan, 143
Grenada, 62
Guardian (UK), 48, 139, 141, 163, 166, 237
Guterman, Norbert, 208

Hadassah Hospital, 84
Haifa, 82–84, 142, 229
Halevi, Yehuda, 59–63
Halkin, Hillel, 59–63, 192
Halpern, Ben, 2
Hampden, Renn, 17
Hanfstaengl, Ernst, 66–67

Hardy, Barbara, 234
Harris, David, 121
Harrison, Bernard, 46, 51n, 66, 126–27, 165–69
Harvard University, 65–67, 124, 140, 151, 155–56, 181
Hashomer Hatzair, 215
Haskalah, 211
Hazaz, Haim, 5, 56, 219
Hazlitt, William, 115
Heaney, Seamus, 156
Hebron, 84
Heidegger, Martin, 186
Heine, Heinrich, 23–24, 62, 203
Heir to the Glimmering World (Ozick), 182–93
Hemingway, Ernest, 174
Herberg, Will, 89
Hermesh (Israel), 164
Herodotus, 27
Hertford College (Oxford), 151–53
Hertz, J. H., xiv
Herzl, Theodor, 50, 210, 229, 237
Heschel, Abraham J., 89
Hilberg, Raul, 76, 98
Hildesheimer, Israel, 210
Hilliard, Constance, 123
Himmelfarb, Gertrude, xiii, 53–58
Himmelfarb, Milton, 24, 53, 90
Himmler, Heinrich, 72–73
Hiss, Alger, 175
Hitchens, Christopher, 201
Hitler, Adolf, 2, 65–69, 71–75, 82, 95, 97, 100, 136, 139, 142–44, 151, 155, 192, 204, 207–10, 237
Hobbes, Thomas, 152
Hollings, Ernest, 121
Holocaust,
  anti-Israel propaganda and, 95–100, 119–20, 160–61, 224, 237
  assaults on memory of, 95–100, 221
  Bellow and, 204–205
  deniers seek repetition of, 99
  Glatstein and, 207–11
  Hungary and, 75–80
  incredibility of, 75–76
  Israel created despite, 210–11
  jealousy of, 147
  Jewish intellectuals ignore, 1–6, 204–205
  Kovner and, 9, 75, 99, 213–17

Holocaust (*continued*)
   Ozick and, 195–99
   Palestinian Arabs and, 71–74
   post-war Europe and, 195–98
   Romania and, 68–69, 197
   warnings of second, 9, 99, 216, 219
   Western culture and, 79–80, 178
   Yiddish and, 207
Homer, xiv, 96
Honderich, Ted, 130–33, 136–37, 168
Howe, Irving, 1–2, 4–5, 7, 89–92, 106, 116, 130, 179, 234
Hutchins, Robert, 65
Huxley, Aldous, 222

Independent (UK), 49, 132, 163, 166
Ingrams, Richard, 237
Intifada II, 123, 129, 133, 163
Iron Guard (Romania), 68, 197
Irving, David, 44, 142
Isaac, Erich, 89, 185
Isaiah, xiv, 27, 31, 34, 53
Israel (Biblical), 27–34, 54, 56
Israel (Land of), 59–61, 107, 228, 232
Israel (State of)
   academic boycott of, 139–44
   America only faithful ally of, 90–91
   Arab hatred of, 142
   Churchill urges recognition of, 57
   Commentary as defender of, 90
   creation of, 1, 3, 6–8, 49, 81, 97–98, 105, 110, 119, 125, 205, 210–11, 229, 231
   "criticism" of, 46, 109, 123–27
   daily trial of, 48–49, 125
   demonization of, 167, 201
   destruction of, threatened, 1, 7, 74, 99, 110, 125, 131, 157, 168
   Diaspora and, 1–2, 105
   English hostility to, 236–38
   holds Jewish future, 59
   Holocaust and, 95–100
   Jewish alienation from, 4–7, 9, 50
   Jewish defamers of, 50, 219–25, 232
   Jewish "identity" dependent on, 50, 159
   "least-liked" country, 125, 152
   liberal abandonment of, 92, 125, 234
   likened by "progressives" to South Africa and Nazi Germany, 126, 160, 166

Israel (State of) (*continued*)
   model for Britain, 55
   new antisemitism centers on, 109
   New Left and, 90
   Obama and, 8, 117–21
   Palestinian terror against, 129–36
   permanent state of siege of, 105
   refugees of 1948 as "original sin" of, 81–84
   "right to exist" of, 49–50, 124–25, 153, 155
   Turkey's hostility to, 118
   war of ideas over, 111
   withdrawal from Lebanon and Gaza of, 163
   Yehuda Halevi and, 62

Jablonka, Eva, 140
Jabotinsky, Vladimir Ze'ev, 110, 229
Jacobson, Howard, 135, 162, 219–25
Jaffa, 82–83
Jager, Elliot, 126
Jane Eyre (Bronte), 184, 187–88, 198
Jay, Martin, 157
Jerusalem, 32, 55–56, 60, 62, 71, 82, 107, 120, 131, 133, 137n, 203, 213, 215, 229, 232, 238
Jewish Chronicle (London), 162
Jewish Frontier, 2–3
Jews' Free School (London), 23
Johnson, Samuel, 8, 105, 201
Joseph, Morris, 20
Joyce, James, 227
Judaism, 4, 15–17, 23–38, 50, 54–56, 59–61, 63, 88–89, 106, 108, 183, 210, 223, 228, 231–32
Judt, Tony, 4, 44, 125–26, 157, 222, 225n, 232
Julius, Anthony, 43–51, 54, 57, 219

Kampf, Louis, 66
Kanin, Garson, 98
Kant, Immanuel, 220
Kaplan, Mordechai, 5
Karl, Frederick, 235
Kastner, Rudolf, 76
Kaufman, Shirley, 214
Kay, Barbara, 159
Kermode, Frank, 183
Kertesz, Imre, 96, 99
Kessner, Carole, 2, 4

King Abdullah, 74
King Abdullah II, 117
King John, 15, 34
Kirkpatrick, Jeane, 91
Klein, Naomi, 162
Klemperer, Victor, 100
Kohn, Hans, 5
Koran, 53, 63
Kovner, Abba, 9n, 75, 80n, 99, 107, 213–17
Kozodoy, Neal, 89, 90, 93
Kristallnacht, 68
Kristol, Irving, 89
Krugman, Paul, 157
Kuntzel, Matthias, 99
Kushner, Tony, 5
Kuzari (Halevi), 59–61

Lambertz, Goren, 124
Landor, Walter Savage, 178
Lawrence, D. H., 152, 174
Lebel, Jennie, 71–74
Lefkowitz, Mary, 145–49
Leibowitz, Yeshayahu 62
Lerner, Michael, 92
Levi, Primo, 6, 96, 99, 205
Lewes, George Henry, 228–29
Lewisohn, Ludwig, 4
liberalism,
 abandonment of Israel by, 92
 angelic sociology of, 130
 critique of, by Lionel Trilling, 173–76
 equated with Judaism, 232
 failure of imagination of, 176
 herd instinct of, 173
 Jews and, 9, 88
 John Henry Newman critique of, 16
 John Stuart Mill and, 27–38
 Stalinism and, 173
 suicide bombing "explained" by, 130, 157
 Thomas Arnold and, 15–21
Lipstadt, Deborah, 44
Literature and Dogma (Arnold), 25
Livingstone, Ken, 129
Loach, Ken, 224
Locke, John, 54
London Review of Books, 124, 126, 155
London University, 17–20, 38n, 50, 141
Long, Breckinridge, 198

Lopate, Philip, 95–97
Lublin, 207–209

Macaulay, Thomas, 15–16, 54, 192
Macmillan, Harold, 7–8, 55, 57
Madame Tussaud, 132
Mailer, Norman, 90
Maimonides, 54, 62–63
Malamud, Bernard, 202, 204
Mann, Thomas, 78, 209
Mapam, 215–16
Margalit, Avishai, 96–97, 100
Mark Twain, 173
Marr, Wilhelm, 109
Martin, Anthony, 145
Masada, 92
Maurice, Frederick D., 31
McDonald, James, 168
McKinney, Cynthia, 121
Mearsheimer, John, 67, 126, 160
Meir, Golda, 2, 92, 105
Melville, Herman, 60
Merchant of Venice (Shakespeare), 45, 48
Merleau-Ponty, Maurice, 204
Middlemarch (Eliot), 179, 182, 187, 230, 233
Mill, James, 18
Mill, John Stuart, xiii–xiv, 15, 22, 27–39, 93, 111, 236
Milne, A. A., 188
Milne, Christopher Robin, 188
Milton, John, xiii–xiv, 21, 24, 51n, 54, 56, 78, 136, 149, 217
Mitchell, George, 117
"Modern Hep! Hep! Hep!" (Eliot), 37, 235–38
Mohammed, Mahathir, 157
Montaigne, xiii
Montefiore, Moses, 232
Mormonism, 159–60
Mortara, Edgardo, 36
Moses, 1, 31–32, 228
Moses, Wilson J., 147
Most, Johann, 154
Moynihan, Daniel P., 91
Mussaoui, Zacarias, 167
Mussolini, Benito, 72

Nachmanides, 108
Nakam (vengeance), 214
Nation of Islam, 146

Nestel, Sheryl, 160
Netanyahu, Benjamin, 117, 120
Neusner, Jacob, 89
New Statesman (UK), 49, 163, 166, 169
New York Intellectuals, 1–5
New York Review of Books, 7, 97, 126, 157
New Yorker, 3, 7
Newman, John Henry, 16–17, 38n, 135, 164, 192
Newton, Isaac, 54
Niger, Shmuel, 198
Nina Balatka (Trollope), 230–31
Nisbet, Robert, 53
Nordau, Max, 210
Norwood, Stephen, 65–69
Novick, Peter, 96

O'Brien, Conor Cruise, 97
Obama, Barack, 8, 113–21, 161
Oliver Twist (Dickens), 43–46, 48
On Liberty (Mill), 28, 31, 35–38, 236
Oren, Michael, 117
Orwell, George, 6, 92, 132, 152
Oslo War (Intifada II: 2000–05), 129, 133
Oxford Union, 49
Ozick, Cynthia, 6, 10n, 95, 97, 179, 181–98, 202, 204–205
Ozsvath, Zsuzsanna, 9, 76–80

Pablo Christiani, 108
Palestine, 2, 4, 7, 10n, 48, 56–57, 60–61, 67, 71–85, 88, 97, 120, 167, 213, 220, 227, 229, 231, 234, 237
Paris, 50, 118, 195–98, 203–205, 228
Paris Review, 196
Partisan Review, 1, 2, 6, 89, 205
Pascal, Blaise, 220
Paulin, Tom, xiv, 8, 44–46, 67, 124–25, 140, 151–57
Peacock, Thomas Love, 222
Percy, Charles, 121
Peto, David, 160
Peto, Jennifer, 159–61
Peto, Jolen, 160
Phillips, Melanie, 57
Phillips, William, 1–2
philosemitism, xiii, 47, 53–58
Pilger, John, 166
Pinsker, Leon, 229

Pinter, Harold, 237
Plantec, Michelle, 146
Podhoretz, John, 93
Podhoretz, Norman, 87–91
Ponary, 214–16
Pope John Paul II, 134
Pope Pius IX, 36
Pope, Alexander, 151
Porat, Dina, 214
Porter, Katherine Anne, 208
Power, Samantha, 117
Prague, 229–31
Princess Diana, 44
"Prioress' Tale" (Chaucer), 45–46
progressive Jews, 125–26
Protocols of the Elders of Zion, 44–45
Pugin, A. W. N., 45
Pusey, Edward B., 17

Rabbi Hillel, 88
Rahv, Philip, 1, 4, 89
Ravelstein (Bellow), 68, 197
Rawidowicz, Simon, 5
Reagan, Ronald, 96
Rebick, Judy, 159
Réville, Albert, 22
Reznikoff, Charles, 4
Ribbentrop, Joachim von, 72
Rice, Susan, 117
Ringelblum, Emanuel, 89
Roach, Kike, 161
Roiphe, Anne, 95
Rose, Jacqueline, 5, 50, 135–36, 166, 222
Rose, Steven, 139
Rosenberg, Harold, 89
Rosenfeld, Alvin, 95–100, 125–26
Rosenfeld, Isaac, 201
Rosenthal, Hannah, 117
Ross, Dennis, 117
Roth, Cecil, 89
Roth, Malki, 136
Roth, Philip, 48, 95, 186, 202, 204, 221, 224
Rothschild, Louisa de, 23
Rothschild, Nathan, 15
Rugby School, 15–16, 235
Ruskin, John, 26–27, 178, 225
Russell, Lord John, 35
Ryerson University (Toronto), 161

Sacks, Jonathan, 109, 165, 237

Index

Sadat, Anwar, 105
Safed, 84
Said, Edward, 66, 97, 132, 156, 188, 229
Saint Theresa, 230
Salvador, Joseph, 31–33
Samuel, Maurice, 2, 89
Sandburg, Carl, 203
Sartre, Jean-Paul, 204
Schmidt, Anton, 213
Scholem, Fania, 215
Seven Jewish Children: A Play for Gaza (C. Churchill), 45–46, 222
Seven Sisters (Colleges), 65
Sewell, Dennis, 168
Shakespeare, William, xiv, 43–44, 78, 148, 156, 182
Shapiro, James, 156
Shlesinger, Miriam, 140
Sholom Aleichem, 209
Short, Clare, 123
Sinervo, Pekka, 133
Sinnott, Michael, 141–42
Slater, David, 143
Smith College, 148
Sombart, Werner, 115
Soros, George, 117, 126
Spain, 60–62, 108, 167, 182, 230
Spinoza, Baruch, 23
Spivak, Gayatri, 132–33, 136
St. Paul and Protestantism (Arnold), 25, 134
Stannard, David, 96
Steele, Shelby, 114
Steiner, George, 5–6, 79–80, 237
Stephen, Leslie, 235
Stern, Fritz, 89
Steyn, Mark, 97
Stowe, Harriet Beecher, 234
Strauss, D. F., 32
Strauss, Leo, 73
Streicher, Julius, 167
Subjection of Women (Mill), 29, 35
Sykes, Christopher, 84
Syrkin, Marie, 2–4, 89
Syrkin, Nachman, 2, 229

Tabachnik, Abraham, 207
Tacitus, 173
Taguieff, Pierre-André, 97
Tancred (Disraeli), 55
Taylor, Benjamin, 201
Tennyson, Alfred, 19
Terkel, Studs, 203
Thackeray, W. M., 44
Thomas of Monmouth, 44
Three Essays on Religion (Mill), 28–29
Tocqueville, Alexis de, 115
Toury, Gideon, 140
Toynbee, Arnold, 232
Transnistria, 197
Trilling, Diana, 174
Trilling, Lionel, xiii, 2, 4–5, 88–90, 125, 133, 149, 173–80, 232
Trollope, Anthony, 44, 187, 230–31
Truman, Harry, 82, 168
Tutu, Desmond, 135
Tyndale, William, 152

Ulysses (Joyce), 227
United Nations, 81
United States, 4, 49, 67–68, 91, 113–19, 133
University College (London), 132
University of Chicago, 65, 68, 73
University of Toronto, 133, 160
USSR, 4, 209
Utilitarianism (Mill), 28

Vassar College, 67, 123, 148
Vilna, 9, 75, 213–17
Vonnegut, Kurt, 129

Wallace, Henry, 204
Walt, Stephen, 67, 126, 160
Walz, John, 66
Wannsee, 47
Warburg, Otto, 143–44
Warsaw, 107, 216
Warshow, Robert, 179
Weingrad, Michael, 140
Weizmann, Chaim, 120
Wellesley College, 145–49
Werman, Golda, 51n
Wesker, Arnold, 224
Wesley, John, 21
Westminster Review (UK), 28, 192
Whitman, Walt, 214
Wiesel, Elie, 75, 89, 92, 96
Wilby, Peter, 167
Wilentz, Sean, 130
Wilson, Edmund, 89
Wisliceny, Dieter, 73

Wisse, Ruth, 4, 88, 92, 105–11, 227–38
Wistrich, Robert, 57
Woolf, Leonard, 49
Woolf, Virginia, 235
Wordsworth, William, 173–74, 217
Wrong, Dennis, 91

Yad Vashem, 96–97, 100n
Yiftachel, Oren, 142–43

Zevi, Sabbatai, 210
Zimmermann, Fritz, 153
Zionism,
   answer to antisemitism, 1, 109
   assaulted by liberals, xiii
   Churchill and Macmillan support, 7–8

Zionism (*continued*)
   demonizing of, 167
   George Eliot and, 227–38
   Glatstein and, 208
   hatred of, as basis of Jewish "identity," 5, 219
   hatred of, as way of life for Arab and Muslim countries, 110
   Herzl and Nordau preach, 210
   Jewish enemies of, 4–9, 48–50, 219–25
   Kovner and, 215–16
   "lifeboat" version of, 225
   medieval form of, 59–63
   psychoanalyzed by J. Rose, 222
   suicide bombing as "critique" of, 123–24
   Weizmann on, 101n